FLYING

WITH

CONDORS

FLYING
WITH
CONDORS

◀ *Judy Leden* ▶

Foreword by
HM King Hussein
of the Hashemite Kingdom of Jordan

———

ORION

First published in Great Britain in 1996 by
Orion
An imprint of Orion Books Ltd
Orion House, 5 Upper St Martin's Lane,
London WC2H 9EA

A CIP catalogue record for this book
is available from the British Library

ISBN 0 75280 133 3

Filmset by Selwood Systems, Midsomer Norton
Printed in Great Britain by
Butler & Tanner Ltd, Frome and London

For Chris, whose love of life is so infectious

'You are never given a wish without also
being given the power to make it true.
You may have to work for it, however.'

Richard Bach

Acknowledgements

I would like to thank

Ben Ashman for showing me how wrong first impressions can be.
Brian Milton for his help and boundless enthusiasm.
Fran Knowles, Judy Mallinson and Ffyona Campbell for their friendship, laughter
 and shared adventures.
Matt Dickinson for believing in the dreams.
Ken Kingsbury who, with his skill in osteopathy, put my body back together and
 kept me in the air.
Peter Terry for removing the blinkers.
Citroen UK, Olympus cameras, Royal Jordanian Airlines and Total Oil who had
 enough faith in me to back my adventures.
Jean and Jack Oldfield for their invaluable baby sitting which allowed me to finish
 the book.

I owe a special debt of thanks to

His Majesty, King Hussein of Jordan for his friendship, compassion and generosity,
 whose love of flying endears him to pilots everywhere.
Sian Carradice for finding time in her hectic life for proof reading.
My Mother and Father for their support throughout my flying career, and for
 being a refuge in the midst of life's storms.
Chris Dawes for his faith in my capability to write a book, his understanding when
 the hormonal swings of pregnancy rendered me irrational and for his ability,
 when all else failed, to make me laugh.

Contents

It is a great pleasure and privilege for me to introduce this book to you on behalf of my dear friend, Judy Leden MBE and 'holder of' the Jordan Star First Class.

"*Flying With Condors*" is an important chronicle of the experiences of not only I am sure one of the greatest hang glider and paraglider of our times but also the story of a remarkable person. Judy is one of the most enthusiastic, humanitarian, modest and one of the bravest, not reckless, individuals I have ever had the honour to meet.

In this book, Judy shares with the reader her incredible achievements with disarming modesty, but her account is a fine illustration of how anything is possible. For example, Judy was afraid of heights yet she overcame this fear to become the greatest woman pilot in the new aviation. This is a story of hope, faith and optimism - a story told with incredible sensitivity yet it illustrates that everything is within reach through sheer determination, commitment and personal courage.

For my part, it has been a distinct honour to contribute in a small way to Judy's achievements through concern for her friend and my fellow Jordanian, Yasmin, who died at such an early age of lung cancer. The *Flight For Life* microlight journey undertaken by Judy from the United Kingdom to the Hashemite Kingdom of Jordan in memory of Yasmin and in aid of cancer research was the most exciting, rewarding and ultimately moving adventure. Furthermore, also in Jordan, we were honoured to host Judy's subsequent world balloon altitude hang gliding drop of 38,900 feet high above the desert in Wadi Rum - yet another exceptional personal feat. I recommend you read for yourselves this account and share with Judy the euphoria of accomplishment.

I hope that "*Flying With Condors*" reaches beyond the heights of success that Judy so richly deserves; Judy Leden is a woman who has in fact "*flown above condors*" - but her inherent modesty prevails.

Hussein I

Introduction

Holding my gaze with its vivid green eyes, a huge condor closed the gap between us. His outstretched wings seemed endless, finishing in a graceful curve at the tips as he flew towards me, head on. I suddenly felt incredibly vulnerable, hanging beneath a fabric wing 2,000 feet above a precipice with nothing but rocks and snow beneath me.

It was a moment I had only dreamed of, to fly with the biggest of all birds of prey, the Andean condor. I had flown with vultures in the past and they had come close to me, curious to investigate such a big and colourful new 'bird' in their domain, but they were tiny by comparison with this fellow. I was eyeball to eyeball with a creature whose wingspan measured ten feet, and I was unsure of his intentions and increasingly nervous.

Entranced by the sight of the condor, I continued to fly towards him when I suddenly realised the seriousness of the situation. We had become so close that a collision seemed imminent. By this time I was unable to move out of his path as my paraglider was not nimble enough to turn away and I had to hope that this bird had a sense of self-preservation and would avoid me. At the last minute, with a speed that belied his size, he furled his wings and dropped past me in a black blur. As soon as he had passed my feet, his wings snapped open once more, and he swooped upwards, deftly turning back towards me to have another look.

Looking over my shoulder, I watched him approach from behind. The blaze of white across his back stood out clearly against his glossy black wings. His gliding speed was faster than mine and he rose above me, disappearing from view above my canopy. I watched his ghostly shadow move silently over my wing, until he emerged once again, silhouetted against the sun. He peered down at me and, having satisfied his curiosity, with an imperceptible adjustment to the curve of his wings, he carved a graceful arc in the air and was gone. As he disappeared across the valley, embarking on his daily foraging expedition, I was left alone once more in the vast Andean sky.

I had come a long way since 1979 when, as an unpromising beginner, I had made my first faltering flights with a hang glider. If anyone had told me that sixteen years hence I would be suspended over a breathtaking precipice under the watchful eye of an Andean condor, I would have laughed in their face, because I have a real fear of heights!

CHAPTER 1

Fledgling

My heart was racing as I lifted the hang glider up. I looked straight ahead to where the ground dropped away to the valley far below. My instructor held the wires, steadying the wing, his wild red hair thrashing in the wind as he went over the instructions once more.

'Hold the wings level . . . keep the nose of the glider up a bit . . . remember your airspeed . . .'

His words were lost as my inner turmoil continued to deafen me. My instinct rebelled against the idea of running off the cliff in front of me, and the idea of stamp collecting suddenly seemed appealing.

'When you're ready . . .'

I hesitated for a moment while my keenness to fly battled with my sense of self-preservation. The latter lost and I took a deep breath and began to move forwards. The glider lifted first its own weight, then mine, and within five paces I was airborne.

I gasped as I cleared the near-vertical edge and the ground fell away. Excitement and adrenaline surged through me and I started to laugh. My exhilaration was tinged with fear and I loved it. Gripping the control bar as if my hand-hold alone would stop me falling, my senses were bombarded as I hung hundreds of feet above the ground with the Welsh valleys spread out below.

I tentatively tried turning right as I had been taught and the glider reacted obediently to my body's movement. Controlling the wing was like riding a motorbike, leaning my weight to the side to turn it, but the sensation of exposure and freedom was unique.

The landing field was getting closer as I sank slowly in the smooth air. I struggled to concentrate on my landing approach as I was distracted by

1

the view and the feeling of flying. I turned to face into the wind as I had been taught and then landed on my belly. I had been so mesmerised that I forgot to put my feet down.

I babbled incessantly. I had flown like a bird, I had tasted free flight and I was hooked!

My love of adventure had been encouraged by my father from an early age. My older sister, Toni, and I were brought up in a small bungalow next to the River Thames near Staines in Middlesex. When we were just eight and ten years old, Dad bought a double canoe and took us one at a time into the middle of the river and capsized it. Having been briefed beforehand, we had to get out of the upturned boat and swim to the shore.

'Ready . . . Steady . . . Go,' said Dad, and the world rotated.

I was nervous. Although by the age of eight I could swim well, I had no experience of getting out from upturned canoes. I held my breath and closed my eyes as I went under the water. I pushed away from the boat, moving my legs clear before I tried to surface, staying as calm as I could, as Dad had instructed.

In less than ten seconds I was swimming towards the bank, breathing hard but feeling quite calm. Having passed the test, Toni and I were then given a single canoe to share and allowed to paddle a ten-mile stretch of the Thames unsupervised.

Dad had given us the 'tools' we would need to get out of a potentially dangerous situation, taught us how to use them and then, the most difficult of all, trusted us enough to release the reins and let us get on with it. It became the most natural thing in the world to react to danger by keeping control and acting positively, to take responsibility for our own survival.

He encouraged us to accept challenges, seeing them as positive experiences. He and his father had escaped from Czechoslovakia during the war when he was nine years old. He was put in an orphanage while his father worked and, as a refugee, had to cope with a new country, a strange language and the appalling reality of the Holocaust, which claimed the lives of his mother and most of his remaining family back home. This harsh beginning had equipped him with great strength and self-reliance, qualities he was eager to pass on to us, and I became confident in my ability to cope with difficult situations at an early age.

I was always a tomboy and early photographs usually show me in dungarees. Living by the river was ideal for an adventurous child and we spent much of our time outside, fishing for sticklebacks in the stream behind the house or swinging from ropes strung from the horse chestnut trees in the garden.

We had very little money during my early childhood. My father's jewellery business crashed and our family home in Woodford Green was forfeited to the bank. Toni and I were blissfully unaware of the anguish that must have ensued as we moved into my grandmother's riverside bungalow.

Toni and I went to St Bernard's Convent School in Slough from the age of nine. Discipline was very strict: no talking was allowed during lunch and we had to curtsey to our teacher at the end of each day. The sudden exposure to Catholic religion had a powerful effect on me. I was one of only four non-Catholics in the class and as such wasn't allowed to go to Mass on Wednesday morning with the other girls. We had to sit alone in the classroom feeling as though we were in detention. I came home and announced to my mother that I wanted to become a nun. The mysterious figures who would glide silently across the school's polished parquet floors enchanted me with their aura of other-worldliness.

My grandmother remembers me as a 'fearless' child, always wanting to jump from the high board in any swimming pool. My only memory of high boards was volunteering to jump from the top platform during a Brownies' swimming gala. I climbed up the steps, looked down at the pool thirty feet below and felt sick. I could not bring myself to jump and, feeling mortified, I climbed back down the stairs to a sympathetic round of applause from the assembled parents. This was the first time that I became aware of my hatred of heights. It sounds idiotic for someone who has a passion for hang gliding, but I cannot walk to the edge of a cliff and look over. However, the feeling is different as long as I am securely harnessed to a hang glider, as I do not have the sensation that I can fall.

At the age of fifteen, I went on a scuba diving course in Devon. It was hardly the tropical paradise I had dreamed of after watching Jacques Cousteau on television. The cold water was so murky that it was impossible to see my hand in front of my face, but the sensation of moving underwater and being able to explore this new world captivated me. This fascination with adventure grew into an addiction which has never left me and I moved on to try skiing, surfing, water-skiing and anything else that came my way. I was a 'dabbler' at things, enjoying the thrills of different sports but never sticking with them, always looking for something new.

This restlessness continued throughout my teenage years. I was competitive and energetic, but did not have an outlet for my drive, and as a result was frustrated. I used a trial and error method to find something that would satisfy my need for focus in my life. I experimented with drugs, religion and adventure in an effort to find a solution.

I rebelled against my father in my teens, and we were often at loggerheads. We are both stubborn and rubbed each other up the wrong way. My mother watched from the sidelines, trying to keep the peace. She is shy by nature and hates confrontation, looking on uncomprehendingly as Dad and I clashed. She was my refuge; we rarely argue and our relationship has always been close.

I studied for my A-levels at Windsor College, but work became increasingly difficult as the alternative lure of the nearby café and pub was always tempting. It was hard to see how drawing an amoeba, or learning the intricacies of organic chemistry, could be remotely relevant to anything I might undertake in later life.

It was during my exam revision that I first heard of hang gliding. I saw a photograph on a friend's wall cut out from a magazine. The picture was of a hang glider flying over the sea in California and underneath the caption read 'It's like sex only it lasts longer!' The idea of being able to fly had never occurred to me before. Conventional aeroplanes didn't inspire me, but hang gliding was different: there were no windows and no control sticks or pedals. The idea of flying with the wind in my hair, in an aircraft that I could carry on my shoulder, fascinated me and I resolved to try it one day.

I discovered a fellow student at college who was a hang glider pilot and photographer. Mark Junak went to all the competitions and I persuaded him to take me along to Brighton to watch the British Hang Gliding League. They were flying at Beachy Head and as we rounded a corner on the approach to the cliffs, a host of multicoloured wings hung in the sky, looking like a swarm of butterflies around a buddleia bush. As we drew nearer, the definition increased and I could make out the pilots and their subtle movements as they steered their gliders around the sky. I desperately wanted to be up there, it looked so serene and, judging by the expressions of the pilots who landed, it was great fun!

It was almost two years later that I made my first high flight off the cliff in South Wales and had my first taste of the addiction which would change the direction of my life, and provide the challenge and fulfilment I had been searching for. At the time, I was at university in Cardiff doing a degree in nursing studies. I joined the hang gliding club and put my name down for the first available course. As the weekend approached, I felt like a child before Christmas, with the yearned-for day never seeming to get any nearer. Saturday morning finally arrived and I drove to Merthyr Tydfil, devouring the scenery of the narrow Welsh valleys with their tight rows of mining houses perched in clumps, each forming their own snug community.

The hang gliding school was based in an upstairs room in a terraced house, wallpapered with pictures of hang gliders and littered with sagging chairs. I sat impatiently while the instructor, Trevor Meacham, took us through an initial theory class before we could move on to the practical side of learning to fly. We finally loaded up the antiquated Land Rover, which belched and rattled its way up the hillside to the training slope of Bedlinog Hill. We were shown how to rig and pre-flight check the hang glider, then rope tethers were attached to the front and to each wing so that Trevor could control the glider if we did something wrong.

My first attempt did not fill me with the heady sensation I'd imagined. In fact I ended up dragging my knees through a cow pat at the bottom of the hill. The tedious process of hauling the sixty-pound glider back up the hill followed, ready to give the next person a go. It was slow, frustrating and undignified, but I loved it.

At the end of the weekend, having reached the heady altitude of ten feet, I returned to Cardiff with a huge grin on my face and an infatuation with flying, the power of which would obsess me for the rest of my life. I could not concentrate on my studies. My days were dominated by the weather forecasts on television and radio, and my mood would alter according to the improvement or deterioration in the prospects for flying at the weekend.

For months after gaining my Pilot One elementary certificate, I would hitch-hike to the school every Saturday morning to spend the weekend flying. The hardest part was always carrying the heavy and unwieldy wing back up to the top of the hill, ready to launch again, and because of this time-consuming business I would generally manage only five flights in a day. During the winter the snow did not stop me, though it made carrying the glider back up the hill even more difficult. At times I slumped under the weight of it, crying with frustration, having slipped for the umpteenth time in the snow as I struggled to haul the wing upwards. Somehow, when I had reached the top and recovered my breath, the half-minute flight back down the hill made all the effort worthwhile. I longed for the days when I would be able to ridge soar, using the wind to keep me above the hilltop until I decided to land. I yearned to be able to fly for hours rather than minutes, and to land back on the top of the hill from which I had taken off.

I was by no means a prodigy, or even a promising beginner. I was nervous and under-confident, always sceptical of my ability. I did not have the courage to launch myself unless Trevor was there, reassuring me each time that I could do it. He was endlessly patient with my frequent doubts and tirelessly encouraging, gradually giving me a glimmer of faith in my ability.

Three months after my first high flight, Trevor decided I was ready to fledge and encouraged me to go out flying with a university group, all of whom had already learned how to ridge soar. I progressed on to the university's Super Scorpion, a wing with starling performance compared with the beginner's glider, enabling me to stay aloft in light winds where before I would have sunk to the landing field at the bottom of the hill.

The first time I flew the new glider, I found myself suddenly rising above the ridge instead of dropping below it. I nudged the glider into a right-hand turn, straightening up to fly parallel to the face of the hill, and found myself soaring for the first time. An ear-to-ear grin spread across my face, though in spite of my excitement it did not feel natural and I was tense in the air, putting far too much effort into holding on. However, I will never forget that first feeling of elation at being above take-off and wafting freely about the sky.

I flew for half an hour and then attempted my first top landing. It almost ended in disaster as I approached too low over the road, aiming straight for a parked car. At the last moment I flew into a small patch of lift, which allowed my wingtip to clear the car roof by eighteen inches. My sigh of relief was immediately replaced by renewed terror as I saw a 'carpet' of high-performance hang gliders lying on the grass ahead of me, with only tiny spaces in between. In my peripheral vision I could see dozens of pilots looking on in horror, working out which of their prized 'hot ships' I was going to destroy on impact. With a second miracle in as many minutes I alighted in a minuscule clear patch between the gliders, to a spontaneous round of applause from the relieved onlookers. I was acutely embarrassed and sheepishly moved clear of their gliders. A sense of enormous achievement washed over me; I could fly, I could really fly!

The rest of the university group were apathetic about flying at weekends as they also wanted to do other things. I could not understand their lethargy as, consumed by my obsession, I wanted to spend every spare minute flying. As I did not have my own car or hang glider, I relied on club outings to be able to fly and my frustration was immense. A fellow flying addict, Richard Newton, came to the rescue. He had been through the school at the same time and, despite living in Southampton, travelled to Wales each Friday night to spend the weekend. He collected me and the university's Super Scorpion on his way through Cardiff and, regardless of the forecast, we would go to Merthyr, hoping to fly. It never mattered how bad the weather was, we were always on take off 'just in case'. There were many days when Richard's van would be nearly upended by a howling gale, or up to its axles in fast-falling snow, but we remained optimistic, with yet another cup of coffee in hand waiting for a glimmer of flyable weather.

Richard was one of the few people who took my dedication to flying seriously. There were hardly any women flying at that time; most of them had started because their boyfriends, husbands or brothers flew and they themselves were not particularly keen. Many of the pilots we met at the various flying sites would not discuss technical topics with me. It was frustrating and I could not understand their attitude.

Richard and I turned up on Pandy, a long easterly ridge near Abergavenny. Although the air was full of pilots wheeling around in the midday thermals, the wind was too strong for me to fly with my limited experience. My frustration was enormous as it looked so good and I desperately wanted to be up there. Mark Junak, my photographer friend, was on the hill and as he knew lots of top pilots, on impulse I asked him if he could get anyone to take me tandem. He found a volunteer in Sandy Fairgrieve, who had never taken anyone dual before but I didn't care. All I knew was that I was going to be up there, higher than I had ever been, secure in the knowledge that I could relax and trust the controls to someone who knew what he was doing.

The wind was strong as we walked to the edge with our harnesses clipped in side by side to Sandy's glider. With several people steadying the wing we launched smoothly, catapulted upwards by the rising air. Once away from the hilltop, Sandy glanced my way. Instead of finding me terrified, all he could see was teeth as my grin spread from ear to ear and remained so for the duration of the flight and throughout the following week.

I was flying properly for the first time, high and happy without the worry of whether I was handling the glider correctly. Feeling completely safe, I relaxed into the sensation of catching thermals and riding them ever upwards by turning a succession of 360-degree turns. Staring with disbelief at Sandy's altimeter, I saw we were over 2,500 feet above take-off.

I was baffled, as Sandy seemed to know where to find the thermals. It was cold and we were both shivering but I could have stayed there for ever. Sandy was tired after forty-five minutes wrestling with the gnarly spring turbulence and we came in to land back on top of the hill, alighting gently in the heather. Although I was on the ground, I was still walking on air, punch drunk.

As we walked back along the hill we met up with one of Sandy's friends, Brian Milton. I had read about him in the hang gliding magazines as the person who had started the Hang Gliding League, and who had instigated several international competitions. He was of medium height with a shock of unruly black hair, animated blue eyes and the voice of a sergeant major. Firing a staccato barrage of questions at Sandy about our flight, he asked him in a somewhat surprised manner, 'Why didn't you go for the British tandem cross-country distance record?'

The concept hadn't occurred to Sandy, but Brian was always pushing himself and others towards new goals.

I was unaware at that time what a significant part in my future success Brian would play. He has the gift of a vivid imagination and boundless energy, always approaching ideas with the attitude that any crazy plan that inspires him is possible, rather than looking for reasons why it might fail. His enthusiasm is coupled with an ability to inspire others and pull them along in his wake.

His words rang in my ears and I became excited at the prospect of the record. Cross-country flying was a distant 'nirvana', a concept I had only dreamed of. The idea of using thermals and the wind to carry me as far away from take-off as possible seemed magical, but first I had to learn the basics. Sandy, however, was an expert and as a tandem pair, my role would be simply to hang on and watch. I was game to try it, but more than anything I just wanted to go up again and fly.

Goaded by Brian's enthusiasm we took off again to try for the record. This time we spent over an hour above the ridge, but the conditions had worsened and we could not get enough height to fly cross-country. Eventually the cold became so debilitating that we had to land back at take-off and Sandy decided not to try again.

Having learned so much from my flights with Sandy, I flew solo from Pandy a few days later and felt brave enough to try my first circles. They were more like notchy hexagons as I hesitantly coaxed the glider round, but the sensation was fantastic as the glider responded to my weight shifting, banking gently as the world revolved around me.

My first accident happened soon afterwards at Merthyr when I made my first solo 'prone' flight. I had learned to fly seated in a webbing and wood harness, rather like a child's swing slung under the glider. The conversion to the more fashionable method of prone flying involved lying face down on an apron-shaped hammock. The more aerodynamic position felt much more 'bird-like' and I flew for half an hour, enjoying the feeling of lying on my belly. I decided to land at my take-off point and flew back over the flat top of the ridge. In the changeover from flying seated to flying prone, the position of the control bar changes and the sensation is quite different and disorientating. I failed to apply my basic theory of feeling the pressure of the bar to tell me the speed of the glider and I slowed it down too much, causing the wing tip to stall. From thirty feet the glider dived sideways and there was a sickening crunch as I hit the ground.

I felt a sharp pain in my right leg and there was no disguising this injury as I couldn't walk and needed help to hop to the car. At the local hospital the porter wheeling me into X-ray took one look at my leg and declared it broken, but I have been blessed with strong and sturdy bones and after the radiologist had thoroughly examined the X-ray plates, I was sent home with my leg intact. The bruising was spectacular. It stretched from knee to hip, turning every colour imaginable, and has left me with a permanent 'dent' in my thigh.

Despite being unable to put much weight on my leg, I went flying again the following weekend. The northwesterly facing ridge at Tredegar had a tiny landing area and my confidence had taken a battering. After half an hour's flying, my leg was numb with the support plate of the prone harness pressing directly on my bruise. I needed to land, but was too afraid to go far enough back to lose height to bring me in to the landing area. Finally, after an hour and a half, in desperation I shouted to the pilots on the ground, 'I can't get down!'

Having watched me overshoot on several occasions, the experienced pilots on the hill realised my plight and waved at me to go further back. Grateful for their help, I followed the hand signals and went much further back than I had before and quickly lost height, landing gently on top of the hill. After resting for a while, I limped self-consciously back to my car.

It seemed always to be a case of two steps forward, one step back as I progressed and then had an incident which dented my fragile confidence. Accidents were usually my fault, but one that really shook me was a mid-air collision with a model aircraft. The man controlling it was practising aerobatics and looped it directly underneath me, so that it hit the two front wires of my glider right in front of my face. Had the wing span of the model been six inches less, it would have missed my glider wires and hit me straight in the face. My hands went automatically to protect my head as the model exploded two feet in front of me. I was flying very close to the hill and my wingtip hit, swinging me head first into the slope. I bruised my face and split my lip. The model glider flier ran down the hill in search of his plane without coming to see if I was injured and was overheard later in the pub boasting of how he had made a hang glider crash.

I desperately wanted to buy my own hang glider. On the rare occasions when other club members came out to fly at the weekend, I had to share the precious Super Scorpion and I hated having to stay on the ground. The university holidays were coming up, so I decided to forego the travelling which I loved in order to work through the summer and earn enough to buy my own glider.

Before the summer holidays I had to take end of year exams. My studies had suffered badly as my obsession for hang gliding had grown. I had always relied on last minute cramming to get me through exams, but the lure of the skies was too strong and I was no longer interested in obtaining a nursing degree. When I went to sit my pharmacology exam, I couldn't answer a single question, which was no surprise as I hadn't even looked at a textbook during the term. It was a new experience for me as I had never failed an exam before. As we emerged afterwards, I knew for certain that even with the help of a miracle I could not have reached the pass mark.

The truth was that I didn't care. I had become a train on a single track with unstoppable momentum, all my energy focused on which hang glider to buy and where that money was going to come from.

I had never settled at university and, apart from my flying, I was desperately unhappy. Prior to starting my course I had spent three months in America, hitch-hiking along the West Coast, returning to New York with two weeks to fill before my flight home. I arrived at Grand Central Station with nowhere to stay and met a group of friendly young people who offered me a bed for the night. Naively, I accepted.

From the moment I arrived at their house I was never left alone and my every waking moment was shadowed. Their friendliness appeared genuine, but the pressure became more sinister as the days went by. They belonged to a cult called the Church of Bible Understanding and at its head was a grey-haired patriarch. His followers at the grassroots level were sincere and led Christian lives, helping others and having very little money, but the higher echelons of the cult were hard-bitten and kept control by brainwashing.

The first few days I stayed with them willingly; they were friendly and welcoming and I happily became part of the group. Each time that I became restless at my lack of freedom, one of my 'friends' would produce a passage from the Bible to show how it was the devil working in me and how I must resist this negativity. The power of this brainwashing was immense and fast acting. I became heavily involved and they put a lot of pressure on me to stay with them and to cancel my ticket home.

It was an old friend who finally helped me snap out of it. I had met him when I first arrived in the States and he was appalled, when we met up again, at my state of confusion and unhappiness. He knew that the only way to rid me of their vice-like grip was physically to distance them from me and he made me promise that I would return to England. I caught my plane home the following week, but a fortnight within a religious sect had had a profound impact.

Although I had left the immediate source of their power, the aftermath of the brainwashing I received stayed with me for nearly two years. I did not fit in when I got home and felt remote from my family and my friends. University life, instead of being the enlightening, friendship-forming, enriching experience I had anticipated, became miserable and lonely. I developed bulimia during this time as I struggled with the confusion I felt inside. This only served to make things worse, as my self-respect plummeted. It was only when I started flying, and had a new and powerful direction to my life, that I could finally banish the influence of the cult.

I did fail my pharmacology exam and returned home from university for the holidays to find a summer job at Heathrow Airport with Fernley Aeroclean, a company which cleaned the inside of aeroplanes. The work was hard but the pay was good and, with the 'carrot' of my own hang glider as my reward, I happily threw myself into the business of sweeping aeroplane floors, cleaning the galleys and emptying ashtrays and rubbish bins.

After two weeks, the receptionist in the office left and, as I could answer the phone, type and do invoices, I was stationed there for the rest of the time. Over the following month I got to know the manager of the operation, who offered me a full-time job as Trainee Operations Manager with a good salary, a company car and a reasonable amount of time off.

This coincided with the arrival of an irate letter from my head of department asking what I was going to do about my dismal pharmacology result. The decision was easy and in a matter of seconds I accepted the job at Fernley's and wrote a letter of resignation to the nursing department in Cardiff. My parents were very supportive, as they knew how unhappy I had been at university, and the following Monday morning I started full-time work.

CHAPTER 2

Spreading My Wings

The feeling of freedom from the pressure of studying and exams was immense and I revelled in the fact that my spare time meant that I could pursue my love of hang gliding without feeling guilty about neglecting my studies. As my financial situation improved, I scoured the pages of *Wings* – the British hang gliding magazine – looking for a suitable beginner's hang glider. I finally opted for a second-hand British-built Cherokee with a chocolate-brown sail, an orange stripe and white wingtips, costing £400. My flying friends thought it a hideous colour but, like a mother with a newborn baby, to me it was the most beautiful glider I had ever seen. I fixed an aluminium ladder to the roof-rack of my company car, padded it copiously with foam and pieces of carpet to protect my new acquisition, and proudly brought it home.

The chocolate Cherokee and I spent many happy hours soaring coastal sites and drifting over the Black Mountains of southern Wales on my days off work. My learning curve was steep and I was finally gaining confidence . I went to Mere in Somerset for the annual hang gliding get together, where the festive atmosphere was rapturously filled with talk of thermals, glider design and endless flying stories.

I entered the 'glide angle' competition in which two pilots took off together and flew out from the hill in a straight line, and the one who went the furthest was the winner, going on to the next round. My knowledge of aerodynamics was pitifully small, and in my ignorance, I thought the way to go further was to fly more slowly. I took off at the same time as my opponent, easing out the control bar, pushing my glider dangerously close to a stall. The air was turbulent with punchy spring thermals and I hit a particularly violent gust.

The nose dropped suddenly, tipping the glider fully vertical. I found myself diving at high speed and felt undiluted terror at being out of control and seeing the ground rising up towards me. I let out an involuntary yell as the glider gathered momentum, then suddenly, with a sharp lurch, it righted itself and continued flying, docile and nonchalant as though nothing had happened.

Gingerly I held on to the bar, not knowing why the dive had happened and fearing that the glider would do it again. I landed trembling, thankful for once to be on the ground. After an explanation from one of the three hundred pilots who had watched my involuntary display, I realised that I had stalled the glider by slowing it down too much. It had been a salutary, but thankfully painless, lesson.

I started flying at a time when training schools were well established. Up until the mid-1970s, if you wanted to hang glide it was a case of making your own glider or buying a kit and learning to fly it by trial and error. For this reason there were lots of fatalities in the early days of hang gliding. With my level of ignorance of aviation theory, I would probably have contributed to those statistics had I not been taught by a school.

I desperately wanted to fit in, to be able to blend in with the flying crowd and be accepted as a pilot without being treated differently because I was a woman. It was important to prove that I could be completely self-sufficient in flying and give no one the chance to say I wasn't up to it. During these early years, I would refuse on principle any offer of help to carry my glider, a rule for which my lumbar spine would end up paying dearly.

The effort I put in for each flight was huge compared with the amount of airtime gained. One of my logbook entries for 1 March 1980 reads: 'Walked up Blorenge (1,800 feet) – rigged – ran – aborted – de-rigged – walked down.'

In January 1981, Brian Milton proposed that a women's competition take place alongside the British League, which comprised the top forty-five pilots in Britain. The normal entry qualification for the League was to be in the top ten of the cross-country table in which pilots enter their best three distances flown during the previous year, but no women had ever reached that standard. Brian has great foresight and recognised the need to give women's hang gliding a boost by encouraging them to compete. That year he set up a separate women's division.

Five women turned up to the first competition in Osmotherley near the North Yorkshire Moors. We found ourselves on Carlton Bank, an imposing northerly ridge, surrounded by all our heroes whose faces we recognised from the pages of *Wings* magazine. Several of the pilots made an effort to make us feel welcome and helped us with tactics.

Jenny Ganderton, who was my age and a geophysicist from London, was flying a medium Typhoon whose performance was way above the gliders flown by the remaining four of us. There had been a quantum leap in hang glider design earlier that year and Jenny had boldly plumped for one of the new generation of wings while the rest of us timidly stuck to our old designs. She floated round the course effortlessly while we struggled to stay up. During two out of the five tasks, I sank to the bottom of the hill, frustrated but with my learning curve becoming steeper with every flight. I had never pushed myself to see how far I could go, or made myself fly out from the ridge and risk going down. I had always played safe and stuck to the comfort of the area around take-off. I was amazed at what I could do with my glider – to fly out to a distant church and come back to the ridge, or to fly so far along the hill that I lost sight of take-off. It was impressive to watch the experts fly to see what was possible.

In the following edition of *Wings* magazine there was one sentence mentioning the fact that five women had competed, but there was no comment about our flying or our results – a symptom of the times. Hang gliding was still definitely a man's world. Jenny was the clear winner and was tipped to be the first woman pilot to succeed in competition flying. I came third and returned with my head full of new ideas and feeling overawed by just how much I had to learn.

I knew I would have to change my glider for one of the new generation with better performance. The constant dilemma that dogged all small pilots was which size of glider to fly. The average hang glider pilot was male, six feet tall and weighed eleven stone. The gliders designed with this in mind were large, heavy and difficult for a lighter pilot to turn. Occasionally, a manufacturer would try to bring out a small wing, but the designers and test pilots would still be heavy and tall, so it would not be competitive but more of a 'toy', with easy handling but inferior per-formance.

My next glider was one of the latter type – a small Comet. Our relation-ship had an inauspicious start when I went to the Isle of Wight to test fly it. I had been working the night shift and went straight from Heathrow Airport to Southampton to catch the ferry, kept awake by the thought of test flying my new hot ship. My first flight was very short: there was no lift and I sank straight to the bottom. I de-rigged and went back for another go. The second try was better and as the wind had increased I was able to soar above the cliffs.

I became intoxicated by the performance of the new wing and flew off along the ridge, not noticing how much height I was losing, nor how the cliffs curved round and were no longer facing into the wind. By the time I turned around to come back, there was no lift and I sank down to the beach below, landing up to my shins in sticky, oily mud. Having found a clear piece of sand to de-rig, I was then dismayed to find there was no route up the 300-foot sheer cliff and had to walk for an hour before I found some steps leading to the clifftop. Undeterred, I rigged again and took off into the smooth air, this time staying close to take-off, having learned my lesson. When I finally went to land at the bottom I was so tired that I completely misjudged the approach and had to make some radical turns to avoid a dry-stone wall, only to find myself heading for the fence on the far side. Ouch! Despite the over-exciting events of the day, I was more than convinced of the glider's superior performance and placed my order.

With my updated equipment, my thoughts turned to cross-country flying. I had watched pilots in South Wales circling upwards in thermals and getting blown along with the wind as they climbed. Instead of heading back to the security of the take-off ridge, they would head off into the unknown in search of more thermals to carry them further, never knowing where they would land or whom they might meet.

The idea of aerial orienteering fascinated me. I had already learned a great deal about where thermals came from, the effect of differently shaped ridges and how to judge the potential of a thermal from the shape of the cumulus cloud above it. The idea of using this knowledge to make decisions which, if wrong, would force me to land, but if right, could lead to great adventures, was an exciting prospect. I resolved to 'go for it' at the next opportunity.

It was May 1981 and I had forty hours of airtime noted in my logbook when the chance came for my first cross-country. It was fitting that it should be from the same site as my first high flight, Merthyr Common. I caught a strong thermal and circled tightly to stay inside it. I climbed quickly, being blown further over the back of the hill with each turn. It was decision time – pull forward now and make it back to take-off, or carry on and commit to the unknown. With a huge surge of excitement, I pushed the glider into the next turn and was on my way.

One and a half miles downwind of Merthyr was Bedlinog, where I had done most of my training. I could see Trevor teaching his latest group of students to do their first short flights and as I reached 700 feet above take-off, I turned downwind and flew towards them. I was still high above Bedlinog when I pulled out and landed on top of the slope, alongside the students. I was so thrilled I thought I would burst.

My new addiction for cross-country flying was insatiable. I read about it, studied the weather and daydreamed constantly. I went 'over the back' several more times during the following month, never leaving the hill with more than 1,000 feet as I could not contain my enthusiasm and wait until I was at cloudbase. The result was a series of small distances, each accompanied by huge elation, whether I had flown four miles or ten. My ambition was one day to manage 'the big one', a long-distance flight which would involve using several thermals and staying airborne for hours on end. Before I could hope to achieve this, I had to learn to be patient. I would have to curb my eagerness and take the time to study the sky downwind to decide if the clouds looked good, using judgement rather than trusting to luck.

That summer, Fernley Aeroclean opened a new branch at Gatwick Airport and I moved down to Crawley in Sussex. Living near the South Downs I could go flying after work, or, if working night shifts, I could take a quick nap and be on Devil's Dyke as the thermals started. The hours at Gatwick were long as I was working twelve-hour shifts, and the stress was intense.

My relief from work was to go flying. It was very different to arrive at the Southern Hang Gliding Club as a competent pilot. Although greeted at first with scepticism, I was soon given the benefit of the doubt and for the first time was treated as a pilot first and a woman second. I still retained my umbilical ties with South Wales and each time I had more than one day off I would drive the three-hour journey to the familiar Black Mountains.

I began to dabble with the idea of sponsorship. Although I didn't fully understand how it worked, having someone else pay for my equipment in return for advertising was appealing. After some negotiations, I managed to get Air Europe to buy me a harness, branded with their logo, and in return had some publicity photographs taken with my hang glider rigged under the wing of one of their aircraft.

Richard Newton and I went to France for two weeks in August in search of some intensive thermalling experience. With two other pilots and all our gear crammed into Richard's long-suffering camper van, we set off for the mountains on the southern edge of the Alps. We flew at Lachens, a steep ridge with strong thermals and plenty of turbulence. The technique for flying cross-country was very different from the system I had learned in Britain. In many ways it was easier, as the valley winds and thermal-producing areas behaved exactly as they were supposed to according to the textbooks. Most of my flights were less than an hour long as each day I made a fresh mistake and went down, having learned something new.

Many of my landings were less than perfect in the rough thermic air, but by now I had perfected the art of avoiding injury by deftly holding back and letting the glider take the force. Richard's landings were better than mine and when one day the wind switched direction and he came racing in downwind, he did not have the same injury-prevention technique and hit his leg on a rock, cutting his knee badly. I took him to the local doctor to act as translator, only to find that during our drive to the surgery, another pilot had flown into the electricity cables and, although unhurt, had caused a power cut in the whole valley. The doctor had to clean and stitch Richard's wound with a miner's lamp stuck to his forehead. Richard and I got the giggles at the ludicrous situation, and even the doctor had to laugh.

As the doctor could not see to clean the wound properly, it was no surprise that Richard's knee became infected and within a few days became stiffer and more swollen. We were due to return home and the doctor, concerned for Richard's health, told him to call in at a hospital on the outskirts of Paris. We arrived the following afternoon and as we walked into the clinic a hostile nurse looked us up and down with distaste. We were dressed in cut-off jeans and T-shirts, hardly a picture of Parisian chic. Richard was limping very badly by now, his injured knee covered with a grubby bandage. Issuing terse instructions, the nurse presented Richard with an anal thermometer! Hopping is not generally associated with speed, but even on two good legs I had a job to keep up with him as he bolted for the door. He decided that the inconvenience of waiting a few hours in pain until we arrived back in Britain would be well worth it.

I returned from France restless and discontented. My longing to be able to fly well had been given a jolt by our trip to the mountains, where I had realised how much there was to learn. I had gained experience which I could not get in the British hills and there were gaping holes in my knowledge. I needed more mountain-flying experience. Work was going from bad to worse, with the resentful atmosphere palpable amongst the cleaners who were constantly being driven to work harder. I decided it was time to move on.

A friend from Brighton knew someone who flew hang gliders in Kitz-bühel. I had never been to that part of the Alps, but it sounded fun and a good place to start. In early January I left Fernley Aeroclean without remorse, bought an old estate car with the remainder of my meagre savings, packed my bags, strapped my hang glider to the roof, bought a road map of Europe and left for Austria.

CHAPTER 3

Reaching New Heights

I arrived at 3 a.m. on the German–Austrian border with no Austrian money or petrol. I had no option but to wait for the bureau de change to open. I parked outside, climbed into the back seat of the car and crawled into my new sleeping bag, pulling the draw-string tight around my neck against the biting cold of the winter air. I slept deeply after hours of non-stop driving while outside the black night sky was teeming with fat snowflakes.

Some time later, I was shocked into consciousness by a blinding light and deafening noise. As my sleep-numbed brain fought to piece together the scene, I realised that I was blocking the tiny road alongside the bank and that a snow plough was trying to clear it. Finding his route barred, the driver had advanced to within an inch of my front bumper, switched his lights to full beam and was leaning on the horn. My fingers fumbled with the string, succeeding only in tightening the bow into a knot. The more I fought to loosen it, the more securely it fastened itself. I managed to get one arm out of the opening while the absurdity of the scene struck me and I started giggling. The more I laughed, the more incapable I became. The tapered sleeping bag prevented any movement of my feet, but I finally managed to slither over into the driver's seat and, with uncoordinated toe twitches on the pedals, kangaroo-hopped the car backwards into a lay-by.

It was mid-morning by the time I arrived in Kirchberg in the heart of Tirol, a picture-postcard Austrian village nestled in the valley alongside Kitzbühel. Every overhanging roof was heavy with its cap of new snow and the streets were already busy with skiers walking with stiff gaits to the lift stations past hunched old men beginning the methodical shovelling of their pathways.

I made my way to the address on the tatty piece of paper that had been given to me in Brighton and arrived at Helmut Lorenzoni's bakery, one of the best-known tourist attractions in Kirchberg, popular among visitors and locals alike. Lorenzoni's make the best cakes in the world; it is a family establishment where Helmut and his wife run the café and bakery with help from their daughter Beate and son, Helmut junior. Both father and son fly hang gliders and they took it in their stride when I walked in and introduced myself, offering me a place to stay until I found a job.

The snow-capped peaks of the surrounding mountains beckoned and I took my hang glider to the cable car and emerged on top of the Hannenkam. Helmut had told me about the wooden ramp, built specially for the hang glider pilots to take off from. I had seen someone flying down earlier, found the place in the fresh snow where a set of footprints disappeared down the slope and brushed away the powder to reveal the wood beneath. I had never seen a ramp before and had no idea how to use one.

A steep ramp is a tremendous help in alpine conditions as the pilot has only to stand at the top, angle the glider's nose downwards and run down the ramp, letting gravity do the work of accelerating the glider quickly, ensuring a clean launch. By now I had flown in every type of weather that Britain had to offer and considered myself a pilot of experience. I knew that the still wind conditions of a ski resort would require a hard take-off run, but I did not know how to use the ramp to help gain the required speed.

I rigged the glider and moved back from the slope to the far side of the ski piste, giving me a fifty foot run up to the ramp. I ran hard, noticing immediately the leaden feel of the glider on my shoulders. Normally it would start to carry its own weight at once, allowing me to build up speed, but this was different. The seventy-five pounds of awkward aluminium sat as a dead weight on my shoulders and felt wrong. I had learned long ago that if a take-off felt a little dodgy, the one thing that could often salvage the situation was to run harder.

I pushed the glider towards the edge and threw myself off. Without sufficient airspeed for the glider to fly, it stalled, executed a graceful arc and deposited me face first in the snow.

At this stage the most sensible move would have been to ask a local pilot for advice, but I have a stubborn streak and loathe being defeated. I decided that my mistake was in not running hard enough. By now a crowd of skiers had gathered to watch as I hauled my glider back up the steep slope, wading through the thigh-deep snow. This time I moved even further back from the ramp, giving myself an almighty long run along the flat. With nostrils flaring, and mustering all the ferocity of a raging bull, I pounded the snow, focusing all my efforts on attaining take-off speed before I reached the edge.

Again, the glider sat on my shoulders, obstinately refusing to carry even its own weight, let alone mine. In a slightly exaggerated repetition of my first effort, I again swung back into the slope, but because of the extra speed, I impacted even further down the hill.

Shaking my head with incomprehension, I dragged the glider back up to the start. The crowd were enjoying themselves, laughing and taking pictures while I struggled. There was only one thing for it – yet more speed. Backing right up against the slope on the far side of the piste, I gathered my strength for 'the big one'. Taking a deep breath, I hurtled towards the edge like a thing possessed. Galloping across the piste, I ran as fast as my short legs, large glider and fresh snow would allow. As I leaped into space I had a brief moment of hope before the feeling of *déjà vu* as the glider began its inexorable turn to the left. With my extra momentum I hit the mountainside 150 feet down with a force sufficient to break one of the uprights. The incline felt nearly vertical and the snow was waist deep. I had to 'swim' round the glider to de-rig, taking care not to lose any of the battens in the soft powder snow.

The crowd had lost interest and dispersed, except for one man who skiied down to help me. Sigi Knoll lived at the bottom of the Hannenkam and was also a keen hang glider pilot. He had watched my antics, loth to interfere, and appeared an unlikely knight in shining armour, being short in stature, in his late thirties and with an impish grin.

Sigi, having flown many times in Britain, was aware of the different take-off technique required and was able to point out the error of my ways. I had not realised that my British method of accelerating along the flat would never work in the thinner, still air of an alpine launch.

The other members of the Kitzbühel Hang Gliding Club assumed I was incompetent. I felt I was back in the days of 1979, as they had no proficient women pilots in the club and my three consecutive failed take-offs put me into the 'hopeless case' category. Thanks to some intensive tuition from Sigi, I never again failed a ramp take-off. He taught me to start running at the top of the ramp and to hold the glider with its nose much lower than I had on my disastrous first day.

I needed to find a job through the remaining three months of the ski season to finance my flying through the summer. I enquired at many of the hotels and restaurants in Kirchberg and Kitzbühel but, being January, their posts for waitresses and chambermaids had already been filled at the beginning of the season.

Sigi came up trumps with a job in the restaurant on top of the Steinbergkogel, a 6,000-foot mountain next to the Hannenkam. The following day, I packed my things and loaded them on to the cable car. From there, the snow scooter dragged my bag, guitar and hang glider in a sled up to the restaurant. The only way to get to it other than by using the snow scooter was by skiing down from the Hannenkam and then catching the chairlift to the Steinbergkogel summit.

As I couldn't speak much German, I wasn't able to help at the self-service counter and was given the job of clearing tables instead. It was hard work, as the lift started depositing the first skiers on the mountain top at 8 a.m. and didn't close until late. I have never minded working hard and the location more than compensated for it. Being perched on top of a spine back ridge, the views in all directions were stunning. Every evening after cleaning up and mopping the floor, I would don my moon boots and down jacket and walk out to watch the sunset, never tiring of the soft orange spangling snow and the elongating shadows of the mountains.

My bedroom was upstairs on the corner of the building, with south- and east-facing windows giving me a view overlooking the highest mountain in Austria, the Grossglockner. Within days I knew the sequence in which the sun caressed the summits in the morning, colouring each in turn with a rich pink mountain glow.

When the wind was favourable, I was able to fly from the ridge just ten paces from the restaurant door, soar above the Steinbergkogel for as long as my numb, cold-nipped fingers and face would allow, and then glide down into the valley below, landing by the cable car where I would leave my glider to be taken up the following morning. I had torn some strips of material which I attached to all the piste markers outside the restaurant to show me what the wind was doing. About twice a week it blew at a perfect strength for soaring the ridge and I would start to twitch and sigh, looking longingly out of the window. The restaurant owner knew my mind would not be on the job and so, if we were not too busy, she would shake her head with incomprehension and let me go flying. It was always good for business, as a crowd of skiers would stop to watch, taking the opportunity to drink and eat at the restaurant with a grandstand view of take-off.

Although the wages were poor, it was easy to save because I was living on the mountain and there was nothing on which to spend my money. Once a week I would venture out with the other four employees, usually to one of the mountain huts where the shepherds live in summer, or to one of the mountain hotels. If the moon provided some light, we would ski down and spend the evening drinking schnapps. There were always some local Tiroleans with their accordion or guitar who needed little persuasion to start the music. Sometimes a couple of toothless old men would yodel in harmony with glazed eyes while the incongruously high-pitched voice emanated from their throats.

I spent three months on the mountain until the ski season ended. The snows melted, replacing the monochrome landscape with one of lush green dotted with alpine flowers. With a modest amount saved and a passable command of German, thanks to constant exposure to the language, I moved down to the valley, rented a room at the local hang gliding school and bought myself a season ticket for the cable car.

Each flyable day I would be up on the Hannenkam, honing my cross-country skills, thermalling up and away to explore the peaks and venture as far from Kitzbühel as I could. When I landed I hitch-hiked back to my car at the bottom of the Hannenkam and drove out to collect my glider. It was a glorious way of touring the Tirol, and of meeting the local farmers, who were invariably friendly, fit and lean with ruddy complexions from the wholesome mountain air.

In May I entered my first international competition – the Tirolean World Masters, held in Kössen on the Austrian–German border. Many of the world's top pilots were among the thirty-five competitors and I was awe-struck at being in such distinguished company and to have the opportunity to fly alongside so many of my heroes. As with the British League, there was a great camaraderie among the hang glider pilots and they welcomed me in their midst. Sadly, there were only two women competing, a pattern that would not change for many years.

The area was typically Tirolean and the trip up the mountain each morning lulled me into a dream-like state as I sat on the chairlift moving above a carpet of wild flowers with only the sound of the crickets and the dull clonking of cowbells interrupting the silence. Conditions were perfect and we flew every day with high cloudbases and turbulent air. On the fourth day Lorenzoni's bakery was hosting a party for the pilots and the task set was a race to Kirchberg. I was sixth across the line and was ecstatic at my best result ever. Helmut junior, desperate to be first into his home town, had landed short of goal. Bitter at being beaten by a woman, he didn't speak to me for three days, but nothing could dampen my enthusiasm. At the end of the contest, Gerard Thevenot of France claimed first place and I finished thirteenth overall and was absolutely thrilled.

Most of the top pilots were driving down to Italy to fly near Lake Como in another competition and I needed little persuasion to go along with them to fly as 'wind dummy', taking off before the competitors to show that conditions were good. I was learning so much in the company of these experienced flyers and was sponging up all the information available about thermalling techniques and glider tuning.

The area around Como was very different from Austria, with poor visibility and huge lakes to cross without being able to see the other side. There was often nowhere to land, just an intimidating web of railways, roads, trees and power lines.

As wind dummy, I took off first while the swifts ricocheted around launch, feeding on the insects carried aloft by the rising air in the best thermals. Each day the task was the same – open cross-country – to fly as far as possible in any direction. Every day I learned from my mistakes and flew a little further.

On the final day of the competition, it all came together and I had my longest flight ever. I was airborne for four and a half hours, during which I flew fifty miles, across the border and into Switzerland. By the time I was nearing the end of the flight I was physically and mentally exhausted. Before take-off, I had tightened up the leading edges of my glider, having watched the other pilots do this to make their gliders fly better. Unfortunately, my glider was already too big for me and tightening up the sail made it a real handful to turn. My arms were so tired I could barely steer for the last part of the flight and with the effort of concentrating for over four hours I could not think straight. The wind was increasing as I flew into a dead-end gully, knowing I would have to land. I flew past many huge fields, big enough to land a jumbo jet in but, fixated on covering the maximum distance and robbed by fatigue of the ability to think clearly, I continued towards the tiny field at the end of the valley. The air grew more turbulent as I neared the ground and I found myself committed to land in a small triangular field with trees lining one side. I flew downwind along the line of trees and was tipped violently towards them. My reactions were too slow and I clipped one of the trees with my wingtip.

I fell thirty feet. Crashing into the ground with a thud, I was badly winded and was soon surrounded by a crowd of excited, Italian-speaking

Swiss, who were determined to stand me up. My only goal at that stage was somehow to gain a breath of air, but gasping like a gaffed salmon, I could not communicate this to them.

My leg was hurt and swollen, but I did not want to go to hospital as I could not speak a word of the local language. I managed to hobble to a nearby house, where a kind lady made me a cup of tea while I phoned for retrieve. Two other competitors came to pick me up and de-rigged my glider. I had damaged it extensively, having fallen through the sail and broken several of the tubes.

It was two days before I managed to get a lift back to Austria. I went to the hospital in Kitzbühel, where they tried to put my leg in plaster, but as it wasn't broken I refused, preferring just to rest it until the pain and swelling subsided. During the following two weeks, I had plenty of time for reflection.

In 1982 the women's world distance record stood at sixty miles, set in Owens Valley, California. I had flown fifty miles in less than perfect conditions and, for the first time, I realised that breaking the world record was within my capability.

My obsessive nature took over. I became like a terrier with a bone and would not let go. I wanted the women's world distance record and it was like a fire burning within me, driving me forward. My life became focused on that target.

I had spent my savings and needed to work again in order to pay for my trip to California. My parents had for some time been trying to persuade me to join the family jewellery importing business. They must have been frustrated to see me drifting around with no useful trade and little income. I felt their offer would mean choosing between flying and working in the business. When I phoned from Austria after my accident, again they offered me a position but this time they made it clear that I could continue with my passion for hang gliding and have the best of both worlds: they would give me two months off the following summer to go out to Owens Valley to attempt the world record.

My father has always said that I am the world's greatest exponent of having my cake and eating it. I certainly hate to make a choice between two things I desire until every avenue has been exhausted that might allow me to have both. Their proposal formed the perfect solution for me, allowing me to save the money I needed for the trip and then to have the necessary time off to try for the record in California. Within a month I was home from Austria and installed at Leden-Imco Ltd, learning the business of selling jewellery.

My father took me to Thailand on his next buying trip so that I could learn the ropes. Our suppliers naturally assumed that I would one day take over the business as is normally the way in Thai culture. Bangkok was a frenzied city, though individually the people are gentle and polite. I was enchanted by the colourful shrines on street corners surrounded by the heady fragrance of jasmine and the extravagant colours of myriad orchids lining the altars.

Our frenetic schedule saw us rushing between suppliers, trying to remember which new samples we had seen where. It was an education to watch Dad at work. He had spent years growing to understand the culture and the way to do business with Thai people and spent long chunks of our precious time verbally 'fan dancing', discussing their families, Bangkok traffic and business in general. We drank endless tea from ornate cups and only after these preliminaries had been performed and a polite interval left, did we gently move on to the problems incurred since the last visit. I watched in amazement as Dad delicately pointed out that the last shipment of silver goods was not saleable because they had used non-silver solder to attach the earring pins. He had been hopping mad at the time and yet managed to show only a hint of displeasure in his voice. As the days passed, so my admiration for Dad grew because of his appreciation of Thai sensitivities, and of the way he had adapted to suit their customs. As a result all our suppliers had a great deal of respect for him and always tried to give him their best service.

I enjoyed working in the business and there was always lots to do. Dad put me in charge of selling and gave me a great deal of autonomy. I was free to arrange my selling trips so that I could visit customers in the Lake District or Wales on a Friday and then spend the weekend flying. I always travelled with the hang glider on the roof and gained experience of lots of different flying sites.

I was eager to find a sponsor to fund my trip to Owens Valley with the aim of extending the sponsorship afterwards to include the following twelve months. I was acutely aware that no company would back me without a return on their investment. If a sports person ranks highly in a mainstream sport like athletics or tennis, they will naturally generate media coverage for their sponsors. For the minority sports, however, this just isn't the case. Hang glider pilots cannot guarantee a potential sponsor that they will receive television and newspaper coverage, no matter how well they do in competitions. Ironically the only way publicity is certain is if the pilot is involved in a major accident, especially if he or she is killed.

To increase my chances, I needed a track record of media coverage and until then the only articles in my scrapbook were a few features in the local press. I decided to do a 'balloon drop', which involves suspending a hang glider beneath a hot air balloon, and towing it up to 3,000 feet. The balloon pilot then cuts the cord, at which point the glider enters a dramatic nose dive to build up speed before righting itself and flying normally. Although it had nothing to do with my record attempt, it would generate media coverage, as I would announce it as being part of my training programme for the high-altitude flying in California. I teamed up with balloon pilot Paul Frewer, who had dropped a hang glider before, and he agreed to fly me, scheduling the drop for January 1983.

On the morning of the flight, the airfield near Wolverhampton was bleak and featureless, though the sky was clear. BBC Breakfast Television arrived to film us, having hired a small plane from which to record the action. Paul was pessimistic about our chances of flying, as the wind was strong, gusting over ten miles an hour. I set up my glider for the cameras anyway and he started to inflate the balloon. To my surprise Paul came over half an hour later with thirty-foot length of rope, telling me to tie the hang glider onto one end.

There is always a tremendous amount of pressure when a film crew has come out on site. The cost of the manpower together with their equipment is huge and it is terribly hard to tell them that the event is not going to happen because of bad weather. If it is foggy or pouring with rain it is easier for them to understand, but winds that are too strong for such slow aircraft as hang gliders are much harder to explain, especially if it is a fine day.

The wind on this occasion was significantly above the safe limit for a balloon drop, especially as it was my first one, but the presence of the TV cameras pressured our decision. Bowing to Paul's greater experience (he had, after all, dropped a hang glider once before), I attached the rope to the centre of the hang glider's keel in a figure of eight and knotted it tightly.

Every spare person around had been enlisted to restrain the balloon, which was pulling at its tethers, anxious to leave the ground. I put my harness on and clipped into the glider. Luckily two friends had arrived to help me and they steadied the wing as I moved the glider alongside the balloon and Paul attached the other end of my rope to the balloon's basket.

The effect of such a strong wind was alarming. In spite of eight people standing on the balloon basket to weigh it down, the whole ensemble dragged at frightening speed across the airfield. As I was now attached to it, I had to chase after the balloon as fast as my encumbering suit, harness and glider would allow. I prayed we would lift off soon, as I could not run any faster.

At that moment, Paul shouted 'Release!' and the eight people, who were effectively acting as ballast, jumped off the sides of the basket. The balloon rocketed upwards like a cork in a bathtub and the force of the ascent ripped my hands off the control bar.

It was a relief to be safely airborne and the ground fell away quickly, revealing the subtle colours of the landscape subdued by a thick layer of frost. The ascent to 3,000 feet was fast and we then levelled out before Paul started to descend in order to prevent the shock on the balloon when he released my weight. This would also reduce the rotation of the hang glider during the drop as at the point of release, the glider has no air flowing over it and is fully stalled. This makes it rotate violently until it is in a vertical dive and can gather enough speed to make the wing fly.

As he started the countdown, my heart was in my mouth. I had heard accounts of balloon drops and I knew that the glider would rotate violently and enter a steep dive upon release. The only question in my mind was, will the glider's in-built dive recovery features prevent it from over-rotating, somersaulting and breaking?

Paul's countdown seemed agonisingly slow and my heart threatened to pound its way through the side of my chest. Finally he came to '... two ... one', and still nothing happened.

I knew he had his knife ready to cut the rope, so why didn't he hurry up and save me the suspense? In the silence I could hear the light aircraft nearby, with cameras rolling, waiting for the action. The only other sound was the thumping of my heart.

'Twang...'

I felt the rope cut and the glider seemed to hesitate for a moment before smartly pivoting around me to point its nose at the ground below. The glider and I went into freefall.

Two seconds later, with a positive swoop, the glider recovered from the dive and flew normally. The balloon was already way below me and I flew down slowly, buzzing with relief, too excited to admire the view. The rest of the flight was uneventful, with the plane droning round me, and I landed neatly in a large sheep field.

'It took all of Judy's four years' experience to land in the strong wind,' said the TV commentary the following morning. In fact, with a stiff breeze it was effortless and I landed as lightly as a feather. It was Paul who had the problems. It is not possible to stop a balloon quickly, and although he chose to land in the biggest field available, he had been dragged unceremoniously along the entire length of it, breaking his instruments and his radio in the process. The TV piece was shown nationwide and while I was painfully inarticulate and self-conscious in the interview, the pictures of the drop spoke for themselves and were exciting to watch.

I enjoyed doing the balloon drop so much that I was keen to have another go. Being in the grip of 'world record fever', I wondered whether I could break the balloon drop altitude record. It would be a project requiring a lot of work and equipment, so I mentally filed it as an adventure for the future.

In March 1983 I attended the first British League meeting in Lancashire, no longer the timid pilot of 1981, but a stronger more experienced flyer with big goals!

I had bought myself an American-made Wills Wing 'Duck' before I left Austria. It suited me well, with its 160 square feet of sail area and easy handling. Its major drawback was that it was designed to be rigged in the light wind conditions found abroad and setting it up was extremely difficult on the ground of a windy English flying site. Once rigged, it would take a minimum of three people to stand it up and attach the flying wires, but it was worth the extra hassle on the ground finally to have a glider which I was so happy to fly.

Jenny Ganderton, my main rival, had gone to live in Australia for a year, and there were some new faces among the five competitors in the Women's League. The combination of a competitive glider, more experience and a hunger to win was a new and successful formula. I was motivated by the idea of achieving my goals and the fire of ambition burned inside me. I had come a long way from the drifting, aimless student who had left school not knowing what to do with her life and easy prey for a religious cult. I was a woman on a mission. My obsessive, addictive traits were coming into their own, focusing all my energies and activities on my three targets for the year: to become British Women's Champion, to break the women's world distance record in Owens Valley, and to fly enough cross-country miles to become the first woman to qualify for entry to the British League.

The first of my goals got off to a good start in Lancashire, where I won the first of the Women's League competitions. I then increased my lead over the following four rounds to finish British Women's Champion in September. My biggest problem was inconsistency: one day I would fly really well, and the next I would blow completely. I notched up a few zero-scores throughout the season, one by landing too close to a military airfield, another by being sucked into cloud and becoming disorientated.

In order to qualify for the British League, I needed to get a few big cross-country flights under my belt as my top three flights in 1983 counted towards entrance to the League for the following year. I desperately wanted to fly in the League as opposed to the Women's League, as I felt my flying was now of a standard where I could compete on a level with men. I had always considered myself as a pilot and did not want to be segregated just because my anatomy was different. In many sports, the physical requirements are such that women have to be classed separately, but in hang gliding, as in horse riding and sailing, physical strength plays a part, but technique is more important.

Notching up cross-country miles to qualify for the League stayed in my mind as I watched the weather constantly. Finally, in April, the conditions looked promising for a cross-country flight from Bradwell Edge in the Peak District. I applied my newly learned patience and held back my instinct to fly downwind as fast as possible. I liked to see the miles whisking past underneath me and found it hard to circle endlessly over the same spot, waiting for the clouds downwind to improve. As I flew towards Chesterfield I had to slow down on several occasions and stick with a feeble thermal, as there were no developing clouds downwind to head for. My speed over the ground was poor, but I saw several people become impatient and fly off, only to land a few miles later.

Despite the penetrating cold, I fought to keep my concentration going, selecting the best clouds, choosing when to wait and when to press on. My last thermal came from the cooling towers of a power station at Gainsborough. It was impressive to look straight down the fat, steam-belching chimneys as I circled away downwind, to land after forty-nine miles at Caenby Corner north of Lincoln. This flight gave me the British women's distance record and it was the sixteenth longest flight made by anyone in Britain that year. It put me well up in the cross-country scores and on my way to a position in the League.

The more certain I felt about breaking the world open distance record, the more sure I was that I could convince a sponsor to back me. My recent balloon drop coverage on national TV helped my cause and I chose my targets carefully, selecting companies dealing exclusively in women's products, who were not currently involved in sponsorship and who would welcome media coverage. I wrote two letters, one to Lil-lets tampons and one to Tampax. In my letter I expressed the confidence I felt that within three months I would almost certainly have broken a world record. Even if the main target (the world distance record) eluded me, there were other records which were certainly within my capability, such as the women's 'out and return' record and the 'declared goal' distance.

I decided on a strategy of keeping the price low, requesting only a camera and a new hang glider from a sponsor. Lil-lets replied after a month, expressing interest in the project. I felt that they were my best bet as their advertising slogan at the time was, 'The small key to freedom', which fitted perfectly with the idea of hang gliding.

They agreed to buy a Lil-lets branded glider on my return and to supply the Olympus camera I needed to bring back photos of my record attempt. Jubilant at having set foot into the elusive world of sponsorship, I stuck the Lil-lets logo onto the sail of my Duck and gathered all the equipment I would need for Owens Valley, ready to depart in June.

I joined forces with Jenny Ganderton, who had written from Australia to voice her intention to go to Owens Valley. She was after the same world record and it seemed sensible to share transport. She was bringing her friend Steve Blenkinsop with her, and we found a fourth member of the party in John Pendry, a lanky and long-haired pilot whom I had known since university.

We arrived in Los Angeles in early June 1983 and bought a huge old station wagon between us, onto which we loaded our gliders and all our gear. We drove east to the hostile desert north of Death Valley and the small town of Bishop, where we would be staying. Straddling the California–Nevada border, Owens Valley is defined on one side by the impressive Sierra Nevada mountain range and on the other by the White Mountains. At its widest point it is seven miles across, and the desert is bleak, arid and featureless.

The extreme temperature difference between the baking desert below and the snow-capped peaks towering above has made it a Mecca for hang glider pilots. The sheer scale of the mountains means that they are perfect thermal producers and therefore lift is predictable above the rocky spines, enabling pilots to fly fast as they do not have to spend time hunting for thermals. The secret of long-distance records is to fly as fast as possible. With a finite portion of the day in which the thermals are usable, the faster you fly, the greater distance you will cover. Cloudbase in Owens Valley is also high, way above the 12,000-feet-high mountains and often reaching 18,000 feet or more.

We stayed in a log cabin at 9,000 feet in the Sierras to help us acclimatise to the high altitudes at which we would be flying. The setting was idyllic, with a mountain stream cascading by just outside the door and surrounded by an amphitheatre of mountain peaks.

The launch area on the White Mountains was very different from the grassy slopes of Britain. The stony ground was studded with resilient sturdy bushes, ready to snag any part of a hang glider which ventured too near on a take-off run. They also provided ideal cover for the numerous rattlesnakes, which thankfully rested quietly during the heat of the day. We were bombarded with all the horror stories that abounded about Owens Valley; terrifying tales of gigantic gust fronts with winds that would tear the roof off a house, turbulence which would flip a hang glider over and break it into pieces so small you could take it home in the boot of your car, and inevitably a dozen different versions of every serious accident that had ever happened there.

It was thus with a certain amount of trepidation that I rigged my glider on the first day. We had been warned about the dust devils which raged through launch, infant thermals vacuuming up everything in their path. Hang gliders, sometimes with an unfortunate pilot attached, could be sucked up, along with pieces of glider padding, sage brush, packed lunches and anything left lying around. Their demented spiralling would often carry their booty several hundred feet in the air before tiring with it and spitting it out over the mountainside. It was a case of waiting to rig until half an hour before you wanted to launch, then muttering a quick prayer for preservation, opening the glider as quickly as possible, and taking off without delay. The thermals were so powerful that they could sometimes catapult a pilot upwards at 2,000 feet per minute (that is equal to climbing the Eiffel Tower in thirty seconds). However, the basic law of physics still applied, and there could be an equal and opposite reaction. At times the air would feel as though someone had pulled the plug, and you could only watch helplessly as the altimeter unwound in sinking air before the next gut-wrenching thermal would intervene to continue the flight.

It was, however, Murphy's Law which was prevalent at launch. Through-out the half-hour of rigging, the dust devils could be heard all around, rattling the stones as they scurried up the mountainside. The temperature was usually over thirty-five degrees, and it took fifteen minutes to put on all my flying clothing – trousers, sweater, two flying suits, balaclava, two pairs of gloves and socks with thick boots. As if on cue, the thermals would then stop for fifteen minutes, leaving me no option but to sit under my glider in the desert sun. I would be as weak as a kitten and soaked with perspiration by the time the thermals started again. I did not dare drink as, with the prospect of a long flight ahead, I could not afford the distraction and inconvenience of a full bladder.

I was very nervous when I took off on my first flight. It was a pleasant surprise to find that the thermals were just like anywhere else, only stronger. In a place like Owens, you expect it to be turbulent so when you are buffeted by the gusts, it is not unexpected. The lift was so positive, hoisting the glider skywards so quickly, it took my breath away.

When I came in to land after my first flight, having covered thirty miles, I headed for a small complex of buildings next to the road. In Britain it is always best to land next to a house as they usually have a telephone, and a kind resident may offer a cup of tea. Landing next to a house in Owens Valley was infinitely preferable to sitting out in the desert, sharing the sand with the rattlesnakes and flies for an hour while waiting to be picked up.

I circled around to lose height and came in to land nearby. Thinking it was strange that there was no sign of life, I took my harness off and wandered over, aware that something did not feel right about the place. A beer sign was clearly visible and I thought maybe my luck was in and it would turn out to be a bar with ice-cold drinks. As I came closer, I saw a red flashing light above the door and a large sign that said 'Men Only'. I had landed next to Janie's Brothel, just over the Nevada border. I scurried back to my glider as quickly as my legs would carry me and packed it away behind the bushes. I sat next to the road, half-hidden in the ditch, and waited for our car. Eyes red from flying and hair tousled, I looked like a Janie's reject and was thankful to see the familiar faces of Steve and Jenny as they rounded the corner in the station wagon.

I made up my mind to go for my first world record, to get one 'in the bag' and fulfil my promise to Lil-lets. I decided on the women's 'out and return' distance and declared a turn point just over twenty-five miles away from launch, which would give me a total of fifty-one miles and double the previous record.

The conditions were uncharacteristically difficult that day, with unpredictable and sparse thermals. It took me five hours to complete the flight. The miles seemed to pass incredibly slowly; there were so few landmarks in the valley with just one tiny settlement every twenty miles, it felt as though I was hardly moving. Only my progress along the steep-sided succession of canyons directly below me confirmed that I was making headway. With my goal finally in sight, I was able to relax. My shoulders were painful with over-exertion, wrestling to keep the glider centred in the turbulent thermals. I found it impossible to relax in the air to give my muscles a break as turbulence could strike at any time, pitching the glider over violently, and so I felt safer with a vice-like grip on the bar. Although this was effective in keeping control, the toll on my muscles was severe. I kept my energy levels up with glucose tablets, taken on the rare occasions when I felt able to let go with one hand for a few seconds. I landed tired but ecstatic, with my first world record under my belt, and I was able to call my parents that night with the good news to pass on to Lil-lets.

Two days later, Jenny and I received an acute reminder of how vulnerable we were in the intense power of Owens Valley. During all our flights so far we had used the thermals on the main ridge, cruising happily above it in the strongest lift. I was heading north as usual when, without any warning, the wind increased dramatically. As soon as I felt it, I turned out towards the valley, only to find myself pinned above the 14,000-foot mountain tops, unable to penetrate forwards.

I pulled more speed as I knew that was my only chance of escape, but the only effect was that the glider descended at an alarming rate towards the mountain top. My options were limited. I could try to land on the mountain peak but my landing speed would be so fast at that altitude, and the air so turbulent with the strong wind, that I would almost certainly break my glider and possibly injure myself. The only other chance was to continue pulling on speed and descend into the canyon below, trusting to luck that the wind would be less as I dropped into the gorge, and would allow me to edge forward and escape.

I resorted to the latter course, leaving the outcome in the lap of the gods. An eternity later, with the canyon sides closing in on me, I began to inch my way painfully forwards, finally emerging into the valley very shaken and thankful to have escaped. The wind was so strong that when I landed, I had to grab the front wires of the glider to avoid being blown away. I did not dare relax my grip to unclip my harness from the glider for over twenty minutes.

Later that evening I met up with Jenny, who had been caught out as I had and was very shocked. She had been forced into White Canyon, the most intimidating and turbulent of all the gullies, only just escaping into the valley. We discovered the next day that we had been lucky. Four pilots had been blown backwards onto the top of the White Mountains. One had been killed on impact, two had broken their gliders and one had escaped unscathed by crashing into a snowdrift. It was a sobering lesson and we never flew so far back on the spine again.

There followed a spate of hang gliders being turned upside down by strong turbulence; at one stage it seemed to be one a day. There were some miraculous escape stories: four had thrown their rescue parachutes and had landed safely; one blacked out as his broken glider spiralled down onto the mountain top below. A search party was sent up to 'find the body', only to meet him limping down the mountainside with a twisted knee and a scratched face. The law of averages gnawed at me and I wondered if I would be next.

I was now concentrating on the open distance record, waiting for the right weather. We shifted our take-off site to the southern end of the Sierra Nevada, a place named Horseshoe Meadows. This maximised our distance potential by giving us a hundred-mile stretch of mountains to fly above, before setting off across the more unpredictable terrain at the end of Owens Valley. The only risky spot was the five-mile crossing from the Sierra Nevada to the White Mountains at the fifty-mile mark. Taking off from Horseshoe Meadows meant that we could start flying earlier as the eastern-facing Sierras caught the morning sun and produced thermals before the westerly-facing Whites. It usually took at least two hours to reach the tricky valley crossing, by which time the Whites were basking in sunshine and producing lift.

The Sierra Nevada was completely different from the more benign-looking White Mountain range. Craggy and rugged, the peak of Mount Whitney dominated the skyline. Standing over 14,000 feet high, it is the biggest mountain in the USA. I had to get a firm grip on my threatening vertigo to stand on launch and look over the edge of the take-off site at Horseshoe Meadows. It faced into a white rocky gully with near-vertical sides plunging to the desert below.

Jenny, Steve, John and myself rigged our gliders. We were thinking about our chance of a record-breaking distance flight when Jenny and I were approached by a local pilot, Rick Masters. 'Today's not a good day to fly,' he said, somewhat ominously. 'It's really turbulent when the wind is in this direction. Last year I watched a pilot being thrown right back into the cliffs from a hundred yards out, and there was nothing he could do about it'.

After my Austrian ramp take-off fiasco, I have always listened to pilots with local knowledge. This man had spent years flying in Owens Valley and if anyone could recognise dangerous conditions, it must surely be him. He made it clear that flying on a day like this would be playing Russian Roulette. Jenny and I de-rigged our gliders, certain we were making the right decision.

We watched nervously as Steve and John ignored Rick's warning and launched, climbing easily in the strong thermals without a hint of the 'man-eating' turbulence. They both flew over one hundred miles that day and neither had experienced anything out of the ordinary, just a typical, rough, Owens Valley day. I wondered whether Rick Masters had deliberately singled out the only two women pilots on launch.

The following day I dragged the others out of bed early. I have never had a problem waking at the first glimmer of daylight and love the early morning rush of energy. My body's batteries then drain slowly throughout the day until I become sluggish to the point of being antisocial in the evening. It is not unknown for me to fall asleep at 10.30 p.m. regardless of where I am, as fatigue catches up with me and I go out like a light. Although the others teased me in the evening, finding it hilarious that they could set their watches by the moment my eyelids started to droop, I always got my revenge in the mornings as I bounced around preparing breakfast while they groaned, grumbled and crashed into the furniture.

We arrived on take-off by 10 o'clock and began our usual rigging routine. When Rick Masters arrived, Jenny and I nodded a cursory greeting and deliberately busied ourselves with our kit, not wanting to hear his scare-mongering stories, trusting instead to our experience to choose whether or not conditions were suitable.

The forecast was even better than the previous day and we took off at 11 o'clock, enjoying a smooth climb to 13,000 feet. The view above the Sierras was stunning. The snow caps stretched endlessly into the distance and the peaks revealed turquoise lakes nestling between jutting crags, often with vivid white ice chunks floating in them. The contrast from our vantage point between the frozen landscape above the peaks, and the dry, flat desert below, was stark.

Concentrating on flying as fast as I could whilst staying high, I reached the crossing point after two hours. Jenny was far behind and I climbed as high as possible before setting off for the White Mountains aware that, as long as I could find a thermal on the other side, I was almost certain to become the first woman to fly over 100 miles and would have my world record.

The nerve-racking glide towards the distinctive slopes of Black Mountain made me clench all my muscles as I tried to blot out the sound of my vario groaning at the severity of the sinking air. My altimeter dial wound its way downwards as I willed myself towards the thermals on the other side. The feeling of frustration mounted as Black Mountain peak rose in front of me and I continued my inexorable descent.

I finally reached Black Mountain at less than 2,000 feet above the valley floor. With the prospect of losing my precious record, I fought to block out my frustration. The only way I kept going was by flying to the best of my ability and keeping my level of concentration. I tucked the glider right in to the mountainside, flying closer than I would normally have dared, knowing my reactions were sharp with all my senses on red alert. I scratched my way down the slope, encountering nothing except sinking air until I was forced to land at the bottom, sweating and cursing.

It was over half an hour later when Jenny reported on the radio that she was climbing prior to crossing the valley. I could see the tiny white dot of her glider as she set course towards me and Black Mountain. She encountered the same drastic sink as I had done and approached at a similar height. She did not find a thermal either but instead of scratching close, she flew out into the valley to land. As she turned into wind, her wing tip lifted, she turned towards it and was scooped up and hoisted slowly skyward by a saving thermal. I watched as she worked her way up to the top of Black Mountain and continued northwards and on to take the world record that I wanted so much.

I felt so frustrated. I had flown as well as I could and had simply arrived at Black Mountain at the wrong time when there happened to be no thermal there. The disappointment was huge, but served to fuel my determination to try again for the record the following day.

It was Steve's turn to drive and after picking me up we drove after Jenny, who finally landed after 115 miles. She had broken the hundred-mile barrier and, as I congratulated her on her flight, I was as jealous as hell that it hadn't been me.

We didn't get back to Bishop until after midnight and it was an even more reluctant and crabby threesome whom I had to bully into consciousness the next day. We arrived on launch and I rigged in double quick time, spurred on by my desire to beat Jenny's newly set 115-mile record. All four of us wanted to try for world records that day so we did not have any retrieve organised. It was a question of sorting ourselves out when we landed and, if necessary, spending the night out in the desert.

I launched at 11.45 a.m., with John right behind me, and we climbed together in the first thermal. He had the bit between his teeth, flew fast when gliding between thermals and soon overtook me. I felt strong and positive and was certain that this would be my day for flying a good distance. I switched my radio off so that I could concentrate fully on the task in hand. For once the crags did not faze me as I circled close in to the rocks to ensure I didn't go down. Two hours later I approached the gap with trepidation, resolving not to cross the valley until I was 'in orbit'.

I climbed and climbed, squeezing every precious inch from the thermal, ignoring the urge to press on. Finally I straightened up, pointed my toes and headed east to my *bête noire*, Black Mountain. I prayed to any gods that might be listening, 'Please, please let me find a thermal – I don't care how rough it is, just let me get high on the Whites'. The sink was not as bad as the day before and I arrived on the far side 1,000 feet higher. A gnarly, rough little thermal was there to greet me and with white knuckles clenching the bar, I was like a terrier with a bone – there wasn't a force on earth which could have dislodged me from that thermal.

High again, and with the worst behind me, I looked north at the perfect, blossoming cumulus clouds sitting high above the mountains and tried to fight back images of my phoning home that night with news of a new record I had set, knowing that I could not afford to get lost in daydreams. The only way to ensure success was to concentrate fully on the task in hand.

Five hours into the flight I approached Boundary Peak, the formidable jagged summit at the hundred-mile point. It marked the end of the White Mountain range and I would have to climb as high as possible before venturing into the desert beyond, where the route became less obvious and thermals much further apart.

Out of the corner of my eye I spotted Steve, the first person I had seen in four and a half hours. He was only 500 yards in front of me and I watched his glider being buffeted by the turbulence preceding a thermal. As he hit a surge of lift, he banked his glider steeply and disappeared vertically upwards as though an unseen hand had grabbed hold of his wingtip and pulled him into the heavens. I had never seen anyone climb so fast and I knew I was in for the most powerful thermal I had ever experienced. Most of me wanted to go for it, but one part wanted to turn and fly in the opposite direction. This was exactly the type of thermal turbulence which could tumble a hang glider that failed to stay in the centre of the thermal core.

I gritted my teeth and flew headlong into the turbulent air with a vice-like grip on the bar. I flew to the point where Steve had 'disappeared' and I was tossed about, fighting to maintain my course. Then, with a huge wrench, I was hoisted upwards with no option but to circle tightly to make sure I wasn't going to get spat out. The needle on my vario jammed against the upper limit on the scale and it screamed at me. Boundary Peak dropped into insignificance below and the view of the Owens Valley unfolded like a map. In the crystal clear air I could see the hundred-mile stretch back to Horseshoe Meadows and in the other direction could make out where Jenny had landed the day before, which was surely within my gliding range.

At 18,000 feet the thermal weakened and I straightened out, heading north. I was bitterly cold. My feet and hands were numb and the biting wind seemed to cut straight through my balaclava, freezing my face. Without oxygen, I was wary of becoming hypoxic and kept checking for the tell-tale signs of dizziness and tunnel vision.

I flew for a few minutes in a straight line in appalling sink and tried to assess my altitude. It took me some time to figure out the dial of my altimeter and I finally came to the highly unlikely conclusion that I was still at 18,000 feet. I was hypoxic after all. The benefits of the sinking air and proportionally greater oxygen density soon had an effect on my mental agility. I realised I was actually a lot lower than I thought and was in need of another thermal.

I was desperately tired, both physically and mentally. The effort of concentrating, coupled with the constant strain of grappling with the glider, had left me drained. My harness was a prototype design and the compression force on my hips was excruciating after six hours' flying. I squirmed about, trying to relieve the pressure, but to no avail.

Another climb, directly over the point where Jenny had landed the day before, assured me of the record and I celebrated with a glucose tablet. Although I did not know where she was, I was confident she had not overtaken me. I generally flew faster than she did and knew that as long as I kept flying until sundown, the open distance world record would be mine. Following the single road that ran north for another hour, I took my final climb as high as I could and watched the sun sink towards the horizon, stretching the shadows of the mountains across the desert.

There were no towns or cars on the road below as I set out on my final glide, maximising my distance in the refreshingly calm evening air. I allowed myself to relax for the first time in seven and a half hours and realised just how exhausted I was. I crunched two glucose tablets to give me enough energy to land as I came in alongside the road. I flared hard but as my feet touched the ground, my legs wouldn't hold my weight and crumpled underneath me. I knelt, exhausted, thinking, 'I've done it!'

There was no elation, just a daze of fatigue and relief. A passing car stopped and the driver asked if I needed help. I blurted out that I had just broken a world record and felt, for the first time, a smile creep across my face. He and his passenger whooped and hollered in celebration and I just sat there grinning inanely, utterly spent. I had the presence of mind to ask them for their names and addresses as witnesses of my landing and they then drove off, leaving me to pack up my glider.

De-rigging proved to be a slow business as my legs wouldn't work, and it was dark before I finished. I called on the radio and made contact with Steve, who had landed five miles short of me. He gave me the news that Jenny had crashed on launch and had damaged her glider but was unhurt and was on her way to pick us up in the car. When she arrived her disappointment was obvious. Her record had stood for only twenty-four hours and she had not had the chance to defend it.

It was 10 p.m. and we still had to find John, who was last heard of high at Boundary Peak at 4 p.m. and who, by now, could be anywhere. It was worse than looking for a needle in a haystack as we worked our way along dirt roads in the pitch black of the moonless night. By 2 o'clock in the morning we were hallucinating with fatigue and finally pulled into a picnic site. We spent what was left of the night sleeping on concrete picnic tables.

We woke early to resume our search, finally discovering John at a café in the town of Gabbs, to where he had walked that morning having spent the night out in the desert. He had flown 186 miles and had set the new men's world open distance record.

My hips ached after their seven-and-a-half-hour confinement, making walking difficult. I could only manage an ungainly waddle as we arrived back in Bishop. I phoned home and Mum's delight finally made it sink in that I had achieved my goal with a distance greater than I had ever dreamed of flying.

My flight was confirmed as 145 miles. When I left England, the record stood at sixty miles. Jenny had almost doubled it and I had increased it by a further thirty miles. There were barely a dozen men who had flown further and it gave women's hang gliding a massive boost in credibility.

CHAPTER 4

Laying the Foundations
for a New Career

'You must be joking!'

My mouth, brain and body staged a simultaneous mutiny when confronted with the take-off at Makapu Point on the Hawaiian island of Oahu. The 2,000-foot cliff jutted vertically out of the Pacific Ocean and the take-off was terrifying. Because the precipice was so sheer, the wind on the edge had no horizontal component at all; it blew straight up, making it impossible to launch a hang glider in a normal fashion because as soon as the nose of the glider poked over the edge, the wind tossed it over in a backward somersault. The solution was radical and made the hair on the back of my neck stand on end. My vertigo threatened to overwhelm me, and I had to fight hard to overcome it.

I had some soul-searching to do. For several years I had had a poster of a hang glider flying this very site adorning my bedroom wall. The bright orange glider soared above the brilliant turquoise ocean, which was dotted with thickly forested islands bordered by golden sands. The broad grin on the pilot's face was one of pure delight and I vowed that one day I would fly there. After breaking the word record I still had a week's holiday left, tickets were cheap from California to Hawaii and I decided to blow the rest of my savings on flying the site of my dreams. Having arrived on Oahu, I rented a hang glider from local pilot, Jeff Cotter, and he had brought me to Makapu Point. I was now confronted with the vision of my poster in glorious 3-dimensional technicolour. I desperately wanted to fly, but I had a major problem with the launch.

There was a flat and narrow 'diving board', which extended over the edge of the cliff. At the end of the board there was a lower platform barely half a metre square where the launch assistant had to stand. Having rigged the hang glider, I followed Jeff's instructions and clipped my harness into the glider. I checked at least five times that I was securely attached before lowering the glider's nose to the ground. I had to step in front of the control bar and, while Jeff pulled the glider's nose towards the edge, I lifted the weight and shuffled awkwardly forwards.

All the angles felt wrong and as we clumsily mounted the ramp, the glider started to sway. We inched our way slowly over the edge of the cliff and the wing rocked with the upward force of the wind. With the sail in front of me I was restricted to looking straight down the precipice. I felt sick.

Jeff kept dragging the nose forwards, briefly pausing so that he could step down onto the platform and tie himself onto the ramp to prevent me from knocking him off his precarious perch. I did not like it and wanted to be anywhere other than stuck in this godforsaken spot.

There was no question of going back now. Reversing back up the ramp would have been impossible.

'Are you ready?' called Jeff.

'Just a moment,' I replied with undisguised tension in my voice.

I was as ready as I would ever be, but I needed to compose myself and quell my pounding heart. I swallowed hard and took a deep breath. 'OK,' I called, trying to sound confident.

Jeff raised the glider's nose and I stepped back behind the control bar, resisting the temptation to close my eyes. I was under the misguided notion that at some stage I would resume a degree of control, but as the wind hit the sail, it started to tremble and so did I! Suddenly, the wires were ripped from Jeff's hands and I was going up in the world's fastest elevator.

I clung to the glider for a few seconds, taking in the fact that the worst was over, and gradually my breathing slowed to a near-normal rate as I laughed with relief and settled down in my harness. The ramp became a mere dot from my vantage point and the sapphire-blue ocean stretched out before me, fringed by foaming surf as the waves crashed onto the beaches, which rose to meet the lush green forests of Oahu.

The panoramic view kept me enthralled for two hours as I flew along the cliffs in the smooth, buoyant air. The delight of being in the middle of my poster scene had me swooping and diving, enjoying the fluid motion of the glider. Hang gliding is my art form; although I have no ability in the earthbound arts of painting and drawing, at times like this I feel graceful and almost balletic, sculpting patterns in the air.

Eventually the cool air became uncomfortable; I was dressed only in shorts and a T-shirt, and I flew out to the beach. The strip of sand looked barely wide enough to land on, but with no sunbathers so late in the day there were no obstacles in my way and I could set up a long, straight approach. I flared hard and the glider obediently stopped dead. I took my harness and shoes off and felt the sand warm between my toes as the surging adrenaline of the flight abated. An hour later Jeff drove by to pick me up, finding me in a dream-like trance, paddling like a child on Brighton beach.

The following day I took a local plane to the neighbouring island of Maui, which is dominated by Haleakala, a 10,000-foot-high extinct volcano. The mountain stands proud in the middle of the island, its sloping sides gradually tapering off into the sea. Although no longer active, the crater is still a moonscape, with huge gaps where its innards have been blown away by past eruptions.

I had made contact with Dave Darling, an ageing hippie who rented hang gliders to visiting pilots, and arranged to meet him the following morning. A friendly local pilot, Dave Neto, invited me to stay at his house while he was away working on Oahu, and I helped myself each morning to the juicy papayas and mangoes which hung heavily from the trees in his garden. The camaraderie between pilots is a part of the sport I have always enjoyed. There is an immediate bond from a shared interest with a fellow flier and many of the normal social barriers can be bypassed. I have enjoyed the hospitality of pilots all over the world, who have invited me into their homes and taken me flying. I have been able to return the favour with those who have visited England and needed a place to stay and a glider to fly. Staying with a local pilot is the best way to experience another country, rather than being based in a characterless hotel.

To fly from Haleakala it was important to arrive on the summit early, as by mid-morning clouds built up to surround the mountain and within a short time obscured the ground completely. Dave Darling had brought me a medium-sized, high-performance Comet to fly and we set off for the long drive to launch.

On the way up, Dave extracted from the glove box the biggest joint I had ever seen and proceeded to light up. I watched with alarm as the car began to weave about as his eyes became redder. I opened my window wide to avoid getting high on the fumes. I wanted to have my wits about me for the take-off and the flight. Dave had obviously found that the combination of marijuana and flying was an agreeable one, but I was not convinced!

The dark, loose rock on the summit was pure lava deposit and crunched loudly underfoot. As I unzipped the Comet's bag, alarm bells began to ring in my head. The uprights looked as though they had been run over by a tractor and had obviously been bent and forcibly straightened many times. On closer examination, there were four large holes in the sail, several of the wires were frayed and kinked, and the battens were bent and misshapen, with the right-hand ones differing from the left by as much as two inches, enough to have given the glider a horrendous turn. These were all problems I could see at a glance – goodness knows what discoveries I would have made had I given it a thorough check over. To me it looked like a death trap.

I really wanted to fly but my sense of self-preservation overrode my enthusiasm. It is often difficult to be objective when you are so keen to fly, but warning signs must be heeded. Over the years I have learned to listen to the voice inside my head if it is telling me to think twice. This has been instilled in me through trial and error; when I have ignored it and flown regardless I have always lived to regret the decision.

Dave shrugged off my reservations with incomprehension and I enviously watched him fly off over the expanding bed of cumulus clouds and drove back down the mountain in the car. The following morning he brought me an intermediate wing that had suffered much less abuse. Clouds were forming as I finished rigging and he took off, leaving me to follow on behind. There was no wind so a fully committed sprint was required to launch. At 10,000 feet, the take-off speed needs to be significantly higher than at sea level. The prospect of not running fast enough, stalling the glider on the abrasive lava and hitting it face first at high speed, was enough to spur my legs into action, propelling the wing into the air.

Once airborne, the view was impressive, with most of the island visible from the crater's edge. The rich volcanic soil nurtured pineapple plantations and other crops until the fields merged into the abundant wild vegetation which in turn gave way to palm trees and then the beach where we were to land.

As I flew over the clouds, my shadow appeared with a circular rainbow around it on the gleaming, gossamer blanket. I flew towards a gap through which the ground was still visible and, with both wingtips hidden in the cloud, I steered along the ethereal ravine with delicate white towers on either side. The cloud closed in, and for a few minutes I lost sight of the ground completely, trusting my compass to keep me flying away from the volcano's slope. Flying in cloud is like driving in dense fog without cats'-eyes or road markings. With no points of reference, it is easy to become disorientated and to fly in the wrong direction.

Finally, I emerged into the dazzling sunshine and, laughing at the sheer beauty of the view, meandered down towards the beach. Dozens of windsurfers were already skimming the waves, making the most of the strengthening breeze, and the sand was littered with sun worshippers on bright beach towels. Steering towards a less crowded area, I landed gently on the soft sand, a perfect ending to an unforgettable flight.

I spent my last days in Hawaii scuba diving, horse riding and walking through the diverse areas of Maui. It was a lovely place to explore and relax before flying home to England.

On my return, I threw myself into the jewellery business. I felt a sense of achievement at having broken the world record, but I was not as contented and satisfied as I had hoped. Having been driven for a year by the all-consuming ambition to fly further than any other woman in the world, I now felt restless and in need of a new challenge.

The third leg of the League was held in mid-Wales, where I took delivery of my new glider, a mylar-coated Airwave Magic 3. I had reluctantly sold my Duck in America. Two months of exposure to high quantities of ultraviolet light and desert sand had taken their toll on the sailcloth, and its performance was impaired. The Magic 3 was my first sponsored glider and, in order that the Lil-lets name should show up well in photographs and on television, the sail was plastered with 'Lil-lets' in huge letters on one side and their slogan, 'The small key to freedom', on the other.

There was barely any wind on take-off on the first day so I rigged the glider standing on its control frame, displaying my sponsor's banner to the best advantage. I returned to the car for my harness and walked back up to take-off with competition director Derek Evans. As we walked over the brow of the hill he caught sight of the glider and his face flushed puce with embarrassment. 'Is that advertising what I think it is?' he asked, scarcely able to believe his eyes. As a middle-aged bank manager Derek could cope with most things, but the blatant advertising of tampons had thrown him.

People's attitudes in 1983 were still reserved when discussing such a sensitive subject as menstruation. Advertising on television was forbidden and magazine advertisements were cryptic. It was something that I had never noticed before, but in trying to get media coverage for Lil-lets, the prudish attitude of the British about something which affected half the population amazed me. Newspapers were endlessly innovative in their ways of avoiding mentioning my sponsor. Many painstakingly doctored photographs, some reversed the pictures to make it less obvious. The majority would not quote the name in writing, or would make a tastefully twee reference to my sponsor, as the Sunday *Observer* did, as '. . . a leading manufacturer of women's toilet wear'!

Lil-lets themselves were often a little naive when dealing with the media's sensitivity. My first live interview on TV AM was an ideal opportunity to display a small logo on my clothing. I asked Lil-lets to supply me with a jacket or sweater bearing their logo. Two days later a package arrived which contained two navy sweatshirts with 'LIL-LETS TAMPONS' emblazoned full length across the chest. Not only would TV AM have balked at this, but I could not have relaxed in front of a camera wearing a sweatshirt like that. Eventually we agreed on a royal blue sweater upon which I had printed a small Lil-lets logo. Even then the producer flinched at it and it was only because they were running late and I wasn't wearing anything underneath that they permitted it.

Sponsorship is now an integral part of sport and the relationship between the sports person, the sponsor and the media is vitally important. It is unrealistic for the media to think that they can cut out all mentions of sponsorship and still have top performing sports people. Most do not win the vast prize money awarded to successful Formula 1 drivers and top golfers, and cannot live and compete without the support of commercial sponsorship. It has been gratifying to see the gradual change in the media's attitudes towards sponsorship over the years and I feel that if it is done subtly, there should be no objections to sports people promoting the companies who pay for them to compete.

My Magic 3 was the first mylar-coated 155-square-foot model ever made. It had been test flown by fourteen-stone Graham Deegan of Airwave on a smooth coastal site. My first flight on it was during the League and the handling was so stiff that I pulled all the muscles in my shoulders trying to get it to turn in the strong thermals. I was not happy. I continued flying the task regardless, using every ounce of control I had to ignore the pain and to keep flying. I was one of only five to land at goal after three hours of agony. I was in tears with the pain when I landed and when I voiced my unhappiness with the handling of the glider to Graham, he looked around the field at the other four top pilots who had made it and couldn't comprehend my complaint.

I came to the conclusion that the problem must be me and I persevered with it for months, but the glider scared me, as I never felt completely in control. The final straw came as I was flying along a tree-covered ridge near Bristol in turbulent conditions and was turned violently towards the trees. Even with full weight shift the glider refused to respond and kept its course towards the hill. It was only by luck that I hit another patch of turbulence, which turned me away from the trees, missing them by inches.

One of the pilots who had watched my hair-raising flight told Airwave of his reservations. They finally asked for the glider to be returned to them. Darren Arkwright, one of the Airwave's test pilots, was given the job of test-flying it on the smooth sea cliffs on the Isle of Wight. Directly after take-off the glider locked out towards the cliffs, requiring all his strength to pull it out of the turn.

'It handles like a truck,' Darren declared as he landed. 'I'm amazed that you're still around, having flown it for six months.'

I was relieved that someone had listened to me at last, and that it was not just me being fussy. They chopped and changed the tubing and sail tension to make it turn, but I simply did not want to fly it any more.

I was not interested in being a 'test pilot' again and resolved that the only thing to do was to fly an average-sized glider that was too big for me and to compensate by getting fitter and stronger so that I could turn it. I would even resort to filling my harness with rocks as ballast if the wind was very strong.

I changed gliders once more and this time chose a Solar Wings S4 racer, which coordinated well in spite of being too big for me. Lil-lets designed the sail and, as they felt the 'small key to freedom' slogan was a bit wordy, they decided I should have daisies instead, which at the time adorned their tampon boxes. I thought a couple of tiny flowers would look quite nice and was ill-prepared for the monstrous six-foot-diameter blossoms which smothered my new wing. One thing was certain – my new glider would never be stolen!

By the end of 1983 my three best cross-country flights added up to ninety-one miles, enough to qualify to enter the National League the following year. My third and final goal for 1983 was achieved.

The first League meeting of 1984 was held in the Yorkshire Dales in March and if I had had any reservations about joining the hitherto all-male bastion, they were quickly dispelled by the friendly welcome I received. There was some good-natured banter and some extra interest in the scoreboard, but in general I was accepted as just another pilot who was qualified to fly among the best. I did not take the League by storm, finishing halfway down the field in the first of five competitions.

The next League meeting was one I shall never forget, not for the quality of the flying, but for the monstrous hills we had to climb in order to fly. Someone had come up with the idea of holding a competition in Northumbria. I have no objections to the area itself – the people are friendly enough and the Cheviot hills are beautiful; but there are no roads up to any of the take-off sites, and the climbs to the top are huge! With a hang glider weighing five and a half stone and one and a half stone of harness, instruments, helmet, map and lunch, I was carrying over two-thirds of my body weight. It would not have been so bad if it had been contained in an ergonomically designed rucksack, but to carry an eighteen-foot long bundle of tubes, thinly wrapped in sailcloth with lots of pro-truding bolts, on one shoulder for over an hour with no respite, is hard work.

I had suffered problems with my lumbar spine for three years, mainly due to carrying hang gliders and aggravated by an occasional bad landing. Sometimes a spasm would become so acute that I could not fly and in two extreme cases rendered me unable to walk. The first time my back went, age twenty-one, I collapsed and when the doctor called he told me to take aspirin, stay in bed until it improved, and to give up hang gliding! I ignored the last recommendation, but I did improve my lifting and car-rying techniques to put less strain on my spine. Prolonged carrying of my glider and harness was very painful, but in Northumberland there was no option.

The first day we thought the local club were playing a joke on us as we stopped at the bottom of Yeavering Bell, a 1,000-foot climb that was so steep that you couldn't even put your glider down for a rest or it would have slid straight back down to the car park. It was a one and a half hour slog, which pushed my 'mind over matter' technique to its limit. The local pilots, half-man, half-mountain goat, beat us southern softies to the top and appeared as fresh as daisies by the time I hauled myself and my own set of daisies to the summit!

Having already been pushed to the limits of my physical strength, it was hard to recover my wits and engage my brain to concentrate on the task ahead. During the four tortuous and pain-racked days of this 'Iron Man' contest, I managed to improve my position to nineteenth place overall.

A few weeks prior to this competition I had received a letter from the

Owens Valley prophet of doom Rick Masters. He had undertaken the organisation of the annual Owens Valley Classic competition that year, entry to which was restricted to elite pilots and was by invitation only.

The criterion he set for invitations was the distance that pilots had flown cross-country. Larry Tudor, the American cross-country ace who had clocked up a 200-mile flight, received invitation number one, John Pendry number two and my 145-mile record gave me number ten, but he sent me an accompanying letter which read:

> I am sending you this invitation as a formality. Owens Valley competitions are extremely fatiguing. In addition, I feel that they are downright dangerous due to the decisions made in the heat of the moment. I sincerely hope that you will decline. Should you decline, I promise to fill the vacancy with one of your countrymen.

I was incensed by this blatant sexism and could not understand his reasoning. John Pendry had all but written his glider off while crashing on launch at Horseshoe Meadows. There had been many other incidents, some involving injury to pilots, but not one of them was female. I had not so much as scratched a fingernail during my six-week stay and this chap was telling me not to come to Owens because it was dangerous and, to make matters worse, wanted me to send a man in my place! I wrote back thanking him for his invitation, accepting my place and expressing disbelief at his blinkered attitude.

He replied to my letter, claiming that I would understand better if I were to 'take into account my proximity to pilots who have been killed, maimed or paralysed for life in this place'. As none of these pilots were female, I still couldn't fathom his resistance to having women flying in Owens Valley so I wrote back again, suggesting he channel his worries into his friends who were flying out there, like Larry Tudor, and advise them not to fly, rather than trying to dissuade strangers like me.

As it happened, fate had other plans and the national team selection for the Eger Cup in Hungary was announced at the Northumbrian League. My name was one of the five on the list. This competition clashed with the Owens Valley Classic and although I really wanted to go to Owens, nothing was more important than being part of the British Team. Reluctantly, I wrote to Rick Masters to tell him I would not be coming. He was no doubt delighted to be able to have his exclusively male competition after all.

After the names for the Eger Cup were announced there was a round of applause as I stepped up to receive my badge as a first-time member of the British team and the first woman to be selected to fly for Britain. Stunned at being chosen for an international competition so soon after joining the League, my feeling of happiness was mixed with pride and humility at the honour of being able to represent my country. I walked back through the crowd in a daze, only vaguely aware of the congratulatory smiles from the assembled pilots. I stared at the badge in my hand and reread the words embroidered on it: 'National Team Great Britain', and bit my lip hard to avoid showing the emotions I felt. I wanted to cry with happiness, but knew I would have to wait until I was alone. As the first woman ever to fly in the British Team, I did not dare to show what would be seen as an obvious female trait, so I propped up my 'stiff upper lip' with all the emotional control I could muster.

The five members of the British Team who flew to Hungary were treated like royalty on arrival in Budapest. The Hungarians certainly knew how to enjoy themselves and threw parties every evening. Their daytime attitude was very different: they would transform into competitive pilots who were out to win, as opposed to the extrovert and generous party animals of the previous evening – they displayed fine stamina.

There were competitors of several different nationalities and the prosperity of their respective countries was reflected in the quality of their gliders and equipment.

The previous year, our team captain Len Hull had been out to the same competition to find most of the pilots flying home-made gliders constructed from very basic materials. On the first day, as Len had unzipped his glider bag and started to assemble his new wing with its crisp sail and shiny, anodised tubing, one of the Czech pilots had watched with tears rolling down his face, partly because he had never seen anything so beautiful but also as he knew it was financially so far out of his reach.

By the following summer when we arrived, the Hungarians were all flying copies of the gliders that had been at the competition the previous year. Although the materials and fittings were still 'agricultural', the wings flew well. The pilots were constantly on the lookout for the latest innovations from the west and as a result all Hungarian fliers seemed to carry a tape measure, notebook and pencil. When one spotted some new gadget or fitting on one of our gliders, there would be a quick-fire conversation followed by an industrious and comprehensive measuring and noting of details. It was certain that the enterprising engineers among them would have a copy made and ready to test within days. It brought home to me that whatever hardships I had endured in my apprenticeship as a pilot, it must have been so much worse for each of these pilots, who had had to make their own gliders before they could begin to fly. They shared the same passion, but had to work so much harder to fulfil it.

Not only were they restricted by their lack of materials, but also by the Hungarian military forces. In Britain we are accustomed to fly wherever we want outside controlled airspace, but in Hungary we were given a narrow 'corridor' each day, outside which it was forbidden to venture. It was hard to navigate over the vast Hungarian plains and the tasks were challenging.

The landings were always an adventure as the hospitality of the local people was generous, although it was very frustrating being unable to converse with them. They were curious to discover where we had come from and how we had arrived in their field with no engine. There was many a time when a pilot was collected late at night who had been rendered incapable of walking by the local wine, supplied in abundance by a friendly farmer. Even when I mistakenly landed in the middle of a maize field whose ripe crop was over six feet tall, the farmer, instead of being angry, beat down a path through the corn so that I could carry my glider to the edge of the field.

One of the Czech pilots competing in Hungary was Tomáš Suchánek, who has since become the best pilot the world of hang gliding has ever known. During that summer of 1984 he was a relative beginner, but within a few years he would prove almost unbeatable, winning three consecutive world championships and breaking several world records.

Our first airborne encounter occurred halfway around a triangle course when flying against a strong headwind. My glider's sailcloth was coated in plastic mylar to increase its speed and glide, and my aerodynamic pod harness was stuffed full of stones as ballast. I thought I was flying pretty fast, when I heard a strange noise behind me. I looked round to see Tomáš closing on me, flying a machine which defied the laws of physics, being held together by copious amounts of sticky tape and constructed of what looked like reinforced sackcloth. The noise was caused by the sail flapping as he coaxed every scrap of speed he could out of the precarious-looking machine while his toes pointed in his old-fashioned harness. I could only watch open mouthed in amazement, as inch by inch he drew level and passed me!

We were not blessed with the high cloudbases and 'thermals the size of

Greater Manchester' which Len had promised us after his experience the previous year, but we had six good tasks and some unforgettable flying. Len secured first place in the competition and Ferenc Kiss of Hungary came second. I came third. I had flown well but I still occasionally suffered from under-confidence. This was not helped by the attitude of some of the other competitors. On the first day of the contest, Len had won the task and many pilots commented on what a good pilot he was and how well he had flown. When I won the following day, I overheard a comment that I had been 'lucky'. Two days later, when I won a second task, I again heard the word 'luck' used as the reason for my success. I was hurt, but it made me more determined to be accepted just like any another pilot. There was still a long way to go to convince pilots from other countries that a woman could fly well and should be treated the same as any other competitor.

CHAPTER 5

Himalayan Highs and Lows

My feet had barely touched the ground on my return from Hungary when I came home after a hard day's work to find a letter inviting me on an all expenses paid trip to Himalayas. The ostentatiously named Grand Himalayan World Hang Gliding Rally was to be held in May in Himachal Pradesh and would be the first hang gliding competition ever held in India. I was to be one of five invited guest pilots.

My imagination was fired by the location in the foothills of the Himalayas. I had long wanted to visit India and the chance not only to see the country, but also to hang glide there, was not to be missed. I talked it over with Mum and Dad the next day, and yet again they agreed to cover for me at work for the period of the competition.

It was in the late spring of 1984 that I flew to Delhi and met up with thirty-three pilots from all over the world. We flew up to Jammu in Kashmir and were taken by coach to Palampur, which was to be our base for the next two weeks. The twelve-hour coach journey was uncomfortably hot, with broken windows creating the effect of sitting in front of a fan heater as the sweltering heat poured into the bus. The views of rural India were fascinating and we were introduced to the truly unique Indian way of driving. The bus would steer a path down the middle of the road, ignoring any oncoming vehicle until a collision was imminent. The driver would then sound the horn and swerve violently, narrowly avoiding pedestrians, mules and sacred cows in his path.

Despite being careful about what I ate and drank in Delhi, I had developed acute diarrhoea, which was to make life miserable for the next six days. We were staying outside Palampur at the Palace Hotel, a colonial-style building with high ceilings and fans which, though much appreciated, only worked half the time as there were frequent power failures. I missed the first practice day as I felt weak and feeble, unable to make any decisions having not eaten for two days.

Transport to launch provided many problems. The Indian Tourist Association had converted the eight-mile mule track which led up the mountain into a road suitable for vehicles, finishing the work the day before we arrived. The army had been drafted in to help with the competition and each morning their eight battered jeeps, with roof-racks hastily welded together at the last minute, assembled at the base of the mountain to transport the pilots and hang gliders to launch.

The Indian attitude towards time was alien and frustrating to most of the western competitors. The vehicles were always late, yet it was always crucial that we took off before 1 p.m. as the weather worsened during the afternoon. The monsoon season was approaching and thunderstorms were common by mid-afternoon. If we did not take off early, we would risk being caught in the fast-developing and hugely powerful storms. The danger was that the force of the ascending air associated with these storms could suck a hang glider into a cloud and carry it so high that the turbulence could break it. There was also a chance of electrocution or oxygen starvation. There could also be extreme turbulence on the outskirts of such a cloud, caused by strong winds.

The second day was set aside for practice and after twelve hours' sleep I felt a lot better and joined the other pilots to wait for our transport. A bus arrived two hours late to take us to the base of the mountain. We hit two walls and a truck on our short journey through the narrow streets of Palampur. The clouds were building ominously by the time we had loaded our gliders onto the jeeps and set off on the one-hour journey to take-off.

Launch was a steep grassy slope at 8,000 feet, bordered by a crowd of bemused onlookers who had walked for hours to watch 'the Birdmen', as they called us. Patiently they squatted in the blazing sun, watching the curious antics of the pilots as they rigged and then flew their colourful wings. Most local people had never seen a plane at close quarters, let alone an aircraft with fabric wings and no engine.

The unmistakable rumble of thunder was drawing closer as I finished rigging, heralding worsening conditions. The alternative to flying was running the gauntlet of being driven back down the precarious track in a vehicle of dubious mechanical integrity. I felt it would be safer to take my chances with the thunderstorms.

Immediately after take-off, I pulled on full speed to hurry my descent.

It was easy to see the landing area, as over 2,000 people had lined the huge field to watch us and were being kept on the perimeter by the army. Many had climbed trees and others perched on roofs to get a better view of the action.

The sky was dramatic, with huge black clouds contrasting with the pale, parched ground below, and a wall of hail was marching down the valley towards me. I spiralled downwards, increasing my descent rate still further, scared by the raw power in the air and wanting to be safely on the ground. I landed and was immediately surrounded by grinning, turbaned soldiers who, anxious to help, began detaching my camera and instruments.

Within two minutes the storm broke with a violent increase in the wind strength and a deluge of enormous hailstones. I could see fellow Englishman Edmund Potter coming in to land, fighting to control his glider in the gusty wind. I ran to help him and halfway across the field I was intercepted by a man, his eyes wide with fear, saying someone had crashed and was hurt. I sent him to fetch a doctor and ran over to where I could see a crowd of Indians gathering around a white glider.

Roman Mennig from Germany was lying with his eyes rolled back and a small trickle of blood oozing from his mouth. I didn't recognise him at first: he looked so different without any expression on his face. I felt for a pulse and found nothing. I had to try to resuscitate him and yelled at the soldiers to help me pull his harness off. About ten of them started to pull the straps in different directions, making the situation worse by tightening it around Roman's shoulders. I managed to get one of his arms out and lifted him to release the other arm, exposing his chest. I intertwined my fingers to give him a double fisted blow to the sternum and as I raised my arms, one of the soldiers was leaning over to get a better view and was in my way. 'Move!' I screamed, and hit Roman's massive chest with all the force I could muster, followed by five hard pulses. 'Can anyone do mouth to mouth?' I called in desperation, not expecting any reply. Deepak Marhajan, one of the Indian pilots, miraculously appeared at my side and he did three breaths to my five pulses.

After a couple of minutes I could feel someone tugging at my elbow. Glancing round, I saw it was one of the army chiefs, who was trying to pull me off. 'We must stand him up,' he said with authority. He had been put in charge of the landing field and felt the need to take command. With no time to explain, I rudely pushed him away and continued trying to revive Roman. 'Try harder,' I yelled, unable to accept his inert form and desperately wanting him to respond and breathe again.

After more than ten minutes there was no hint of response from Roman and Deepak and I had to give up our futile efforts and let the soldiers take the body away. I went to find Roman's best friend, Josef Guggenmos, to break the news gently before the army could get to him. Together we found where they had laid Roman's body at the side of the field. People were staring at him, so I took his emergency parachute out of his harness and covered him with it while Josef knelt alongside and played Roman's favourite song on his harmonica.

Soaked, filthy and stunned, we returned to the hotel.

This was the first time I had seen someone die. Having done two years of a nursing degree, I had been taught what to do on finding a patient who had had a cardiac arrest, and I would often mentally rehearse the resuscitation technique. During these imaginary rehearsals, the patient would always recover after heart massage and mouth to mouth. He would then thank me for saving his life and all would be well. The reality of having to admit defeat and give up our efforts on Roman left me shattered.

Taking part in an adventure sport, I have always been aware that injury or even death can be only a mistake away. With experience and good tuition the chances of an accident are minimised, but there is always the 'sod's law' situation where a poor decision or bad luck can intervene. In the early days of hang gliding, when pilots were self taught, the accident rate was high. With the advent of qualified instruction and modern, safer gliders, this had reduced dramatically, until hang gliding became one of the safer forms of sport aviation. Fatal accidents are rare and I have never seen another. There is still a small degree of risk, but for those pilots who taste the joy of free flight, it is a chance worth taking. Losing a friend is always hard and witnessing Roman's death haunted me for a long time.

A post mortem later revealed that Roman had broken his neck on impact and had died immediately. The pilots called a meeting that evening to decide what to do. Roman had been excited about the competition and had had his jacket embroidered with the logo of the 'Himalayadventure', with the same design printed onto his colourful harness and glider bag. We felt he would have wanted the competition to go ahead and together we decided to continue to fly in his memory, but it was a very subdued group of pilots who headed up to launch the following morning for the first day of the contest.

The course set for the first two days was a ten-mile triangle with each corner marked by a white cross. Normally pilots would have to photograph the turnpoints from the air to prove they had been round the course but in India, where manpower was easy to obtain, two judges were positioned next to each turnpoint to watch the competitors round the pylon and then wave a flag above the white cross to signal to each pilot that they had passed correctly. Unfortunately, the flags they were given were also white and from several thousand feet up it was impossible to see the white flag against the white cross, which caused some confusion. The competition was run on a one-on-one basis, where each pilot flew against a different competitor each day and the tally of wins and losses was counted. The pilot with the greatest number of wins at the end of the contest would secure overall first place.

In the middle of the launch area, standing out from the rest of the pilots wearing the usual T-shirt and shorts, was a dapper, grey-haired man in polished shoes, smart trousers and a shirt and tie. Jack Donaldson's ambition was to hang glide in the Himalayas and the fact that he was seventy years old didn't deter him. We all looked on in admiration as he launched, marvelling at his courage. His take-offs and landings weren't good and on his third flight he dislocated his arm in the landing field. Although that put an end to his flying, he remained unfailingly cheerful, having fulfilled his dream.

Navigation was difficult as the whole area seemed to be a uniform shade of brown. The usual method of referring to towns and roads was impossible, as we had no maps. Most of the time we used turnpoints and goals that were visible from launch, but occasionally we were sent further along the mountain range to land at a point that was distinctive in some way and easily found from the air.

Landing anywhere other than the official landing areas was a problem as there were many power lines and most of the area was terraced, creating narrow ledges to allow cultivation. This meant that if a cable-free area was found, the pilot would be faced with the prospect of landing on a narrow 'shelf', and many broke their gliders by misjudging their approach.

Even more dangerous were the crowds of people, who seemed to appear from nowhere. No matter how deserted an area appeared to be, there were always people around. One of the American pilots worked for twenty minutes, circling in weak lift trying to get back up, only to lose his thermal and be confronted by his earmarked landing field filled from end to end with a carpet of people. He had no option but to land in the middle of them and he hit three of the spectators, knocking one child unconscious for ten minutes.

All the army jeeps were sent to the official goal, so if you landed elsewhere it was up to you to find your own way home. With no telephones, it was a test of initiative, and each evening there was a succession of pilots arriving back at the hotel on the roof of a local bus or in carts drawn by skinny horses.

Each evening the meal was always enriched by entertaining accounts of everyone's adventures, recounted as we ate by candlelight because of endless power cuts. It was as though we had been spirited back a hundred years, as waiters wearing white jackets and bow ties would serve the food from silver platters. The image was occasionally shattered when a western dish, such as omelettes, was served. Not knowing how to transfer these strange items from his tray, the waiter would resort to fishing the individual egg 'pancakes' out by hand and slapping them on each dinner plate.

I won my first two rounds and on the third day I was drawn against world record holder, Larry Tudor. I felt very sick and weak on launch, having endured 'the runs' for six days and having eaten very little. I had to push modesty to one side as I dashed behind the bushes at frequent intervals and tried to ignore the curiosity of the crowd of onlookers.

As I was too feeble to lift my glider off the jeep, a kindly American pilot carried it for me and helped me to rig. I managed to get into my harness while he carried it to the take-off slope. I wanted to wait a while to let my stomach rest but Larry was impatient to get going. I offered to forfeit the round, but he assured me I would feel better in the air, as he had suffered from the same problem the previous day. Mustering what strength I could, I launched into a good thermal. The fresh air was a welcome relief from the heat and, as Larry had promised, I felt a lot better.

The task was a twelve-mile race to Palampur town with one pylon in between, and we climbed above launch to 9,500 feet. We flew together for the first four miles then Larry, mistakenly thinking we were close to goal, started to race, pulling the bar so far in that he lost a lot of height. I did not understand his tactics, but had been told at the beginning of the competition by Chris Bulger that the most important trick for flying one-on-one competitions was to 'stay with your man'. Chris was a gifted young American pilot whose accomplishments in competitions showed he knew what he was talking about, so I mirrored Larry and pulled the bar in fully.

I knew we still had several miles to go and we needed more height, so eventually I chickened out of our suicidal speed dive and flew to a small ridge where a group of birds were circling. I was rewarded with a rough but strong climb back to cloudbase, leaving Larry struggling to find a thermal 3,000 feet below.

I concentrated hard on reaching the finish line, oblivious to everything else around me. Suddenly I had an eerie sense of being followed. I turned around to find myself face to face with a large vulture flying less than three feet from the back of my wing. I froze as he extended his talons towards the sail. After a couple of seconds, he retracted his legs and continued to follow me. This exercise was repeated several times and I realised that rather than trying to attack me, he actually wanted to fly with me. His glide speed was slightly faster than mine and to avoid overtaking me, he put his legs down to create more drag until he had slowed down into the right position again.

The competition was forgotten as I watched this bird accepting me in his own environment. We flew into a strong thermal and as I started to circle, the vulture moved to my wingtip and mirrored my pattern. I could see every fleck in his eye and every subtle twitch of his feathers as we tightened our turn and climbed together to cloudbase. Finally I set out towards the goal with my personal escort behind me. It was not until I was safely across the finish line that he turned back towards the mountains.

I landed at the university sports ground, a football-pitch-sized stadium surrounded by grandstand seating, houses, power cables and a crowd of 2,000 people. The approach to the field was radical and entailed hurtling across the front of tiered seating to give the maximum length of run-in, then performing a steep turn to avoid hitting the crowds before straightening up to land. There were additional obstacles in the arena, such as a poor soldier whose brief was to stand in the middle of the field under the blazing sun and hold a windsock ... all day.

An Indian TV crew rushed up to me for an interview. Their technique was somewhat unorthodox. Thrusting the microphone inches from my mouth, the command was, 'One ... two ... three ... TALK!' I was then expected spontaneously to hold forth on hang gliding until their tape was full. The army had their work cut out to keep back the curious crowd, who constantly jostled for a better view, occasionally pushing so hard that someone in the front row fell onto my glider. A tiny, wizened old lady pushed forwards from the throng, lightly touched my arm and then reverently pressed my hand to her forehead as if to assure good fortune. With a shy smile, she pressed a crumpled one rupee note into my hand and was gone.

I returned to the hotel to discover the local doctor standing in the corner of my room whispering, 'Mr Jeff, Mr Jeff.' The muscular frame of Jeff Wilkinson was lying unconscious on my bed. Apparently he had landed in the middle of nowhere and had collapsed. Luckily some kind locals had brought him to the hotel and had carried him to the nearest bed.

A quick discussion with the doctor revealed that dehydration was the problem. I knew that without an intravenous drip the only way to treat him was to get some fluid inside him quickly. I started by patting his face gently and calling his name. It had no more effect than the doctor's efforts to wake him and eventually I resorted to hitting him across the face as hard as my depleted strength would allow and shouting at point blank range into his ear. He came round just long enough to drink two mouthfuls of water and then collapsed again. I repeated this routine every ten minutes, each time forcing him to take a little more. Within an hour he was awake and staggered to his feet, utterly confused as to what had happened but well on his way to a full recovery.

I was recuperating slowly from my sickness, though still eating very little. It was hard to sleep as it was so hot and humid at night and the sight of yet more curry at breakfast was enough to extinguish any glimmer of hunger.

My next round draw was against Gerard Thevenot, another of the world's top ten pilots and one of my flying heroes. I was looking forward to learning from him as we flew the thirty-mile task to a goal at Daremsala, but it was not to be. I lost a lot of height after take-off and had to scratch around in weak lift while Gerard climbed to cloudbase on the next ridge, cruised down the range and out of sight.

Finally I clawed my way back up and flew along the course, enjoying the view of the dramatic mountains. At 11,000 feet I met up with Josef Guggenmos, who was unmistakable in his fluorescent orange harness. He was just in front of me when a vulture that seemed to have a fetish for orange appeared behind his wing. The bird flew in perfect formation and appeared to be totally besotted with him. As we started to circle, the bird moved into position behind Josef and when I got in the way, inadvertently flying between them, the bird indignantly wove its way back to Josef's wing, casting me a 'go and find your own mate' look over its shoulder. The bird then escorted Josef all the way to goal.

Flying was cancelled for the next two days as huge storm clouds could be seen over the mountains, with towering anvils of ice. I went into Palampur and was immediately surrounded by people. A toothless old lady wearing a widow's white sari approached me, grinning broadly. She was a tall, striking matriarch who obviously enjoyed the fact that there were two women flying amongst 'the Birdmen'. She clasped my hand warmly as she smiled, pointing to herself and saying 'Mama'. I reciprocated with my name and she led me by the hand to her house, which was refreshingly cool after the heat and dust of the streets.

She barked instructions and a chair and small table were set upon the bare mud floor. I was brought a glass of pink water, which I drank with a smile, trying not to think about the consequences of the untreated water on my poor abused innards. Neighbours and friends came pouring into the house when they heard one of 'the Birdmen' was available for close inspection and soon the room was full. I had been given a photograph by the local newspaper reporter which showed me landing at the university. I gave it to Mama, who beamed broadly, possessively clutched it to her bosom pronouncing 'Mama's', and would not let anyone else even look at it.

The clouds finally cleared, allowing a short final task which was the same as that of the first two days, a small triangle finishing at the university sports ground. This time there were 7,000 people lining the field and I could hear the roar of the crowd from 3,000 feet as I flew in having won my round to claim third place in the competition. The contest was over, with Gerard taking first place and Chris Bulger second. I was thrilled with my third position and was awarded an enormous, gaudy silver platter and £1,000 prize money.

The following morning we were sitting on the veranda of the hotel, packed and ready to leave, waiting for the buses which were due to arrive at 9.30 to take us to Delhi. At 11.30 one bus turned up with only three vacant seats on board. There was no other transport arranged and we all had planes to catch within thirty-six hours. Heated arguments broke out between the organisers of the competition and the pilots and eventually another bus turned up to take the remaining people.

The twenty-four-hour journey was arduous but eventful and was interspersed with an array of mechanical problems. The gear stick fell off, so we picked up a young boy who was employed to sit alongside the driver and kick the remaining stump in the appropriate direction according to which gear the driver required.

Jack Donaldson had contracted dysentery and I was very worried about him. There was no way of getting medical attention or of finding a suitable hospital and I felt very vulnerable on his behalf. He was past caring, with his eyes sunken, and he was muttering deliriously. He could not rest in the tiny seats, so we took him to the broad bench alongside the driver's seat and I perched on the edge of it to prevent him rolling off while he got some much-needed sleep. Once home in England, Jack was hospitalised for three weeks and had to have a kidney removed. He then gave up hang gliding in favour of a safer pastime: land-yachting! He made a full recovery and no doubt he still wore his shirt and tie for his new hobby.

We had to stop at one stage when we found the road blocked by an overturned bus, which had crashed and been left for some time obstructing the narrow mountain road. Our driver just shrugged his shoulders and disappeared to find some tea. The American pilots, aware of their planes to catch in Delhi, climbed up the hill, emerging some time later at the helm of an enormous bulldozer, which they had found at a nearby quarry. It was commandeered by a local man, with a dozen people shouting instructions. The crippled remains of the bus were finally moved and we were on our way once more. We made two further unscheduled stops, one for a flat tyre and the other because we ran out of diesel. We finally arrived at the Punjabi border, only to be turned away as there were escalating problems between the local Sikhs and Muslims and no trains or buses were being allowed through. After backtracking a hundred miles it seemed nothing short of a miracle that we arrived in Delhi just in time to catch our planes.

India had been an extraordinary adventure, combining the extreme lows of Roman's death and the worst physical illness I had ever suffered, with highs of experiencing the most wonderful camaraderie between pilots and the hospitality of the people of Palampur. There had also been the unforgettable experience of being accepted as a bird by a bird in its own environment. This had opened up a new dimension for me in hang gliding. I wanted to fly with other birds of prey, to watch them at close quarters from the privileged viewpoint that only a hang glider pilot can experience. I began to dream of flying with golden eagles and peregrine falcons, but above all with Andean condors. To me they embodied everything I loved about hang gliding with their perfect soaring technique, flying above the spectacular mountains of the Andes.

CHAPTER 6

The Sky's the Limit

March 1985 marked the beginning of the competition season and I was approached by an Italian hang glider manufacturer, Polaris, who were trying to woo me into changing gliders once more. Their new design was called the GZ – a 175-square-foot monster of a glider weighing ninety-five pounds, with an enormous control frame. They flew me to Italy to test fly it and baited the hook with promises of paying my competition expenses, cash incentives and providing two new gliders. I would not commit to the glider until I had tried it out in Britain and I insisted they built me a lightweight version with a small control frame, as the sheer dimensions of the standard model made it impossible for me to carry it or to take off.

When the glider arrived in England it had a smaller control frame, but they had obviously decided that I was being a wimp and over-fussy about the weight, so it remained just under seven stone. The first time I lifted the GZ onto the roof of my car I put my back out, leaving me confined to bed for a week, and it was a month before I could fly again. A lighter version was made but, despite its huge sail area, it did not climb well in thermals and I was always lower than everyone else. In the end I gave it back to them, having learned the invaluable lesson that it wasn't worth losing out on glider performance no matter how good a deal a manufacturer was offering.

By the beginning of the 1986 competition season, I was back on an Airwave glider, this time a new 155-square-foot Magic 4. The glider suited me well: the size was perfect and the handling and performance were excellent. I was overjoyed to be so confident with my glider and it showed in my results. At the first League meeting of the year among the familiar hills of Merthyr Tydfil, I won a task outright, putting me in second place at the end of the competition.

The first Women's European Championships were to be held in France in the summer of 1985. It was the first time an all-women's international competition had ever been held and a British team of five was selected.

A month beforehand, we held a women's competition in Britain to bring together and encourage women in the sport. After years of being in such a small minority, it was wonderful to see so many keen women pilots outnumbering the men on the hill. There were several new and inexperienced pilots there and I really wanted to encourage them, as I knew what difficulties they were experiencing. I spent my time talking to them about different gliders and flying techniques, helping with any problems. As a result, when we flew a simple ridge run I was in 'pedestrian mode' and was beaten by Heidi Fawcett from Scotland.

The next task was open cross-country, my speciality, but again I made a mistake. The conditions were poor and Jenny Ganderton and I had waited for a long time to find a thermal which would get us high enough to leave the hill. When the thermal died two miles behind launch, we both flew to a small ridge facing into wind in the hope of being able to pick up another thermal. It didn't happen and we both sank to the bottom of the ridge and landed, only to watch in frustration as several other pilots, some of whom had never even been cross-country before, flew in a straight line away from take-off and beat us.

Heidi collared me in the pub that night, clutching her well-deserved second place trophy. I had not met her before, but as a feisty, red-haired Scot, she was not fazed by such an irrelevance, and told me some home truths about my attitude.

'If you go to France and flit around the hillside talking to people as you did today, you'll lose the European Championships,' she said bluntly. Her directness was softened by her gentle voice and lilting Scottish accent. Looking me straight in the eye she continued, 'If you concentrate on the competition and take it seriously, you will win – it's up to you.'

For the first time I found myself thinking about the completely separate, mental side of my sport. I had learned and developed the necessary physical expertise to climb well in thermals and to maximise the performance of the glider. I had studied meteorology and had a good idea where thermals formed and could recognise the shapes of the cumulus clouds which would give me the best climb rate. Now I was confronted with the fact that there was an extra dimension which I had never even noticed – that of sports psychology.

I began to prepare for the Europeans with dedication. I was fuelled once again with the same obsession I had experienced in breaking the world record in Owens Valley. Taking on board what Heidi had said, I concentrated hard on my goal and would not be distracted. I badly wanted the title of European Champion and could see the advantages that this would bring in my search for a full-time sponsor.

Lil-lets had terminated their sponsorship at the beginning of the year. It had been immensely hard to get coverage for them, as not only was their product a sensitive subject, but also their publicity department did not know how to promote hang gliding. On more than one occasion I found myself writing press releases and dropping them through the doors of national newspapers in Fleet Street at 2 o'clock in the morning. The partnership had run its course, Lil-lets had benefited in media terms from me, and the experience I had gained from the media and how to deal with a sponsor would serve me well in the future.

The site for the European Championships was Séderon in the southern French Alps, a beautiful area famous for its lavender, grown in vast purple swathes along the valley floor. I arrived a week early to explore the area and to get myself in the right frame of mind for the competition. I went with fellow team member Louise Anderton, whose sense of humour ensured that we had a great time, combining late nights and meeting new friends with some excellent flying practice around the Séderon valley. We set ourselves tasks to fly and enjoyed exploring the area, taking pleasure in the novelty of lavender-scented thermals.

By the time the competition started, I felt full of energy and satisfied with my flying. I had a deep and immovable feeling of self-confidence, not a brash big-headedness, but a sense of composure and eager anticipation of the contest to come.

As the pilots arrived, it was obvious that there was a wide range of ability, from world record holders down to an Italian woman who had never flown cross-country before. The camaraderie was strong and it was uplifting to see a group of physically strong and determined women who had all been through a similar struggle to me and had emerged as keen pilots.

I was placed as favourite to win the championships because of my experience in the British League and my world distance record. As I had never met or heard of many of the other sixty competitors, I reserved my judgement, as they were an unknown quantity.

The contest was scheduled to last four days and we needed to fly a minimum of three tasks to validate the competition. It was an anticlimax when, on the first day, the wind was so strong we didn't even drive up to take-off to look at the conditions. By the second day the wind was calmer and an open distance task was set. Rosi Brahms, a muscular German pilot, flew the furthest distance of thirty miles and I landed just a hundred yards behind her.

The following day's conditions were poor with sparse, weak thermals, and the organisers set an over-optimistic triangle task. I had put my back out the previous evening while carrying my glider. By the time we reached launch I was in agony. The wind was light and continually switched direction, which meant that we had to keep moving to a different part of the mountain top to take off. I needed help to carry my glider and swallowed some aspirin before taking off.

I made the same mistake as I had in the women's competition in England by thermalling away from take-off and then stopping to soar a ridge downwind to wait for another thermal. In these fickle conditions this tactic didn't work and I continued to fly back and forth in vain until the sun set and I landed at the bottom, having been overtaken by several pilots who had just flown off downwind. The winning distance that day was twelve miles. With one task left to fly, a warm and friendly Italian pilot, Ornella Magnaguagno, was in first place, and I had dropped to third.

A boisterous party was held that night, with wine and dancing. A few more aspirin quietened my back down sufficiently for me to participate and a few glasses of wine proved an excellent anaesthetic. I danced into the small hours along with the other women. The following morning I gingerly climbed out of bed, expecting to be incapable of walking through having aggravated my injury, only to find that whatever had been out of line had slotted back into place. Whether it was the dancing gyrations or the alcohol-enhanced deep, relaxed sleep that had fixed it I did not know, but the relief was immense.

At last on the final day conditions improved to produce classic-looking cumulus clouds and the excellent weather we had been hoping for. A race was set to Laragne, twenty miles away, and I sat under my rigged glider to decide tactics.

I wanted to win and was prepared to cut it as finely as I could, relying on the hope that the other pilots would fly the race more conservatively. With my ruler and map I worked out how many thermals I would need and what height I needed to be before I could leave the last thermal and be sure of making it across the goal line. The conditions were similar to those I had experienced in Owens Valley. I decided that if I adhered to my plan I would either win the European Championships or blow it in style.

I took off early and climbed to cloudbase before crossing the valley to connect with the ridge which ran all the way to goal. I had been watching the cloud development for an hour before taking off and I headed straight for the spur which was producing the most consistent thermal. I was rewarded with a fast climb back to cloudbase and then flew in a straight line all the way to the end of the ridge to goal.

I arrived thirty-five minutes after taking off, but it took me a further ten minutes to locate the goal line. Instead of the usual conspicuous fluorescent line, the marshals had set out a white material strip on top of the white stones of the dry river bed, and from 2,000 feet above it was almost invisible. They had parked their car in the shade of a nearby tree, so there was nothing to give away their position. I knew I was in the right place and my frustration mounted as I searched, wasting precious time and height. Finally I saw the faint line of the material and crossed it with an official time of forty-five minutes. The next pilot took an hour to complete the course and I won the title of European Women's Champion. This was another major achievement and at last I began to have faith in my ability as a pilot.

I returned to England for the League final in the Yorkshire Dales. The day before the competition the weather was perfect for cross-country flying and I broke the British women's distance record by flying 115 miles, landing near the mouth of the Humber. I was accompanied part of the way by a group of top French pilots, who had come to fly with the League.

The French team had arrived looking like a collection of tropical birds, wearing fitted, colourful flying suits. The standard British flying suit of 1986 was either navy or royal blue and totally shapeless. Raising more eyebrows than any other Frenchman was Richard Walbec who, having discovered the drag-reducing properties of a tight lycra outer layer, had adorned himself in a pale pink stretch catsuit with multicoloured spots.

Three hours into the flight, while flying across Grimsby, I watched Richard land in the middle of the town and a huge crowd gather on the playing field around him. When I asked him later if he had been given a cup of tea, he looked puzzled and replied. 'No. Zey all stared at me strangely and zen 'urried away.'

I couldn't help laughing as I imagined the scene: a man descended from the skies wearing a pale pink spotted body suit only to be greeted by a group of Grimsby folk. I'm surprised he wasn't arrested!

The British Team selectors had taken note of the improvement in my flying. A squad of eight pilots was selected to receive intensive training from which the next world championship team would be chosen. Mine was among the eight names read out and my aspirations moved up to an entirely different grade. I was in with a chance of competing at the very top level alongside the men. I sensed a resistance from some of the selectors to the idea of a woman on the 'A-team', but I obviously had enough supporters to get me onto the squad and it was now up to me to continue flying well.

The next world championships were due to be held in Australia in January 1988 and I would need to prove myself by doing well at the pre-world championships the year before. It clashed with the biggest jewellery trade fair of the year and Dad needed my help. With great self-sacrifice, my mother said she would stand in for me despite her hatred of trade fairs.

I was delighted when Louise Anderton decided to join me on the trip to Australia. We had talked a lot about travelling when we were in Séderon, but she seemed firmly entrenched in her regular job at Barclays Bank. When I told her of my plans, she handed in her notice, withdrew the money she had saved for a deposit on a house and booked herself a plane ticket to Sydney.

We arrived just before Christmas to discover that our gliders had not been put on the plane and wouldn't arrive for another week. We managed to keep ourselves occupied by exploring the beaches of Sydney and buying a vehicle for our travels.

In Australia the skin cancer awareness campaign was as its height and, as Louise had red-blonde hair and fair skin to match, she was constantly approached on the beach by people horrified to see a woman exposing just-arrived-from-England skin. Louise would try to explain that she was only going to stay outside for twenty minutes and that she was smothered in sunblock, but they would not be deterred. She was lectured every day by well-meaning strangers telling her she shouldn't be in the sun, and shops would offer her after-sun skin repair cream when all she wanted was to buy a packet of crisps!

We met Bill Moyes, one of the founding fathers of modern hang gliding who started flying in 1962 whilst exploring ways of spicing up water-skiing by holding onto a kite. He would be towed at increasing speed behind a boat until he was airborne. He began doing stunt shows and proved to be something of a cat with nine lives after a series of horrific accidents. He tells great stories of his close shaves, pointing out the relevant bits of his misshapen body which were bent by each particular fall. Bill set up Moyes Gliders in Sydney, which is still one of the top manufacturers in the world.

Bill is generous to a fault, but he does have a problem with accepting strong women, especially those who invade his macho terrain of hang gliding. He has turned this into an art form and revels in teasing any female flyer to the point of fury. I found that the only way to counter this was not to react, but to stand my ground firmly and always keep a sense of humour. I liked Bill and admired his courage, realising that all his attempts at being brusque and intimidating disguised a big heart underneath.

We spent a lot of time with Bill and his wife Molly at their house next to the beach. Molly is always good humoured and never flinches at the unending procession of visiting pilots who invade their house. Bill took us to a car auction, where Louise and I bought a VW Kombi van whose engine had been modified to cope with the heat in Australia. It was ideal for carrying gliders and large amounts of luggage.

We drove it back to Bill's house and checked it over, discovering that there was hardly any oil in the engine. We filled it up, but as we drove up the road blue smoke billowed from the exhaust as all the new oil came pouring straight out again.

We drove to Bill's car workshop (his other business apart from hang glider manufacturing), where he gave us a set of tools and told us to start taking the engine to pieces. We helped ourselves to dirty overalls out of the laundry basket and set to work. Neither of us had ever taken an engine out before so Bill kept popping back to tell us which bits to extract. When it became more complicated, he sent one of his mechanics to help and I ended up passing him the tools, which was much quicker as he knew what he was doing. Bill found the sight of Louise and me struggling to get to grips with the basics of the engine in our filthy overalls endlessly amusing, but he always made sure we had the help we needed.

In a couple of days we replaced the rings and rectified various other problems. On Christmas morning we discovered Bill with his hands deep in the engine putting the final touches to it, saying it would be a lovely Christmas present to see us driving off into the sunset and out of his hair.

We left Sydney with the van's engine purring contentedly and made our way towards Mount Buffalo, the site of the pre-world championships, to get some practice before the competition. As we drove into the snowy mountains the forests became more dense and we were on the lookout for kangaroos, which had a tendency to jump out in front of the van without warning. Flocks of sulphur-crested white cockatoos clowned in the trees, hanging upside down like bats and screeching loudly.

We based ourselves at a campsite in the village of Bright, surrounded by mountains with a clear, bubbling river nearby where the swimming holes were cold and refreshing after the heat of the day. Anxious to fly, we sprang out of bed the following morning and raced up the mountain road to the top of Mount Buffalo. Both Louise and I stopped dead in our tracks as we caught sight of the take-off.

The top of the mountain was a huge granite slab which dropped vertically for 1,500 feet. My vertigo returned and the concept of running off the edge terrified me. Louise's fear of heights was worse than mine and we found going towards the edge intimidating to say the least. A wooden slatted ramp had been built onto the edge of the granite. Louise had never taken off from a ramp before and all she knew was that I had crashed three times in Austria when attempting it for the first time.

I was more fearful for her than for myself and once we had rigged our gliders I walked away from her. I did not want to help her launch, preferring to leave it to one of the other pilots on take off, as I knew she would feel my apprehension. I busied myself round my glider whilst keeping one eye on her as she approached the ramp.

As she lifted her glider, I could not watch. I turned my back and looked in the other direction. I heard the rhythmic thump of her feet as she ran and then a terrifying gasp. I whirled round, expecting to see her glider's wingtip as she was slung against the granite, only to see her floating serenely away from the cliff after a perfect launch. Apparently as she went over the edge she had looked straight down the rock face and had let out the involuntary yelp. By the time I was ready for my own launch, I was a nervous wreck. Needing to get a grip of myself, I took a few deep breaths and tried to rationalise my fears. The only cure was to get in the air and with a fully committed sprint I hurtled off the edge of the cliff.

I soon recovered my composure as I saw the pattern of the mountains taking shape. Many were covered in dense eucalyptus forests, whose deep green leaves gave way to the scorched fields in the valleys below. Cultivated forests of fast-growing pine trees lined some of the slopes, their regimented rows looking incongruous next to the unruly native gums.

I flew for four hours along a triangle course, meeting up with a wedgetail eagle *en route*. Its hooked beak gave it a bad-tempered expression and it was much larger than the vultures I had flown with in India. As he flew above me, I watched his shadow float across the top of my sail. I looked back to find he was following my circle pattern, three feet behind my wing, giving me a full inspection. Unlike the Himalayan vultures, which liked to thermal in company and climb at the same rate, this bird was following his own pattern. As he came out of his next circle we were on a converging course. I watched spellbound as he cruised majestically past, gently brushing my wingtip with his, before proceeding on his way. I continued round my triangle, ending up back at the campsite where we were staying. If the flying continued like this, I knew I was going to love Australia.

A couple of days later, we reluctantly returned to Sydney to collect the other two members of our party, Palle Jensen and Digby Rolfe. We decided to enter a competition at Corryong, some fifty miles from Buffalo, which would provide an ideal warm-up for the pre-worlds.

The campsite at Corryong was basic, with no washing facilities, but the Murray River flowed alongside and was sparkling clean, though very cold. The usual washing procedure was to jump off the bridge upstream and swim as fast as possible to the bank before you froze in the icy water.

During my first flight at Corryong my previous enjoyment of the wedge-tail eagles was put into context. Here they were nesting and far more territorial, attacking any hang glider who had the audacity to intrude on their patch. Often, the first I would know of their presence was when I heard a loud twang as they caught the top rigging wires with their talons and the whole glider shuddered. Sometimes they would give a couple of warning passes before striking, screaming in fury and just missing the glider with their claws outstretched. They would then climb for another strike but this time the sickening sound of tearing sailcloth would fill my ears as the eagle angrily grabbed the leading edge of the glider on its way past.

I found myself in the company of wedgetails up to six times per flight and began to feel victimised as I had far more eagle attacks than anyone else. I came to the conclusion that it was the bright red and orange colour of my glider. I felt like a sitting duck, unable to out-manoeuvre them. I tried imitating their aggressive cries, squawking even louder than they did, thinking I might frighten them off, but I only succeeded in making myself hoarse.

In the end I just had to put up with it, thankful that they struck the glider and did not go for the pilot, whom they assumed to be the talons of the thirty-foot wingspan bird. Every now and then I enjoyed a small taste of revenge when an eagle tripped over my top wires and would come tumbling over the front of my glider. His wings and feet would flail wildly and there seemed to be a look of confusion on his face. The birds they normally attack don't have 'trip wires' above their wings.

At night the campsite was teeming with wildlife. There were possums in the trees, which we fed with museli bars by torchlight. Their cuddly appearance and long bushy tails belied the noises they made when foraging for food. Their guttural gulping, slurping and grunting sounded fiendish when at point-blank range outside our tent. It was like the sound effects from a horror movie and we resolved not to feed them in future to stop them coming for more snacks in the night.

I was flying well and feeling confident, and after the first two days of competition I was in first place. My muscles were sore and I needed to relax more in the air. I achieved this by the unorthodox method of cutting my finger to the bone just before take-off on day three. Unable to grip the bar as hard whilst flying I gave my arms a much-needed rest.

We flew one more round and I held on to my position to win the competition. It was the first mixed event I had ever won and although I was really pleased, I felt some discomfort as I could feel the dented egos of the men around me. I still had problems understanding why they saw me as different and made such an issue of the fact that I was a woman.

Although the calibre of pilots was not as high as it would be the following week at Mount Buffalo, it was a good start and put me in the right frame of mind for the competition to come.

We moved back to Bright for the start of the pre-world championships to find that most of the world's top pilots had arrived and the number of competitors was up to 150. We were split into three groups and each flew from a different site. Our group was allocated to Mount Buffalo for the first day and, in spite of the strong wind forecast, we drove up the mountain.

Because of the length of time it would take to launch fifty competitors from the normal launch point, a group of pilots had spent the previous week building a second ramp at the back end of the granite gorge. The original ramp was enough to set my nerves jangling, but at least you could not see the 1,500-foot drop from it. Not only did the new launch ramp leave nothing to the imagination, it was also perched twelve feet above the ground on a wooden platform, so you had to climb up some precarious steps with your glider to reach it. I christened it 'scary corner' and resolved to have nothing to do with it.

As the competitors were rigging near the original launch, two free fliers prepared to take off from scary corner. With the wind blowing from behind, their technique needed to be perfect. The first pilot didn't have his wings level and as he ran off, the glider lurched to one side. With such a sheer cliff below, however, he got away with it.

The second was not so lucky. He also allowed one wing to drop, either through sloppiness or fright. His wingtip caught on the rock face and began to drag along it. The friction slowed the glider down and rotated it towards the cliff. There was silence on launch as everyone watched in horror, the only sound the scraping of aluminium on granite. His legs hung limp as he looked straight down, knowing he was about to die.

The glider seemed to pause, prolonging the pilot's agony before the tumble down the cliff which seemed inevitable. This coincided with him reaching a small gully which cut into the rock face. An opportune thermal lifted the back of his glider and flipped him into the gully, planting him upside down in a tree. He was undoubtedly the luckiest man alive.

Our task was cancelled because of the strong tailwind, but the other groups who were flying nearby hills facing into the wind managed to get a round in. Two members of the British team, Darren Arkwright and Bruce Goldsmith, had a lucky escape when their driver rolled their station wagon after picking them up. Miraculously, no one was hurt, but their gliders were a mess. The weight of a large car plus occupants sliding along a tarmac road on its roof bearing the lightweight frames of two hang gliders does aluminium tubing no good at all. After hours of tube bending, sleeving, pop riveting and the application of copious amounts of sticky-back sailcloth, their gliders were finally declared airworthy.

After a poor first round, I improved my position with each subsequent day. I overcame my tendency to follow other people, which had always been my downfall when flying with good pilots. As soon as I started ignoring the others, using them only as thermal markers, my results improved dramatically.

The penalty for not making it to goal was high and so I flew conservatively, trying to ensure that I got there each day. I felt outclassed by some of the top pilots, who managed to produce top scores every day. While I was concentrating on getting to goal, they had the confidence that they were going to get there and were just concerned about flying faster than their opponents. I wanted to make sure I made it through the cut, as only the top sixteen from each group would go on to the final rounds.

The last task of the heats was a seventy-five-mile race to goal at

Khancoban airfield just past Corryong. Having taken off into a booming thermal, I was flying alone above Lake Hume, a man-made reservoir. The skeletons of trees reached skywards out of the watery depths and flocks of pelicans coasted regally on the surface.

I reached the ridge on the far side of the lake, where I found a monstrous thermal which hoisted me above the haze to 12,500 feet. The terrain sank below me until I could see all the valleys and routes spread out like a map. A wispy cloud formed between me and the sun, displaying all the colours of the rainbow shining through the water droplets, which became a mass of radiating colour.

Three hours later I arrived at goal, which put me up to sixth in my group and comfortably into the finals. I was the only woman to make it through, which gave Bill Moyes the opportunity to enhance his reputation as the world's number one sexist. He teased me at the goal field, saying, 'We can't have the cut yet – there'd be a woman in the final for the first time and that'll never do!'

After a week of competition flying I was beginning to suffer physically. I had flown every day for the past three weeks, averaging four hours' flying each day, and my muscles were sore. Worse than this was the problem of late nights and erratic meal times. Because many of the goals were miles away from Bright, by the time a car had come to pick me up and brought me back, it was well past midnight. Supper was a bonus and often consisted of a packet of peanuts and an ice-cream from a late-night shop. Usually, I was too tired to eat.

The rest day, which was to be held before the start of the finals, was cancelled (to the disappointment of my shoulders and arms) and we went straight on with the competition. I was now surrounded by the best of the best of international hang glider pilots.

The first day of the finals was very windy, which was the worst scenario for me. Unlike the gliders of most of the men I was flying against, mine was tuned so that it handled well, which meant the sail was slack and its top speed was reduced because of this. They all seemed to have an extra five miles an hour, which made all the difference against a strong headwind.

Eventually I became frustrated with my painfully slow progress and left the ridge to go around a turnpoint. I found myself far too low and landed short. I lost a lot of points, making my take-off position (which depended on each pilot's ranking) much later the following day, and I spent a frustrating hour watching conditions deteriorate before it was my turn to launch.

It was the last day of the competition and I finished with a paltry ten-mile flight, dropping to forty-second overall. I was disappointed after my performance in the heats, but I still had a lot to learn about keeping my concentration and not being fazed by whom I was competing against.

Louise and I spent a week with the Moyes family at their holiday home in idyllic Shoal Bay north of Sydney. Bill bossed all his guests into enjoying themselves, ensuring they were all out of bed and on their way to the beach with surfboards by 6 a.m. if the waves were right. His authoritarian approach backfired with Louise, when he caught her putting sunblock on her skin before going swimming. 'What do you think you are, a beach belle?' he yelled at her.

Instead of telling him where to go, Louise obediently put away her lotion and went into the sea. She spent forty-five minutes without skin protection and went beetroot from head to foot; even her eyelids were burned.

I was needed back at work, but Louise had developed the travel bug and had decided to stay until her money ran out. As she drove me back to Sydney to catch my plane, I felt very sorry to be leaving. I had been impressed with Australia, the huge variations in landscape, the beautiful beaches, friendly people and the consistency of the flying, which had been second to none. Whilst I had enjoyed my stay I had no idea that in three years' time I would be moving out there to live.

CHAPTER 7

Crash Landings and
Gold Medals

For the first time in years the back pain which had plagued me was gone. Through pure luck I had discovered a skilled osteopath, Ken Kingsbury, who started work on my spine. Ken is a surgeon who travels around the world with the British judo team and what he doesn't know about fixing injured bodies isn't worth knowing. He diagnosed a rotation of the fifth lumbar vertebra in my spine, which had been out of place for five years. Within two weeks he had manipulated it sufficiently to stop the pain. I had forgotten what it was like to live without backache and could not believe my new-found freedom of movement. It took a few more sessions before the muscles adjusted to holding my back in its new straight position, but finally I was pronounced 'fixed'. Ken was the first person I had ever met within the medical profession whose attitude was unreservedly positive towards sport and, instead of telling me to give up hang gliding, his aim was to get me back in the air as soon as possible.

I trained hard in the gym to get myself as fit as possible and tuned my glider for greater speed, ready for the first League meeting of 1987. Even though my chances of making the world championship team had been lessened by my poor Australian performance, there was everything still to play for with a full competition season ahead.

I was asked by the BBC to teach Peter Duncan how to fly cross country for an edition of *Duncan Dares*. We spent a week in the Brecon Beacons, during which time the weather treated us to a display of extremes which defied belief. Normally in April the weather is variable, but you can be sure that some of the conditions will be perfect for a beginner's first thermal flights. On this occasion, Murphy's law prevailed as we sat through fog, hail, rain, snow and, as a finale, a small hurricane which brought down all the phone lines and closed the Severn Bridge. We admitted defeat and headed home.

I was driving back from Wales in the fast lane of the M4, when my car hiccuped twice. As I pressed the accelerator pedal to clear what I assumed to be a fuel blockage, the engine revved but had no effect on the speed of the car. Cursing the fact that I would have to call out the RAC and would be late home, I pulled over to the hard shoulder. As soon as I stopped, steam started pouring out from under the wheel arches. Within two seconds, the paint on the bonnet started to bubble and I realised with horror that it wasn't steam, it was smoke!

Flames licked from under the bonnet as I leaped out. The only thing on my mind was my brand new glider attached to the roof-rack. I ignored my handbag alongside me on the passenger seat with my diary, address book and set of work keys, and rushed to undo the strap holding my glider to the roof. The front end was tied to an aluminium support which was bolted to the front bumper, but I could not reach it as the heat of the fire was too intense. Using force borne of desperation, I pulled the glider so hard that it broke the support and I carried my precious wing up the embankment.

Hugging my glider, I watched numbly as the flames engulfed the car, burning it from end to end within ten minutes. All my favourite flying equipment, collected over seven years, went up in smoke: my harness, parachute, suit, maps, instruments, radio, and gloves. I had only three weeks to replace it before the first League. I was shocked at the speed and intensity of the fire. I spent so many hours in the car, travelling for work and for flying. The last thing I expected was for it to combust spontaneously on the motorway. Although a thorough examination was carried out on the thirteen-month-old car, no cause could be found as there was so little left of the engine to examine.

I had to replace all my equipment if my preparation for the forthcoming competition season was not to be in vain. Over the next two weeks I begged, borrowed and bought enough replacement gear to be able to fly again.

The weekend after the car fire, I went to Derbyshire to do a photo shoot with freelance photographer David Higgs. He had constructed a long pole which stuck out from the glider's nose like a giant proboscis. With the camera attached to the far end, the picture would be taken looking back at me and the view behind.

We went to a site in the south of the Peak District called Bunster, just west of Dovedale, which I had never flown. I was instructed to fly as high as I could and then to do some steeply banked turns while David fired the camera from the ground using an infra-red remote control.

The wind was light, making it difficult to stay level with the hill, let alone gain thousands of feet above it. I flew four times, landing back on top for David to replace the film, adjust the exposure and tamper with the temperamental infra-red release. During the fifth flight, the wind picked up and changed direction slightly and I was able to soar easily in the now buoyant air.

The remote control went wrong again and I heard the motordrive methodically fire off the entire film immediately after launch and I came in once more to top land. David replaced the faulty remote control with an electronic one with a wire leading from the camera to a button on the control bar which I could operate myself.

By the time he had taped it in place and reloaded the camera, the wind had increased a little more. As I took off, the air felt alarmingly different, unpredictable and turbulent. After five minutes of wrestling with the glider I became really unhappy with the conditions and called David on the radio to say I was going to land.

It was a struggle keeping the glider pointing into wind as I descended towards the big open field at the top of the hill. Without warning, at sixty feet I hit a patch of violent turbulence and the glider tipped nose down in an accelerating dive directly towards the ground.

I pulled on more speed to try to get the wing to respond, but I was too low and the turbulence was too severe. The glider sail blotted out the sky and all I could see was the mixed greens of the grass and fast-approaching trees.

At twenty feet the glider began to pull out of the dive, but by then it was too late as the ground came rushing up to meet me. At the last moment, unable to salvage the situation, I had to resort to self-preservation tactics and I curled up in a ball with my right arm over my head. My last thought before I hit was 'This is going to hurt.'

The impact was hard as I hit the ground at over thirty-five miles an hour. I was badly winded and initially I could only lie and gasp for air, upturned like a stranded beetle.

I was aware of bits of broken tubing everywhere and small rips in my glider's sail. On later inspection I had broken off the entire nose section – both leading edges and the keel, within six inches of the nose plates. My arm had hit the keel and had broken it further down. Every other tube on

left Toni (3) and me 18 months. In almost all our childhood photographs, Toni is in a dress and I am in dungarees. *(Tom Leden)*

below Learning to fly near Merthyr Tydfil, 1979.

foot The first women's league, 1981. My first 'flying suit' consisted of a pair of salopettes and a wooly jumper!

top Taking off from Steinbergkogel above Kitzbuhel, Austria, in 1982. I was living 10 paces from where this photo was taken.

above Ten miles under my belt, with 136 still to go. Breaking the women's world distance record in Owen Valley, California. *(Judy Leden)*

left Lil-lets sponsored glider. I was ill prepared for the monstrous six foot blossoms which smothered my new wing!

Gendarmes and customs officials bemused by yet another English eccentric on a beach in Calais after crossing the Channel, 1989. (Nick Caddick)

above Jack Donaldson (aged 70), having just fulfilled his ambition to hang glide in the Himalayas (he never flew without his shirt and tie). (Judy Leden)

left Collecting my MBE with Mum and Dad, 1989.

overleaf
Photo (David Higgs)

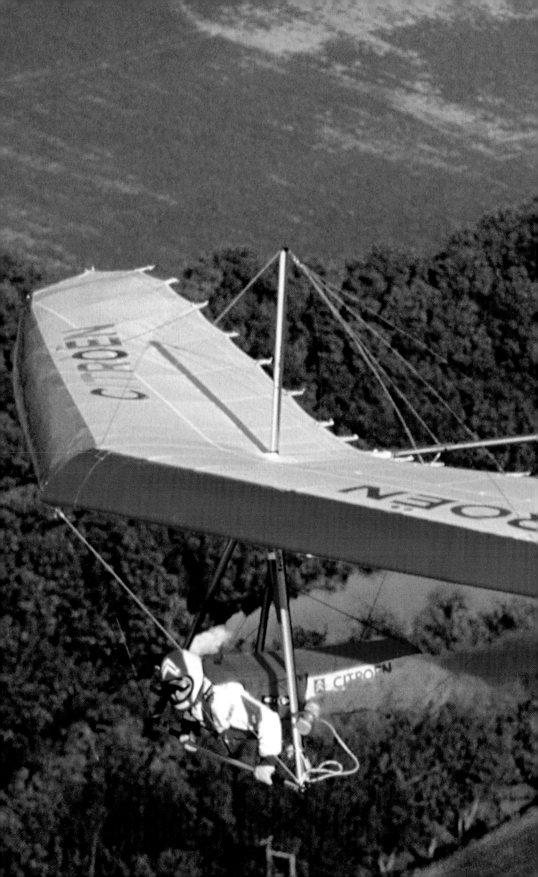

Cotopaxi Volcano. *(Matt Dickinson)*

---

left
above Looking into the jowls of Cotopaxi crater. *(Matt Dickinson)*

below Sunrise during my first ascent of Cotopaxi. I had been climbing for
five hours and was thoroughly hypoxic. *(Judy Leden)*

---

overleaf
12,000 feet over the Aletsch Glacier in Switzerland. In the background
are the Jungfrau and the Eiger. *(Brendan Monks)*

Publicity stunt for Citroen – a synchronised balloon drop with Sharon Wright, a freefall parachutist, at the Bristol ballon fiesta. *(Simon Ward)*

left Taking off on the last day of the Women's World Hang Gliding Championships Kossen, Austria, 1991. *(Judith Bolton)*

below Talking tactics with Kari Castle, Kossen, Austria, 1991. *(Judith Bolton)*

foot Relaxing before launch, Kossen,1991. *(Judith Bolton)*

right Aertowing during the 'Flight of the Dacron Eagles', Kenya. *(Matt Dickinson)*

main picture Taking off in front of Mount Cook, New Zealand. *(Paul Chisnall)*

below Celebrating the victory with Mum, Kossen,1991. *(Judith Bolton)*

Lining up for take off aboard the trolley (alias 'Chitty Chitty Bang Bang'). *(Richard Meredith-Hardy)*

Curious onlookers, Kenya. *(Richard Meredith-Hardy)*

left On tow in Kenya with few landing options as all the trees below have three inch thorns! *(Judy Leden)*

below left The Dacron Eagles – Tim at the back, Judy, Louise and Mark. *(Gavin Crowther)*

below Yasmin Saudi. *(Niall O'Connor)*

overleaf
Pilot's eye view, on tow in Wadi Rum. Below is the canyon Ben towed me through. *(Judy Leden)*

the glider had been either broken or bent, with the strange exception of the control frame, which is usually the first to go. The impact was so fast that the glider had only touched on the control bar before somersaulting, destroying the tubing but spreading the impact and probably saving my life.

David ran over and unclipped my harness from the glider, freeing me from the wreckage. I sat up with difficulty and tried to assess the damage to my body. I felt badly bruised all over, but miraculously did not appear to have broken anything. With my hatred of hospitals verging on pathological, I refused to go to casualty, but I did agree to stay at David's house rather than driving home. His wife ran me a hot bath and I went straight to bed.

I woke up the following morning to find that my spine had seized rigid from the neck downwards. I had huge bruises on my right arm and both legs, with a stabbing pain in my ribcage. I managed to get out of bed by rolling off the mattress onto my knees. Standing up slowly, I staggered to the car and drove home. I was worried about my back and, afraid that I might have fractured it, swallowed my loathing of casualty units and drove to Ashford Hospital. After the statutory two-hour wait, I saw a doctor who diagnosed a cracked rib and internal bruising. I was asked to do a couple of movements and he declared my spine undamaged.

I went home feeling very shaken. Not only had the crash knocked the stuffing out of me physically, but the accident had dented my confidence in the sport I loved. All the knocks and scrapes I had had before could be pinpointed to pilot error; I had either misjudged weather conditions or made a mistake in my piloting skills. I visited Bunster time and time again in my mind and, given the same set of circumstances, I would have done exactly the same. I felt I could not learn anything from the experience that would prevent me from repeating it in the future. The conclusion I came to was that the turbulence was caused by wave rotor. The hill in front must have been causing interference in the air which only formed when the wind was at the precise strength and direction as at the time of my accident.

I had to put it in perspective. I had clocked up over 1,000 hours flying time and this was the first time I had been in a dangerous situation which was totally out of my control. It was just 'one of those things', the equivalent of driving along a motorway and a car coming through the central reservation in front of me. There was no question of giving up flying; the pleasure I enjoyed from it was worth the small risk involved and going by the 'lightning never strikes twice' theory, I resolved to carry on.

My poor, jinxed glider went back to Airwave with a plea for a super-quick repair in time for the League the following weekend. By the time I arrived in South Wales on Friday night, the glider was already there, looking none the worse for its two near-death experiences, and was in considerably better shape than I was.

A subsequent visit to Ken Kingsbury revealed that I had four vertebrae out of line, one in my neck, one halfway down and two in my lumbar area. Just walking was painful and the thought of carrying a hang glider and harness up a hill filled me with dread. My posture was worsening daily as my shoulders rose to protect my damaged neck and I developed the 'backache walk', with my lower spine fused rigid with muscle spasm.

It would have been sensible at this stage to have gone home and had treatment for my back, but my stubborn streak was riding high. I had worked so hard to be ready for the League to increase my chances of selection for the World Championship team and could not give up without a fight. It had not occurred to me that once in the air, I would be unable to fly properly in my current physical and mental state.

As luck would have it, all four days involved long, hard climbs to take-off. I had help for the first three days, but it was still impossible to find a way to carry even half the weight of a hang glider without a lot of pain. Apart from my back, my cracked rib was very sore and to lean sideways to counter the glider's weight on one shoulder was painful.

I had had plenty of experience in practising the technique of 'mind over matter'. Flying hang gliders is often uncomfortable and after hours in the air, or when flying whilst injured, it can be very painful. As with many other sports, it is possible to train your mind to continue through the pain and I needed every mental resource I could call upon to keep my mind from the physical trauma of carrying my glider during those four days.

Once I reached take-off, I found that I could launch and I could thermal and climb when the vario chirped to signal lift, but I could not make decisions. My brain was overloaded with the stress of the previous three weeks and, in addition, I did not trust the air after my experience at Bunster. I was a mess!

My first landing unnerved me. I chose a huge field, clear of all obstructions which might cause turbulence, and set up a straight final approach like a jumbo jet. My knuckles were clenched white on the bar as I anticipated the Bunster-like turbulence. It was a relief to land without being bounced around and I realised that I would need some time to get my nerve back. It was no surprise that my results were abysmal – I finished in forty-second place, sixth from last.

It was two weeks later that I finally managed to see Ken, who watched me walk into the room hunchbacked and stiff.

'What have you been doing – and after all our hard work!' With patience and sympathy he gently started work. It took several sessions before he was satisfied that my vertebrae were back in alignment and I could walk upright again.

I needed to get my confidence and health back quickly as after the success of the Women's European Championships, the French were now organising the Women's World Championships, which were scheduled for July.

A team of five was chosen, including Louise, Jenny and myself with the addition of Kay Simpson and Kathleen Rigg. The two-month interval before the championships allowed me to return to full fitness by the time I left for France.

The small town of Millau, fifty miles northwest of Montpellier, was the base for the competition. It was a landscape of high plateaus and deep narrow gorges and the conditions were quite different from any other place I had flown. The week I had set aside for practice beforehand was invaluable for learning the idiosyncrasies of the area.

I had brought my own car with me and a friend, Colin Hood, had agreed to drive retrieve. After my experience in Australia, I knew my performance suffered if I did not get a full night's sleep and so preferred not to risk trusting the organisation's retrieve system to get me home, and paid for this luxury myself.

The opening parade saw all the teams walking behind their flags through the streets of Millau, with the procession led by the local brass band. Unlike the low-key European Championships, there were a lot of French media covering the Championships and again I was down as the favourite to win the title and was harassed daily for interviews and comments.

The first day started with a flurry as everyone was keen to fly and we all rushed to set up our gliders on the Puncho D'Agast take-off site. The task was set with a turnpoint twenty miles away and then open distance in any direction. We had to be patient while the conditions, which originally looked so promising, took a long time to develop.

It was 3 p.m. before the first wind dummy managed to claw his way above the mountain, followed by a scramble as pilots raced to launch. The clouds quickly grew and I knew I had to fly fast to get as far as I could before the inevitable thunderstorms started. As I neared the turnpoint I heard thunder behind me and had to make the decision about which direction to fly. It seemed that every path was blocked by cumulonimbus clouds. Colin sat patiently below, waiting at the turnpoint for me to make up my mind.

The route with the least threatening clouds was to the northwest and as this was one direction I had not expected to follow, I had no map with me. A quick check with Colin confirmed there were no airports or military bases ahead and I set off, concentrating on staying as high as I could and keeping a good look out for threatening clouds developing along my path.

I climbed up the side of a cloud bathed in heavenly sunshine and saw in the distance the awesome sight of a growing cumulonimbus with an exploding anvil shaped head fluorescent in the sunlight, its beauty disguising its sinister nature. There was a large lake ahead and I called Colin again with as much information as I could give, as I had no map.

'I will be flying down the west side of a large "L"-shaped lake. I am probably on my final glide and when I land, I will telephone my position to the organisers.'

I then enjoyed a glorious half-hour floating along in buoyant air, descending gradually and having the time to admire the view and update Colin on my progress.

I landed at a farm at the far end of the lake, where the farmer was convinced I had come on horseback despite my flying suit and radio. I took him outside to show him the glider and he walked round it several times to convince himself that there was no engine. He paced out the wingspan and then stood enthralled as I put on the harness and showed him the instruments and parachute. He stood shaking his head and muttering sceptically to himself.

Colin arrived, having used some inspired guesswork as to where I had landed, and drove me back to Millau. I had flown forty-five miles, twice as far as the nearest competitor, Ornella Magnaguagno, my Italian friend from the Europeans.

The assembled media circus had decided I was going to win and descended on me the following day at launch. There were still seven days of competition left and anything could happen, but they had made up their minds. I was constantly distracted by requests for interviews.

On day two, thunderstorms were already building as we rigged. The task was shorter, but it still looked ambitious as the sky deteriorated by the minute. At the task briefing I questioned the wisdom of sending us off along the course when conditions were already looking unsafe and the biggest thunderhead of all was positioned right above the first turnpoint. The meet director looked at me and said, 'The task is set, the launch window is open.'

With hindsight I should have made a stand and refused to fly. It has always bothered me that meet directors can overlook basic safety in the interests of getting scores on the board, especially if there are TV cameras about and the pressure is on. In a competitive situation, the pilots get so psyched up that their normal parameters for flying can be extended far beyond their capabilities and they take off in conditions which are obviously dangerous if they are told to do so. Over the years I have become wiser and am more vocal if asked to fly when conditions are dangerous, but at the time I wanted to win and if we had to fly, I was going to take off as soon as possible. I made sure that I was first in the air.

Because of the wall-to-wall storm clouds, there was no sun getting through to warm the ground. With cloudbase only 2,500 feet above launch, I headed towards the ominous gloom covering the first turnpoint, with Jenny in hot pursuit. I made a desperate glide for the only non-threatening cloud around and flew into a strong thermal underneath, which took me back to cloudbase.

By now the menacing cloud above the turnpoint had decayed and as I took my photograph I was losing height fast. I landed after a meagre twelve miles to win the day, with Jenny coming second with six miles.

We arrived back in Millau to find that one of the last competitors to launch, Catherine Boussemart, had been turned upside down by the increasing turbulence. Being a fairly inexperienced pilot, she had taken too long to throw her reserve parachute and it did not have time to open. It was her lucky day, as she impacted on a scree slope and, other than some bruising, was unhurt. The other casualty of the day was Lillian Leblanc of Greece, who encountered turbulence as she was landing and crashed, gashing her lip and badly bruising her elbow.

The following day was forecast to produce even more thunderstorms but we were taken up Puncho D'Agast and told to rig. We had our reservations, as the clouds above looked as though they could 'unzip' at any time, but competition is competition and so we did as we were told.

It grew dark as a huge storm developed in front of launch and it started to rain. The deluge increased until the whole of take-off was awash. The water carried all the surface dust with it in wide brown torrents and turned the white sails of the gliders a blotchy rust-red.

Competitors and officials piled into the organisers' bus, only to bundle out again as the wind increased to a ferocious gale that lashed the trees and started to lift the sodden gliders, threatening to flip them over. With eyes narrowed against the force of the rain, we flattened ourselves on top of our wings to keep them on the ground. When the storm finally abated we were soaked to the skin and shivering with cold. Without waiting for the official announcement, we unilaterally packed up and went down the mountain.

The following day brought fresh conditions with no storms in sight, much to everybody's relief. The northerly-facing Brunas launch was producing pleasant British soaring conditions in the moderate wind. The task was a fifty-mile race to goal, which proved ambitious as the thermals did not work properly until 3 p.m.

I left the ridge when I had worked as much height as possible and then clung to every bit of rising air I could find. Without finding another thermal, I landed after fifteen miles and was beaten by Ornella and Jenny with the outright winner being Carol Thomay of the French team, who had outflown us all with a distance of thirty-five miles. I held on to my lead, with Jenny moving into second place.

The weather looked promising the following morning but, true to form, played cat and mouse with us as we swapped sites. The wind obstinately refused to obey the forecast and we finally ended up on Puncho D'Agast in time for a 5 p.m. launch window.

By this time the conditions were weakening and again I took off first, closely followed by the other competitors who were all airborne within thirty minutes. I circled patiently in the first thermal, prepared to wait as long as necessary to drift with it over the plateau. Along with Jenny and Kathleen, we maintained our height for some time.

Jenny's patience finally gave out and she left in search of something better over the high plateau. Each time I had tried this technique I had always been forced to land. I kept an eye on Jenny just in case and to my disbelief she seemed to drop down to tree-top height, and then started circling upwards. For five minutes she seemed to hang on to a scrap of nothing and then, slowly but surely, she started to climb well. I straightened up and flew to where she was, watching her angle of bank increase as the thermal became stronger. I arrived, 300 feet beneath her, and found nothing. She had found a small bubble of lift, and I was left behind to land in a field with a distance of fifteen miles. With frustration I watched her as she climbed away from me, clearing the edge of the plateau to land after twenty-one miles.

I was still ahead in the scores, but Jenny was hot on my heels. By the final day Ornella was lying in third position and showed her determination by going for the same 'shit or bust' tactics I had used on the last day of the Europeans. The task was open distance and to maximise her chances of going a long way, she took off as soon as the window opened, gambling the chance of going down early in the unreliable conditions against going much further than anyone else through gaining an hour's start.

I was confident that she could not overtake me and waited for the conditions to become more consistent before launching at 2.30 p.m. I climbed with a huge gaggle of twenty gliders and from my vantage point at the top of the thermal it looked like the Battle of Britain as they all swarmed erratically beneath me.

At last I could relax in conditions which were both pleasant and challenging. With cloudbase at 7,000 feet the views were superb, with agitated rivers carving their way through narrow gorges and the beautiful French countryside stretching out in every direction. The time passed quickly and I radioed occasional messages to Colin to report on my progress. I landed at 7.30 p.m. after sixty-one miles, with Jenny just three miles behind. Ornella's gamble had paid off and she won the day with a flight of seventy miles.

On 13 July 1987 I took the title of Women's World Hang Gliding Champion. As I received the gold medal along with possibly the most garish trophy I had ever seen, I had inadvertently reached a turning point in my life. Whilst I recognised the benefits of being Women's World Hang Gliding Champion in searching for a potential sponsor, I was not satisfied competing only against women. The standard of flying was higher amongst men and I learned more from them. I was aware of the ambivalence of my viewpoint, as I wanted to be able to hold women's world records and to be European and World Champion. At the same time, in my heart of hearts I did not feel that the men's superior physical strength made enough difference to warrant keeping the sexes separated in competitions.

It came as no surprise when the team selection for the World Championships in Australia did not include my name. My results at the beginning of the year had been poor after my accident and the rest of the squad were flying well. The ambition remained and there would be more chances in the future. I still had a lot to learn and when I had proved myself, I felt that my chance would come.

The men against whom I was competing for a place all worked in the hang gliding industry and could fly whenever they wanted. I felt at a disadvantage by having to hold down a full-time job, in spite of the lenient concessions from my parents.

When I arrived back at work, Dad wanted me to settle straight into the backlog of work which had piled up during my absence, but the phone kept ringing with journalists wanting to interview me about my success in France. Tensions were mounting, so we met to thrash out a possible solution.

The business was busier than ever and needed an increasing amount of my time. The freedom they had given me had not got flying 'out of my system' as they may have secretly hoped, but had inspired me even more to push for the top. If I was going to try for full-time sponsorship, now was the time, with several world records and the Women's European and World Champion titles to my name. We agreed that I should make a concerted effort over the following months to find a full-time sponsor and if I was not successful, then I would commit myself to the business and fly for pleasure in my spare time. Again I marvelled at my parents' constant encouragement to follow my ambition, rather than to try to tie me to what surely represented a more secure and safe future.

CHAPTER 8

A Career out of Hang Gliding
– Surely not?

I devised a strategy to woo a sponsor and turn professional. It was one of the biggest challenges I had come across, to approach a company 'cold' and emerge with a contract that would allow me to fly hang gliders full time. I decided to go in with a positive attitude, confident in the value of what I had to sell.

My first port of call was to Brian Milton, my media and sponsorship guru. Our brainstorming session resulted in a wealth of ideas and a new, more professional c.v.

I spent hours in the library with a directory of British companies, listing those whose marketing strategy fitted with adventure sports. I had a list of over a hundred by the time I had finished and then set about the daunting task of telephoning them all.

I have always disliked the idea of bombarding companies with a sponsorship proposal, as the majority will simply not be interested. It wastes money sending paperwork out and means you cannot give the personal touch to those which may have a genuine interest. I therefore preferred to produce a glossier and more detailed c.v., which I sent out only to those who asked to see it.

I had been selling jewellery for five years and if people did not want to buy my earrings, I did not take it personally. This time it was different, as the product I was trying to sell was myself. Being a self-publicist did not come naturally to me and extolling my own virtues and achievements was difficult. Sometimes people I spoke to on the phone were pleasant but explained that their budgets were allocated or that they chose to sponsor schoolgirl gymnastics, etc. . . . Others were rude and dismissive and after these calls I had to fight to regain my confidence to make myself pick up the phone again, remembering that the next one might be the one that said, 'Yes!'

By the end of three draining days I had a sore ear and a list of thirteen companies who had sounded positive and wanted to see my c.v.. By far the most promising had been the contact with Citroën UK. After my car fire I had bought a Citroën BX and was delighted with it, which gave me the idea of contacting them. I spoke to Jim Mather, who was in charge of special events and promotions. He was immediately excited by the idea and we talked about the BX, hang gliding and what Citroën might be able to gain from backing me. I promised to send my c.v. and put down the phone feeling that we had shared a good rapport.

The next morning the phone rang and Jim was on the line asking where my c.v. was. I smiled at the thought of a potential sponsor phoning me! It arrived on his desk the following day and a meeting was set up for two weeks later. I went to see Brian in a mixture of excitement and panic. We went over everything from the paperwork I should take with me to what outfit to wear. Brian recommended a somewhat baffling 'glamorous but vulnerable' look.

The big day finally came and I dressed for the occasion. I am not a great one for skirts, preferring trousers and sweaters, but I pushed the boat out and donned a skirt, blouse, boots, jewellery and even a little make-up. I arrived at Citroën's head office in Slough armed with my press cuttings book and three pieces of paper. One gave a breakdown of my equipment costs for the forthcoming year, the second showed my expenses for the competition season and the third suggested some 'media events' designed to attract publicity for Citroën.

Jim Mather came to meet me. His air of unabashed enthusiasm was tangible as he showed me into his office and his eyes shone brightly with the challenge of a new project. I gave him some time to look through my cuttings file and then handed over my two budget sheets. 'This is what I want from you, now let's talk about what I could do for Citroën.'

I think it is imperative to appreciate the sponsor's needs as well as one's own and Jim seemed impressed that I had thought about Citroën's point of view. We discussed the possibilities at length. By the end of our meeting, I knew he was sold on the idea and it was a question of whether he could convince his bosses. He felt that the image of hang gliding was right for the company, associating their cars with the aerodynamics and smoothness of flying. He could see the attention-grabbing potential of my projects, especially as I was a 'woman in a man's world', which provided an added area of interest. To him it was a genuine 'first' and it fitted well with the pioneering spirit associated with Citroën.

It was a nail-biting few weeks as I waited for them to decide whether to back me. Finally Jim phoned to say that the answer was 'Yes!' The contract would commence from the start of 1988 and would run for a year. The icing on the cake was the offer of a brand new car for twelve months.

I was walking on air and it took a few days for the news to sink in properly. Mum and Dad were delighted for me as they knew this was what I really wanted, but were a little apprehensive as they would be losing me in the business and it would be hard for them to find and train a replacement. It was also a step into the unknown, a job with no career structure and no security.

My life began to appear in shades of red and white, Citroën's corporate colours. Artwork was produced and my new hang glider's sail was emblazoned with the Citroën logo. It arrived along with matching harness, helmet, flying suit and clothing.

It was the start of a busy year, as I headed for Venezuela to take part in a competition in March. It was my first trip to South America and I learned basic facts the hard way, as I had sent my glider by air freight instead of taking it with me as accompanied baggage. It took six hours to get it out of customs with the aid of a local pilot who was an expert negotiator. There was lots of talking and subtle slipping of dollars into sheaves of paper before my glider finally appeared.

The competition base was La Victoria, four hours' drive inland from Caracas. The hills in the area had suffered badly from deforestation and the streams flowed a different colour each day depending on which effluent the local factories were producing. Despite this, the mountains were beautiful from the air and the flying conditions were excellent, with strong thermals and great distance potential.

The air was full of turkey vultures, which made excellent thermal markers but which were ugly and untidy fliers, often flying with their legs hanging down. There was an enormous rubbish dump next to the nearby town and there was a constant 'cloud' of vultures circling in the permanent thermal above it. The smell was ghastly, but it was a godsend to any pilot who found themselves low in that area. The only exception was an unfortunate Swiss pilot who, banking on the guaranteed thermal, flew low over the dump only to find there was no lift and he landed smack in the middle of it, sinking up to his waist in the stinking, fetid mulch.

Crowds of barefoot, happy children would surround me whenever I landed and would help to de-rig the glider, keeping up a constant stream of chatter. A dozen of them would then pick up the folded wing and carry it to the road, centipeding along tiny dirt lanes with grubby hands holding on to the glider bag.

La Victoria proved to be a place where privacy is unheard of when landing a hang glider. I had been in the air for hours during one of the practice days and my bladder felt as though it would burst unless I landed soon. Everywhere I looked there were huts and small settlements which, as in India, would disgorge quantities of children as I approached. I then spotted a large area which didn't seem to be inhabited apart from a couple of concrete buildings in the distance. I wound off my remaining height and landed, scrabbling to get out of my harness and flying suit and relieving myself behind my glider. As I was in 'full flow', I heard voices approaching. They were not the usual excited chatter of children, but rather the deeper voices of men.

I managed hurriedly to finish and had just pulled my trousers up when a small group of soldiers, each wearing at least one gun, appeared round the side of the glider. They stopped dead at the unexpected sight of a woman pilot, but soon recovered and started firing a barrage of angry sounding questions at me. I applied my most friendly I-am-no-threat-to-anyone smile and said in my defence, 'No hablo espagnol.' To my relief, several of them smiled back, but the one with the most stripes on his sleeves continued his verbal assault and, with growing comprehension, I heard the words 'Zona Militar'. He motioned for me to accompany him, so I left my glider and harness where they stood and followed nervously.

I was taken by tractor to one of the concrete buildings I had seen from the air. Here a man with even more stripes on his shoulder shook my hand and I apologised to him via an interpreter for landing in the prohibited area. With an ease that surprised me I used the fact I was female and 'lost', babbling about it being my first time in Venezuela, how difficult it was to read the map and repeating my apology again. My self-preservation instinct told me that this would be the most plausible explanation for them to accept and in this situation my principles had to be swallowed.

Finally he was convinced that I meant no harm and sent five of his soldiers to help me pack up. One seized my radio and held it importantly, while another discovered my 'commando knife' attached to my harness and enjoyed himself taking out the contents – fishing line, matches and compass – before testing the sharpness of the blade on his thumb. It was with much hilarity that they finally dropped me off at the motorway junction outside their base to be collected by my Venezuelan pilot friends.

There were thirty-two competitors on top of the mountain on the first day of the competition. I was clipped in and ready to take off but had to wait as a strong thermal had just ripped through launch while two pilots steadied my glider. One of them looked upwards, let out a sharp cry and ran away. The other followed his gaze and he, too, vanished leaving me to battle with my glider, which was thrashing about in the strong wind. Glancing upwards I saw the reason for their panic as Carlos Perez, one of the Venezuelan pilots, had been turned upside down in the thermal above my head and had thrown his emergency parachute. He was now descending fast and straight towards me.

Still clipped into my glider, my movements were restricted. I tried stepping to the left and to the right, but his trajectory seemed to adjust to follow me. With only seconds to go before he hit, I adopted a fatalistic approach and stayed still, prepared to side-step if he seemed about to land on my head. With a loud 'crump' he deposited himself just in front of me, missing my glider by inches, and stepped neatly out of his glider unharmed. He borrowed another glider, hurriedly repacked his parachute and was airborne again within an hour.

There were lots of small fires burning on the hillsides and stubble fires where the sugar cane had been harvested. Although reliable thermal generators, they were unpleasant to fly in as, apart from the smoke, burning embers were often hoisted aloft in the rising air and created quite a hazard for a glider's sail and a pilot's face. There were also bits of blackened straw and sooty chunks flying about and it was like a scene from *Star Wars* as I was bombarded, often landing with my face and glider peppered with black marks.

Retrieve was provided but only from the main roads. In the case of landing elsewhere, it was up to the pilots to use their initiative and get themselves to pick-up points. Thankfully, the local buses seemed to drive along even the tiniest of dirt tracks and although it was a bone-shaking ride in a vehicle with no apparent suspension, it was a lot better than walking.

By the last day of the competition I was in the lead by a big margin. Several of the wives and girlfriends of the Venezuelan pilots were supporting me and urging me on to win, but some of the men found the concept hard to handle. The way the competition's rules worked, I could have not flown the last task and still won outright. Just before take-off, they announced that the scoring system had been changed! Needless to say the alteration allowed a huge increase in the points for the final task so the pilots behind could catch up if I flew badly. In spite of their efforts, however, I managed to hang on to first place.

On my return to England, I barely had time to wash my underwear before being summoned to attend a meeting with Jim Mather to plan a publicity campaign for the year. I could not guarantee to get Citroën a good return on their investment if I only flew in competitions because the British media were not interested in minority sports, no matter how good my results were. We needed to plan a major stunt to attract publicity and, after looking at all the options, we plumped for the idea of crossing the English Channel by hang glider. This had been done once before by Ken Messenger in 1979, when he was towed by a hot air balloon to 18,000 feet over Dover and then released to glide across to land at Calais.

The job of organising the publicity was given to Citroën's public relations company, Wyndham Leigh, and I was introduced to the motivated but highly strung director, Sean Lees. He organised a photo shoot with the *Independent* to launch the story.

Sports Photographer of the Year, David Ashdown was given the job of getting the shot for the article. The result was a striking picture dominating the back page with a summary of the Channel crossing plan. Citroën were delighted and Sean was inundated with enquiries from the media for more details. It brought home to me the value of stunts as a source of publicity. Crossing the Channel would not take a fraction of the skill it needed to win the Women's World Championships and yet the excitement over a woman crossing the Channel by hang glider was colossal.

The real skill of the flight lay in detailed planning and red tape-cutting to remove all the obstructions that barred the way. Tony Hughes, twice European Hang Gliding Champion, was brought in to coordinate the logistics.

To maximise our chances of success, the flight would have to be done with a following northwesterly wind. This would not only help me to land in France but would also ensure the balloon could reach Calais and not land short of the coast.

To compensate for the lack of lift over the sea, the balloon would have to tow me to a minimum of 9,000 feet before dropping me. The biggest problem was that this would take us into the frenetically busy air lane which lies directly above the Channel, used by many of the aircraft leaving and approaching Gatwick and Heathrow. Tony and I visited the air traffic controllers to discuss the project with them.

Their operations centre was a hall of hushed activity, dimly lit by the glow of radar screens, over which controllers hunched, totally immersed in an array of slowly moving dots. We were given permission to do the flight, but on the condition that we took off at 5 a.m. to be out of the air traffic controllers' hair by the early morning aircraft rush hour. This meant that we had a window from May to August when it would be light at 5 a.m., during which we would wait for a perfect northwesterly wind with clear skies.

Sian Carradice, Sean's assistant, was delegated the job of organising the publicity for the project. Sian seemed at first glance to be a wild woman. With a huge mass of unruly blonde hair she seemed most at home on her fuel-injected, turbo-charged motorbike, on board which she terrorised the roads of London. She was often outrageous, but combined this strength of character with sensitivity and an insatiable sense of fun. Her enthusiasm for the project was enormous and she infused all the journalists she spoke to with the same excitement. As she spoke excellent French, her brief also included organising everything we would need on the French side of the Channel.

As a publicity stunt, we set up a practice run for the cross-Channel flight in March. Sean had managed to get ITN involved, with the offer of an exclusive story and they turned up one frost-laden morning in a field near Newbury with a helicopter from which to film the event. The balloon pilot for the cross-Channel flight was Ron Griffin, who was based in Newbury. He flew hang gliders as well as balloons and gave me confidence as his take-off technique was smooth and gentle, very different from the dramatic snatch launch of my first balloon drop.

The flight went perfectly, with a pause before Ron cut the rope to allow the cameramen in the balloon basket and the helicopter orbiting us to get into the perfect position for the best shot of the release. The only dodgy moment for me was after the drop, when the helicopter pilot decided to move in so that the cameraman could get a close shot. He flew straight across my path and I hit his wash. The whole sail deflated with a loud crack and I went weightless in the harness, hitting my feet on the keel. Although I cursed him at the time, the shot was excellent and the footage was shown on the lunchtime, early evening and 10 o'clock ITN news programmes and was also transmitted internationally.

Citroën were delighted, though after seeing the coverage they wanted me to put more Citroën branding on the glider. Each time the Citroën logo came into shot, the editor had cut to a different angle where Citroën could not be seen. In order to ensure that the company who was making the flight possible received some exposure, we would have to make the branding so obvious that they couldn't cut it out. I had to make sure that Citroën was written on the left- and right-hand sides of the wing and on both top and bottom surfaces of the sail.

Newspaper and magazine articles were appearing regularly thanks to the efforts of Sian and Sean. Although many of my fellow pilots may have looked upon my new lifestyle with envy, watching me go from international competition to competition, it certainly wasn't all roses.

My publicity work often involved flying when no one else would bother. A London *Evening Standard* photographer wanted to shoot me flying on a day when the wind was so light I could not soar and top land. He was pressed for time so I had to fly from the top of Dunstable Downs with his heavy camera and counterweight on board, dressed in my warm suit and land at the bottom only to lug it all back up again. I ended up doing this three times to get the right shot. After the first flight, the photographer came halfway down the hill to help me carry the harness. My gratitude for his help turned to alarm as the exertion turned his face puce as he sweated and gasped. I took the glider up and then went back to relieve him of the harness. After that, he stayed at the top and I carried the glider, harness and cameras up on my own.

In another publicity stunt for local television I set a 'world record' for the maximum number of tow launches in an hour. It was a meaningless exercise, being hauled into the air by a winch sixteen times in a row, but Citroën were pleased with the coverage. I scared a rabbit on my last landing as it caught sight of me in the air and, thinking it was about to become my lunch, it ran first to one side, then the other and then, resigning itself to its fate, sat still and let out a shrill and eerie scream. I landed alongside and it looked at me in seeming disbelief before grabbing its wits together and bounding off towards its burrow.

TVS wanted to do some filming on Firle Beacon on the South Downs, which involved interviewing me while I was flying. This meant I had to carry a camera mounted on the wing, a huge transmitter, battery, recorder and the accompanying yards of cable to connect them all. For a foot-launched aircraft in light winds it was a massive load, and I barely cleared the fence halfway down the hill. Before I had struggled my way back to take-off height, the interviewer was chirping questions in my ear, blissfully unaware of my desperate battle to stay airborne.

Tony Hughes and I made daily contact with the weather forecasters at the meteorological centre at Bracknell, who were keeping an eye out for a possible northwesterly airflow for the cross-Channel attempt. Normally the conditions we were looking for would occur after the passage of a cold front, but each time one passed something would happen to spoil the pattern. Either the front would pass too quickly and the wind would swing too far to the west, which would have caused the balloon to drift towards Scandinavia, or there would be total cloud cover forecast.

I took time off from our waiting game to enter a big international competition in Switzerland. It was held in Fiesch, ten miles south of the Eiger, and the most beautiful area I had ever seen. The take-off was a large sloping meadow overlooking the Rhone valley, dominated by the unmistakable shape of the Matterhorn.

Soon after take-off on my first flight, I found a strong thermal and circled tightly, gaining 200 feet with each turn. As I approached the top of the ridge the huge Aletsch Glacier was revealed behind it. Curving in a vast arc, the frosted blue river of ice cut through the rocky valley around the Jungfrau. The mountains above it were crowned with craggy 'dorsal fins', too steep for the snow to settle. It was a magical place and each day I found myself laughing out loud at the outrageous beauty of the area. I felt very small and insignificant when flying alongside such imposing mountains. I often lost sight of all the other competitors, each a tiny dot against the vast scale of the peaks. Each flight was a voyage of discovery, exploring virgin snow fields and stumbling upon tranquil lakes high up on hidden ledges.

There were several small glaciers which emerged from valleys high in the mountains, which in summer produced a long cascading waterfall into the Rhone valley. As the ice moved slowly downwards under the relentless pull of gravity, great overhangs would form over the cliff edge and would occasionally break off with a thunderous boom, crashing into a million crystal shards on the rocks below.

The tasks we were set often read like an up-market ski brochure, with turnpoints at Saas Fee, Crans Montana and Zermatt. Among the British team was a new star pilot, Robbie Whittall, who was leading the British League and who went on to win the competition in Fiesch. At the age of nineteen he was already an accomplished pilot, having trained with John Pendry, who was the reigning European Champion. With great courage backing up his natural and learned talent, Robbie's flying was inspired and would be recognised the following year, when he went on to win the world championships.

I was in thirteenth position on the last day, when I made a huge mistake. I flew down a narrow dead-end gully, convinced there would be a thermal there. When I didn't find one, I was committed to landing in a tiny area at the far end. The slope was strewn with large boulders and the air was turbulent and unpredictable. I was only twenty feet off the ground and heading for a patch of grass when the glider turned violently to one side, heading straight for the biggest rock of all. Too low to correct the turn, I knew I had to pull off the best landing ever to get away with this. I flared as hard as I could and the glider's nose rose obligingly, but I was in the worst position possible, with my glider dropping vertically onto the rock and my body slamming into it.

I displaced both elbow joints and they were extremely painful. Brendan Monks, a photographer from the *Daily Mirror*, had flown to Switzerland especially to take wing-mounted photographs for a colour spread the day after the competition finished. I simply could not let him down.

The following morning my arms were in agony, so I swallowed some painkillers and enlisted the help of Colin Hood, who was again driving retrieve for me. He helped me rig my glider and then I showed the photographer how to mount the camera on the wing positioning it at the correct angle for the best shot. I then threaded his remote cable release through the sail to hide the wire and taped it to the control bar within reach of my thumb. I was in terrible pain when I launched and prayed for a gentle but fast rising thermal to give me a quick climb with minimum arm wrenching.

I lost over 1,000 feet before I found some lift big enough to circle in, finally rising above the Aletsch Glacier and able to line up the shots and press the button. After an hour my arms gave out and I landed, unable to move them at all, but the photographs were excellent, clearly showing the magnificence of the landscape.

Only seven days later, the British League would hold a competition in the Haute Provence Alps, giving me little time to recover. My elbows were most painful at night, when spasms would run up to my shoulders and down to my fingers. When they still hadn't improved after four days, Colin drove me to St André les Alpes, the base for the League, and I went to see a doctor. He examined me and took X-rays and then laughed out loud when I said I wanted to fly on Sunday.

'Impossible,' was his unambiguous reply.

'You don't understand,' I answered. 'I will be competing on Sunday no matter what, so please do what you can to fix my arms.'

He shook his head and said that the only possibility of flying would be if the arms were immobilised completely for the three remaining days before the competition. He put plaster casts on both my arms from wrist to shoulder and I felt very conspicuous walking around town.

When Sunday arrived, the casts were removed and Colin again helped me rig and to put my harness on. My arms felt weak and painful, but the stubborn goat in me insisted on flying. It was peak thermal time in one of the most turbulent areas in Europe when I launched.

The pain was excruciating and I flew straight down with barely enough strength to make the turn into wind to land. In tears I realised my stupidity. Having come to my senses, I went back to England and visited Ken, who with his usual good humour began the task of putting me back together.

A month later we had a perfect-looking weather window for the Channel crossing. A cold front followed by perfect northwesterlies had been marching towards us as we watched the synoptic chart each evening with bated breath. Everyone was put on twenty-four-hour standby – the balloon pilot, his crew, ITN, the helicopter, the press, French customs and police, the rescue boat in Calais, the coastguard, British customs and the air traffic controllers. Sian was despatched to France on her motorbike to make sure everything over in Calais was in order. We made a final call to the met. office in Bracknell.

'If you don't go tomorrow, I give up on you,' said the long-suffering forecaster.

Everyone met in Folkestone that afternoon under overcast skies, but confident in the clear band of air which was marching inexorably towards us. After a shortened night's sleep, we rose at 3 a.m. Rushing straight to the window I was dismayed to see no stars, and a blanket cover of cloud. I was worried, but it seemed impossible after such a definite forecast. Everyone assembled at the Stour Centre in Ashford, anxiously looking skywards at the ominous layer of stratus cloud.

Tony and I rigged the glider while Ron inflated the balloon. I was carrying oxygen in case we were allowed by the air traffic controllers to go above 12,000 feet and the cylinder was attached to the glider using copious amounts of gaffer tape. Cameras were applied to the wing and I was wired for sound. I did an interview with ITN and donned my warm suit for the cold flight to come.

Tony shut himself away with a car phone to establish a better picture of what was happening with the weather. The helicopter, which had already taken one of the ITN cameramen to France, reported that the cloud was

4,000 feet thick. The impossible had happened. The fast-moving cold front had stopped right above our heads.

The wait was sickening, knowing that the chances of it clearing were virtually non-existent before the end of our launch window at 7 a.m. Finally, we had to admit defeat and I de-rigged the glider in tight-lipped silence. It was such an anticlimax, a waste of Citroën and ITN's money and time, and a huge disappointment for everyone. We returned to the hotel for breakfast, after which Ron disappeared to consult the charts and the met. office to see if the weather would be good enough for another attempt the following morning. After an agonising wait, he emerged with a smile saying, 'We'll give it a go.'

The next morning the sky was clear and it was a much happier group of people who re-enacted their movements of yesterday. A camera crew rushed off to catch the hovercraft to Calais as the customs official checked us out of England. It was time to go and after a brief pause for some photographs for the press, I clipped into my glider. The line was connected to the balloon and Ron fired the burners, slowly taking up the slack between us. The rope went tight and gently I was lifted into the air as Ron coaxed a higher rate of climb to get up to release altitude before we reached the coast. There was nothing for me to do except watch the hypnotic twinkling lights of Ashford below.

At 4,000 feet the noise of the burner fell silent and I could hear the muffled sound of Ron talking to the air traffic controllers. With no heat going into the balloon, we were gently losing height. It was not a big problem as we still had a fair way to go before we reached the coast, but I could not understand what was taking so long. Finally Ron's voice came over the radio to me with the devastating news, 'We have been refused permission to climb and have been instructed to abort the flight; I have to release you.'

I shook my head in disbelief. I could almost see France from where I was but there was no point in arguing. I knew Ron would have done everything possible to change the minds of the air traffic controllers, and I prepared to drop.

Ron cut me free at 3,500 feet and I landed, feeling bewildered about what had gone wrong. I met up with Ron again at the hotel and he explained that the air traffic controllers thought we were heading towards the special rules area above the Channel. Ron argued that our course was veering with increasing altitude and that we would be running parallel with it, but the controllers disagreed and ordered the attempt to be aborted.

The ITN crew had already arrived in Calais only to be met with the bad news. They drowned their sorrows in a slap-up breakfast with Sian and then between them they drank the bottle of celebration champagne which was to have been opened by me on the beach.

Back in Ashford we felt frustrated and helpless but adamant that, having come this far, we would sort the problem out and try again. Our permission for the flight had run out for the year and we would now have to wait until the following May before we could attempt the crossing again.

CHAPTER 9

From England to France on a Wing and a Prayer

'It is imperative that you phone the office immediately', read a terse message handed to me at the final League meeting in September.

My first thought was that Wyndham Leigh needed some press information and I mildly cursed them for not being able to leave me undisturbed for four days to concentrate on the competition. I phoned Sean, but he knew nothing about it. I then rang Jim Mather, thinking Citroën must need me to do something urgently, but he hadn't called either. Suddenly I had a feeling of dread as I realised that the message must have come from the offices of Leden-Imco. From that moment I knew something awful had happened to one of my family.

My hand shook as I dialled the number and when the company secretary answered and recognised my voice she blurted out 'just a minute', and put me on hold. It was the longest thirty seconds imaginable, until I heard my mother's voice thick with emotion. 'It's Dad – he's had a heart attack and he's in intensive care.' Within seconds, I was sobbing into the phone, my mind awash with irrational and irrelevant thoughts. How could it be? He was only fifty-eight and walked miles every day with his beloved dogs. He was so fit, everyone said so.

I told Mum I would drive straight down to London. After half an hour in the car I started to think more clearly. Poor Mum was obviously very shocked and I stopped at a phone box to call her back and suggested she get a friend to drive her to the hospital and warned her that Dad, being in intensive care, would probably look ghastly with tubes going into him and monitors all around.

I continued along the M1 with nothing to do except think of Dad and the situation he was now in. The business had been stressful over the years and this had undoubtedly contributed to his heart attack. The build-up to the Christmas rush would have started and he would be worried. I decided that the best thing would be to help run the business while he was ill. I had finished my work with Citroën for the year and the media side of things had gone quiet as the Channel crossing was on hold. It was over a year since I had worked at Leden-Imco, but I knew all the customers and suppliers and they trusted me. I would start as acting Managing Director at Leden-Imco the following day and together Mum and I would hold the fort.

I arrived at St Stephen's Hospital to find Dad looking better than I had dared hope. His face was flushed pink with anticoagulant drugs and Mum was at his side, much happier now she had seen him. She and I left later that evening and planned what to do. I decided to move into their house for the next few weeks to help Mum look after the dogs, my grandmother and then Dad when he came home.

It was a rude shock to be thrown back into the maelstrom of Leden-Imco at the height of the busy season and to be learning a completely different role within the company. The eight employees were more like a big family as they rallied to help with any problems, sharing the concern about Dad. He had booked a trip to Thailand, one of his regular visits to see suppliers and to buy new samples. I took his place and ventured alone to Bangkok for the first time. All the suppliers happily accepted me as his stand-in, concluding that I was now fulfilling my filial duty of taking over the family business.

After two weeks, Dad came home but was severely limited by angina. He was booked in for angioplasty to expand the restricted artery in his heart in a week's time. Two days before the appointment he woke in violent pain; we called an ambulance and I went with him to the hospital. He was ashen grey and when the doctor on duty said to me, 'It's just a bit of angina', I could have hit him. It was confirmed later that he had in fact suffered another heart attack.

Mum and I went to work in a daze, sick with worry and unsure of Dad's prognosis. We visited him that afternoon to find that his face had a deathly pallor and his eyes were glazed. He was too tired to talk to us and barely even registered our presence. Mum and I muddled through the next few days, trying to be productive at work, visiting Dad, walking the dogs and generally supporting each other. Gradually he began to improve and started on the long, slow road to recovery.

The following weekend I went flying to clear my head. I find it impossible to sit still and relax if I am stressed. When I am flying, all my senses are totally absorbed in something totally different, giving my mind a break from whatever is troubling me.

Citroën had bought a microlight earlier that year, a flexwing 'trike' with a Citroën-emblazoned hang glider wing and a two-seat three-wheeled carriage underneath. I felt very lucky to have a machine which Citroën serviced and stored. All I had to do was fly it! I had held a pilot's licence for microlights since 1986, though until Citroën bought the trike, I had flown very little with engines, preferring the quieter method of soaring hang gliders.

That weekend I flew the microlight from Popham Airfield near Basingstoke. On the way, I picked up a hitch-hiker, a young music student from Germany called Ingrid who was on her way to an evening concert in Southampton. She asked what the odd-looking thing was that I had on the trailer. When I told her it was a microlight she went into raptures. She had always dreamed of flying but had never had the chance.

'If you've nothing to do, why don't you come for a flight?' I suggested.

Her eyes searched my face, wondering if she had heard correctly. 'Do you mean it? Really? Could I?' she blurted, her eyes wide with eagerness.

Together we rigged the microlight and I left her grinning with anticipation while I went to the control room to sign us out. I then helped her into the back seat and fastened her safety belt, watchful for signs of nervousness, common in people sitting in the tiny exposed seat of a microlight for the first time. I climbed into the front seat, with her knees under my armpits. I always watch out for the telltale signs of apprehension as, if a passenger were to lose their nerve in the air, the consequences could be dire. In spite of my caution, Ingrid still smiled with excitement so I taxied to the start of the runway, applied full power and took off.

Immediately, she started babbling with excitement, pointing out the tiny cows and toy-town houses below like a child on Christmas morning. The air was turbulent and I wrestled with the wing to keep us in a straight line, worried that my tension might transmit through to Ingrid. I need not have worried, as each time I turned around all I could see were teeth!

We flew down to the Isle of Wight, round the Needles and were just turning back when I spotted the local paragliding school training on the hill above Freshwater cliffs. I knew Mike McMillan, a friend from the League, would be teaching there so I flew low above the hilltop and we waved. I saw Mike sprinting up the hill, signalling for me to land on the cliff path. There were no obstructions and the air was smooth, so I lined up to land. As we rolled to a stop, Ingrid's eyes were wide with astonishment.

'Come and have a fly, Judy, conditions are perfect,' Mike said.

I had tried paragliding once before when Derbyshire enthusiast Gerald Williams had persuaded me to have a go. Gerald had been flying a parachute off the hills of the Peak District for years, but it had such poor performance that he could not soar, landing each time at the bottom and carrying it up again. He would emerge breathlessly over the rim of the hill and would collar anyone who would listen, extolling the virtues of this 'sport of the future'.

At the time it looked far too much like hard work, and a backward step as, to be able to soar a canopy, the wind strength had to be perfect. If it was two miles an hour too light, the pilot would end up at the bottom of the hill, and two miles an hour stronger meant the parachute would be blown backwards. Many people sniggered at his exploits, but Gerald has had the last laugh watching paragliding grow exponentially in recent years.

My first flight under Gerald's supervision was luckily in a wind of perfect soaring strength and was unforgettable. I stayed up for fifteen minutes above Mam Tor, hanging way underneath a bright green canopy that felt as wobbly as an unset blancmange. From the ground, all Gerald could hear was me giggling as I turned to and fro, almost grazing the hill with my feet.

More than a year later, the sport was catching on fast and Mike's school on the Isle of Wight was one of the biggest. Ingrid and I followed Mike to the training hill and he gave me a lurid stripy canopy to fly. Ingrid sat on the slope with an expression of disbelief on her face. I launched cleanly and soared the gentle slope for ten minutes, laughing from start to finish. Conscious that Ingrid had to get back to Popham to collect her rucksack and hitch to Southampton in time for the concert, I landed, thanked Mike and we walked back to the trike and took off once more.

By the time we reached Basingstoke, she had fallen silent, happy to drink in the surroundings and the sensation of flying, with a fixed grin on her face. We packed up the microlight and I dropped her off at the motorway junction. Her parting words were, 'They'll never believe me', and I imagined her meeting up with her friends with the opening line, 'Guess what happened to me on the way to the concert.' She would go on to describe flying above the clouds, round the Needles, paragliding and the Dinky toy cars. She was right – they probably wouldn't believe her!

Over the following months I gradually handed back the business to Dad, who was recovering well. Our relationship had changed during his illness as our parent-child roles were reversed and he temporarily relinquished responsibility to me. I was acutely aware that things could have turned out differently and I cherished the closeness we now had, the appreciation that only comes from the very real threat of losing someone you love and then being given a second chance.

The Royal Aeroclub awarded me a silver medal for my competition achievements which was presented to me by Prince Andrew at the annual awards ceremony in 1988. Also present were Richard Branson and Per Lindstrand who were collecting a huge trophy for their crossing of the Atlantic Ocean by hot air balloon. I had seen the film of their epic voyage and knew Per was a man who remained cool under pressure. I mentioned to Per about my wish to break the balloon drop altitude record and he agreed to pilot the balloon.

As so often happens with these things, all went quiet for a few years while we were involved in our own projects, but the idea sat simmering in the back of my mind. It was another five years before the opportunity arose to develop the idea beyond just a daydream.

In the meanwhile, I was still doing press events for Citroën, making appearances at dealer promotional evenings, and giving occasional TV interviews. We signed up for another year and had several meetings to plan forthcoming events. By January of 1989, the media were again becoming excited about the Channel crossing. The Civil Aviation Authority had patiently reissued our permission, which started on 14 May and lasted until August. I was determined that I would do the flight this year for the sake of my credibility. We could not afford to risk repeating the fiasco of the aborted launch. This time it would have to be right.

Tony and I began our obsessive daily weather watch and on 12 July we finally got the perfect forecast. The Bracknell forecasters had again been patient with our constant enquiries, but they were keen to have us out of their hair once and for all. Everyone met at 5 p.m. at Broome Park, a hotel and outdoor leisure complex ten miles north of Dover. I felt nervous, not about the flight, but at the thought that the weather was going to thwart us again.

Members of the team arrived throughout the evening: Tony, the balloon crew, Sean and Sian together with Susie MacKean from Wyndham Leigh. The helicopter pilot flew in and parked his Augusta 109 outside the front door, and finally, the ITN film crew joined us. I rigged the glider to allow an over-zealous customs official to check everything before he was entirely satisfied that I was not smuggling illegal contraband to France!

After ITN had attached a lightweight video camera to the wing, we all moved inside for a final briefing. Susie's job was to be aboard the rescue boat which would be waiting off the coast of Calais, ready to fish me out of the water in case I didn't make it to the shore. The air traffic controllers had only given us clearance to 9,000 feet over Dover and at this height, if the winds were not favourable, there was a significant chance I wouldn't make it to the beach.

Landing in water with a hang glider is the stuff nightmares are made of. With so many wires, tubes and strings, and the pilot encased in a restrictive heavy harness, it is easy to drown. I took Susie aside as her role aboard the rescue boat was to listen to the radio. If it looked as though I would land in the sea, I would contact her immediately and she was to make sure the boat reached me as soon as possible. Her normally smiling face was serious with the thought of the responsibility and together with Sian and a London *Evening Standard* photographer, she left to catch the midnight hovercraft to Calais.

I went to bed sometime after midnight and lay awake mentally rehearsing what I would do if I landed in the sea. I woke up at 2.30 a.m. gasping for air after a terrifying nightmare that I was drowning. I did not want to sleep any more and pulled back the curtains to reveal stars from horizon to horizon. The trees were still and the air had the crisp, fresh feel of a northwesterly. My fears evaporated and were replaced by excitement that today, finally, we were going to do it.

We met at the take-off site at 3.15 a.m. Most people were bleary eyed, but my fatigue was banished by eager anticipation of the flight ahead. Ron, the balloon pilot, was cool and calm as always as he checked the wind forecast from Bracknell. He inflated the balloon, which then stood fat and motionless in the still morning air, lighting up like a beacon as Ron intermittently fired up the burners to keep the envelope turgid.

I put on my warm clothes, life jacket and harness before doing various TV and radio interviews. Tony, meanwhile, tied one end of a rope to the keel of my glider and the other end to the balloon basket. I clipped my harness in and, after final checks, we were ready to go. Ron gave me the thumbs-up and set the burners roaring. The basket rose alongside me and out of sight above the glider's sail. The slack of the rope disappeared as I walked underneath the basket following Tony's directions and waited for the tug of the rope to pull me up.

The glider was plucked gently from me and, as my harness straps went tight, it took my weight smoothly. I seemed to leave the ground one toe at a time and gave a jubilant wave as we accelerated upwards. The sky was clear and washed with orange in the east as the sun rose. A thin film of mist had settled in the hollows and played among the lower branches of the trees. To the south, I could see the coast clearly and the port of Dover already busy with ferries and early hovercraft. The Channel looked calm, glinting benignly and beckoning to us.

The drift was almost perfect, taking us straight along our desired track, and I could feel my excitement mounting. At 2,000 feet Ron stopped the burners and paused to talk to air traffic control. I had a feeling of *déjà vu* as we stopped climbing for a moment and then, as the balloon cooled, slowly began to descend. There was a sudden reassuring burst from the burners and again we started to rise.

Ron called me on the radio to say that the controllers had cleared us to climb to 7,000 feet. This was good news in that they had confirmed we could continue, but bad news in that 7,000 feet would not be high enough to make it across to France. My excitement turned to anxiety as I crossed my gloved fingers and hoped. At 7,000 feet there was another short period of silence while Ron requested permission to go higher. We were nearing the coast and the point of no return.

'We have permission from air traffic control to climb to 16,000 feet', came Ron's magical words over the radio and I cheered with delight. There was no stopping us now. The burners were on again and we climbed quickly to gain maximum height before reaching the white cliffs of Dover, which would be our release point.

We decided not to go above 14,000 feet as neither of us had oxygen and the burners were less effective in the lean, thin air. Above the white cliffs, Ron started a descent with the ITN cameras in position in the helicopter alongside. The silence was eerie after the noise of the burners had stopped and there was nothing to do but wait and try to control my nerves, which were now jangling at the thought of the imminent release. I had never been dropped from so high up and I worried whether the glider would rotate too fast and tumble. I had to trust the in-built stability of the wing to pull the glider out of the dive the right way up. Easier said than done.

Ron checked that I was ready and started the countdown from ten. We were down to 13,500 feet and I held my breath, waiting to be cut free. I heard the twang as Ron's knife sliced through the rope and for the briefest moment the glider hesitated before plunging towards the earth far below.

My harness went slack and my feet hit the glider's keel. All I could do was to hang on and wait for the glider to pull out.

I fell 300 feet before I regained control as the glider swooped out of its vertical dive. Relief flooded through me and I looked around to find France. The northwest coast was laid out like a map in the distance with Cap Gris Nez jutting out and beckoning to me. Resisting the urge to do a celebratory orbit of the balloon and risk losing precious height, I aimed straight towards the beach near Calais, where I knew Sian and the crew were waiting.

Conserving height was my main aim as I had heard stories of horrendous patches of sinking air over the Channel and there were twenty-four miles between me and the safety of dry land. With the following wind, I slowed down to maximise my glide. Although the French coast looked so close, I knew distances could be deceptive when the air was so clear. The shipping lanes were busy with boats of every size and shape. Cutting across their paths were the Channel ferries, trailing their white plumes of wash behind them.

Away in the distance was my rescue boat. Susie had taken her briefing seriously and had insisted that they were in position five miles off the Calais coast by 3.30 a.m., 'just in case'. The poor diver on board was in his wet suit with oxygen tanks on two hours before we even took off!

I was over halfway and still had plenty of height to spare and I began to pull the bar in. After all the build-up of, 'Will she make it or will she land in the sea', I did not want to pass over their heads at 5,000 feet. I was confident of reaching the beach and my tension had evaporated, replaced by sheer exhilaration as I absorbed the incredible view.

Sian let off two flares to show me the landing position and I pulled the tops off my two coloured smoke canisters, trailing red and white streamers as I circled over the beach. Susie, diligent to the last, insisted the boat stay in position just in case. She wasn't going to desert her post until my feet had touched the ground. My landing on the sand was perfect and Sian ran up with a bottle of champagne. I was so happy and relieved finally to have completed the flight. It had taken only forty-five minutes to accomplish from take-off to landing, but a massive six months in the planning and a further fourteen months spent waiting for the weather.

The local gendarmes, surely hardened by now to the eccentricities of the British and their dotty ways of crossing the Channel, looked bemused.

'Mademoiselle, we have been waiting for you for a year and a half,' said one, while the other smiled uncomprehendingly, and shook my hand.

The diver from the boat, having finally been released from his vigil by Susie, had swum ashore and slopped up the beach in his flippers to greet me. I shook the champagne bottle with vigour and popped the cork, spraying it high in the air. As we drank a celebratory toast, I was brought sharply back to earth by a plaintive call from Ron. 'Balloon to rescue boat, over...'

In my elation, I had forgotten that Ron was still flying and he had met unfavourable winds. His instructions from air traffic control were to descend until he was clear of the busy airway and then to continue to France as planned. Unfortunately, the lower level winds had backed round to the west and were pushing him along the Channel, parallel with the coast. He was halfway across when he found a shallow northwesterly flow sandwiched between the westerlies and was sitting in it, praying it would last, concerned about his ever-diminishing fuel level. He now thought he might make Calais but needed the rescue boat to be on stand-by in case his unreliable northwesterly flow should disappear and commit him to a sea landing.

In order to appear live on the ITN lunchtime news, I boarded the helicopter and flew back to London, leaving Tony and Sian to finish off the champagne and pack away the glider. We took off in a flurry of sand, arriving at Lydd airport to clear customs. On our final approach to land, we were relieved to hear that Ron was safely over land and due to touch down in Calais any minute.

I phoned home to tell my grandmother I had made the crossing and was now safely back in England. She had hated the whole idea of the Channel crossing. It must have been hard for her at ninety-three, born before the age of the motor car, to comprehend why her granddaughter feels the need to hang glide and gets involved in dangerous aviation projects. Usually she kept her reservations to herself, saying a superstitious 'Take care' each time we said goodbye. She was far more vocal about the Channel crossing, saying she hoped the authorities would stop us from doing it. She did not want to know when we were going on stand-by, just to be told when it was all over. She was not surprised when I telephoned that morning as she had, despite herself, been keeping an eye on the forecasts and knew the winds had been perfect for the flight.

We called in at Broome Park to collect the door of the helicopter, which had been removed so that the camera crew could get unobstructed pictures. Sean was there to meet us, beaming, having broken the news to the media at 6.30 a.m. We flew on to Fairoaks and then completed the journey by car. Stuck in the morning traffic on the way into central London it was strange to think that only two hours earlier I had been flying freely across the English Channel in a hang glider.

John Suchet met me at ITN and made me feel relaxed with a very friendly welcome. The film of the flight was followed by a lengthy live interview with me, dressed in my Citroën flying suit under the sweltering studio lights. The afternoon continued in a haze of unreality as I sat in the offices at Wyndham Leigh answering journalists' questions and writing thank-you letters to all the people who had helped us with the project.

Citroën were thrilled with the coverage. There was a large photograph in most of the daily papers the following morning, and lots of television and radio coverage, later valued at over £750,000.

I was relieved finally to have the shadow of the Channel crossing behind me. It had influenced so much of my life over the preceding eighteen months and now I was a free agent again. I deliberately missed the weather forecast that night, exulting in my new-found freedom. It had been less of a test of flying skill than of the ability to cut red tape and to organise a project of such proportions. This time I did not have the same feeling of emptiness at a goal achieved, but rather an overwhelming sense of relief that I could now get back to the business of flying hang gliders.

CHAPTER 10

All in my Mind?

An ominous brown envelope had been sitting on the kitchen worktop for a week. It had that 'income tax demand' look about it with 'On Her Majesty's Service' written across the top.

It was one of those rainy, windy days designed for catching up on paperwork and I finally opened it. Inside was a simple letter with the heading and crest of 10, Downing Street. Momentarily confused as to why my meagre tax dealings should warrant a letter direct from Mrs Thatcher, I went on to scan quickly through the text.

Among the official-speak, certain parts leaped out at me ... Birthday Honours ... Her Majesty ... Member of the Order of the British Empire. I was stunned. This had come out of the blue and I wasn't sure I had understood correctly. I phoned my Mum and read her the letter. Her voice went husky with emotion, triggering mine to do the same as I realised I was to be awarded the MBE for services to hang gliding.

The honours list was published on 15 June and Mum, Dad and I were invited to Buckingham Palace dressed up in our best outfits. It was a wonderful day, full of the best of British pageantry from the Beefeaters guarding the Queen on the dais, to the fanfares from the balcony.

I felt that I had reached a hiatus in my competition performance. In women's contests, I had reached the top and my confidence was absolute, but when flying against men I was not consistent, often making mistakes through trying too hard, losing my concentration and feeling intimidated by the big names. The best result I had achieved during my five years in the League was fifteenth overall, though I felt in my heart that I should be able to make the top ten.

Looking objectively at the top pilots, we had all mastered the physical skills of flying; we could all climb well in thermals and could glide at the right speed for any given wind strength. Each one had a reasonable understanding of meteorology and the formation of thermals. I became more convinced that what separated the champions from the also-rans was their ability to make decisions under stress, coupled with being able to remain calm and analytical, and to concentrate for long periods.

I wanted to delve further into the field of sports psychology. I had read a couple of books which seemed to strike a chord, but I needed more personal advice as the demands of competition hang gliding are so different from those of cricket, athletics and golf, which were the usual examples used to illustrate the books. A hang gliding task often lasts for hours without a break and a competition can span many days. The pilot frequently has to deal with fear, not just of losing the contest or spraining an ankle, but of making mistakes that could lead to serious injury or even death.

I wanted to consult a sports psychologist directly, to see if he could help me identify the problems which were blocking my progress. I contacted the Central Council of Physical Recreation and was put in touch with Peter Terry. Peter worked predominantly with players of more conventional sport like tennis. Before he could help me, I had to teach him what was involved in flying a hang glider and how competitions worked.

During our first two sessions he listened patiently as he came to grips with terms like thermalling, gaggle flying, cloud formations and optimum speed to fly. Once Peter was in the picture, we were able to discuss the more specific problems of wandering concentration and tension in the air. I soon realised that the solutions to my difficulties could be found within me. Peter helped me to isolate a problem and then change the way I dealt with it. For example, I had always tried to concentrate fully throughout a competition task, which inevitably resulted in fatigue after a couple of hours. He taught me that there were times when full concentration was necessary and times when I could afford to relax my mind, occasionally even forcing myself to think of something completely different in order to rest my mind from the flight, then deliberately locking back onto the task in hand when the time was appropriate.

I stopped looking where my opponents were and thinking of what they were doing, instead concentrating on my own flying and what I needed to be doing. The results then sorted themselves out and I made sure I was enjoying myself, another vital factor in doing well in competitions. It is not possible to perform to the best of your ability if you are unhappy and distracted by outside issues.

I was able to put my new-found skills into practice when I was invited to complete as a guest in the Balkan Games in Bulgaria. It was the first time I had been to an Eastern bloc country since visiting Hungary five years before. Bulgaria was very different and I was not prepared for the depressed state of the country and its people.

I stayed at the house of the only female hang glider pilot in Sofia, Dessy Vamporova. This caused problems with the authorities, as they liked to keep checks on foreigners, which is much easier to do when they stay in hotels. Together with another pilot, Dimitar Dimov, she spent some time in the run-down offices of the local authority, making sure the paperwork was in order to allow me to stay.

Everyone I met over the age of fourteen smoked cigarettes. There wasn't a non-smoking section on the aeroplane on the way over as there was simply no demand. During meals people would smoke not only between courses, but even between mouthfuls.

The cars all looked similar, with their old, functional design; there were no 'luxuries' like wing mirrors. Windscreen wipers had to be detached and carried inside the car as, when left in place, they would be stolen because it was impossible to buy new ones. The queue for petrol was often thirty cars long.

There seemed to be some confusion about the competition. The air force in Bulgaria was much more restrictive than in Hungary and some days would simply state that we could not fly. The local pilots were so frustrated after their hard work, but there was nothing they could do about it. An increasingly familiar sense of tired resignation would appear on their faces and in their voices.

The centre of Sofia was busy, but the shop windows were bare, in stark contrast to the over-indulgent west, where each shop competes with the next to part customers from their money. There was no array of colourful and brightly lit goods to tempt potential buyers; instead the supermarket shelves were almost bare, with the goods that were available wrapped in grey paper and marked 'flour', 'sugar' and 'soap powder'.

I felt sorry for the elderly people in Sofia, who had no comforts to ease their old age. They shuffled along the pavements, carefully avoiding the loose drain covers and uneven paving stones. There seemed to be no tasty foods with which to treat themselves and no luxuries to indulge in occasionally.

The local hang glider pilots were as keen as anywhere else in the world; they just had to fight harder to be able to fly. Unlike the Hungarian pilots, most were flying gliders made in the west, bought through government-sponsored sports programmes. It must be such a contrast to feel the freedom of flight and yet be subject to such restrictions in the course of normal life.

On the first day of the competition, all non-Bulgarian pilots were issued with 'Paddington Bear labels' stating who we were, what we were doing and where to send us back to. Although I learned a few basic words of Bulgarian, it was not enough to wrestle with the phone system, so I would give the label to a local person when I landed and they would contact the competition headquarters.

The Stara Planina mountain range runs like a spinal column along the length of Bulgaria and most of the competition flights took us along it. The trip to take-off was never smooth and was usually courtesy of a grinding, heaving Russian truck. The sound of the gliders bouncing on the roof was worse than that of the dentist's drill to a hang glider pilot as the crunching of the gear box punctuated the roar of the engine. As we reached the bottom of the hill on the first day the driver turned to me and said, 'When you drive fast, eet is leetle shake', and with that he pushed the accelerator pedal to the floor and sped up the hill.

It was a relief to take off and fly. The views were different, but I immediately felt at home once my feet were off the ground; no more rules, no smoke, no jarring truck journeys – bliss.

Landing after a cross-country flight was a great adventure. Often the country peasants would stare in disbelief before approaching me. I always enjoyed watching the rural scenes whilst waiting to be collected by the competition truck. On the second day I saw a herd of goats being driven back into the village where I had landed. Each knew its own house and peeled away from the group as it passed the front gate. They were followed by a man walking his pig along the road, looking for all the world like a pensioner taking his labrador for its daily constitutional.

Each day I put my new mental skills into practice in the air. My concentration was better than it had ever been and I was relaxed and happy. The results took care of themselves and at the end of the three-day competition I was in first place.

On my return to England, I wanted to fulfil a promise I had made to Dad when he was in hospital. I would take both him and Mum for a ride in the microlight. They had always been supportive of my flying and I wanted to be able to share a taste of what it was like to fly and to give them an insight into why I loved it so much.

We drove down to Popham with the microlight on the trailer. The air was cold but the wind was light so it wouldn't be too turbulent. I took Mum first. As I was rigging, she became increasingly quiet. I knew she was nervous but I was confident that once we were in the air she would love it, as for most people the anticipation is much worse than the actuality of flying in a microlight.

She fastened her seatbelt and said nothing as I took my seat in front of her. I started the engine and told her to put her hands on my shoulders. I always get my passengers to do this as I then know where their hands are and don't have to worry that they may grab hold of the throttle or choke by mistake. I can also tell how nervous they are by how deeply they dig their nails into my neck. I cut the preliminary chatter to a minimum and taxiied to the runway. As we took off, Mum's grip did not tighten, remaining feather light so I could hardly feel the weight of her hands. I was impressed with her composure.

'That's all there is to it,' I said reassuringly as we climbed away from the airfield. There was a resounding silence from the back seat.

'Hello . . . are you still there?' I asked.

'Yes,' came the tight-lipped reply from the back and I realised that, far from being relaxed as her hands indicated, she was in fact frightened to the point of immobility. I kept up a soothing patter, pointing out things of interest whilst making sure I kept flying straight and level to minimise the movement of the trike. There was a strong inversion, making the air very hazy, so we climbed up above it, breaking into the glorious clear blue sky above. It felt like a different world as the sun reflected off the haze, totally obscuring the ground below. She began to relax a little as we looked down on the tops of the sparse cumulus clouds.

After twenty minutes we landed again and over a strong cup of tea in the airfield café, Mum confessed to me that she hated heights and that her flight had been a rather terrifying ordeal. She was adamant that she had wanted to understand what it was that inspired me, and was glad to have had the experience, though she enjoyed it only once her feet were back on the ground. It was courageous of her to agree to go up with me, but I couldn't understand why she had never told me that she suffered from vertigo. Unlike me, her fear of heights robbed her of the enjoyment of flying, whereas as soon as I was in the air, it did not bother me.

Next it was Dad's turn and I was a little concerned as it was only a few months since his heart attack and I did not want him to become stressed in any way. He has always been a bad passenger in a car, preferring, like me, to be in control. However as soon as he stepped into the trike, I knew he would be fine. He accepted that I knew what I was doing and sat back to enjoy the ride. We swooped over the tops of the cumulus clouds and grinned our way round the magical aerial playground. For him it was like being back on his old motorbike, but with a lot more ground clearance. He had not been scared at all and loved every minute.

CHAPTER 11

Never Say Die

My world distance record had finally been beaten. It was six years to the day after my epic flight in Owens Valley and American pilot Katherine Yardley flew nineteen miles further to claim the new record with a distance of 164 miles.

I was always pleased to hear of other women who were driving themselves to fly further and to compete. Katherine had seen me take off the day I broke the record in 1983, having watched my preparation frenzy. She later saw the photographs I had taken on that flight, so far away from my start point that it was out of sight, obscured by the curvature of the earth. From that day on she had been fuelled by determination to do the same, and had now succeeded.

With a renewed sense of challenge, I started to plan how I could get the record back. I had heard great reports about the distance-flying potential of the flatlands of New South Wales in Australia, which enjoyed hot summer weather, high cloudbases and no obstructions along the way.

With no hills to take off from, the best way of getting airborne was to tow up behind a car using a 2,000-foot length of rope and a crude tension gauge. The role of tow driver was crucial, as my life would be in his or her hands and I preferred to have someone I knew and trusted to drive the car. Sarah Fenwick fitted the bill perfectly. Well organised and confident, Sarah had been working at Airwave for some years and knew a lot about flying, though her own experience was limited. We didn't know each other well, but I had a gut feeling that we would get along.

With Citroën's backing, I bought us each a ticket to Sydney for early January. On our arrival we were lent a car by Citroën Australia and we headed straight for Forbes, a small and characterless town six hours' drive west of Sydney. Its only 'tourist attraction' is the grave of outlaw Ben Hall on the outskirts of town, and the newsagent proudly sells postcards depicting his headstone.

The tow paddock was a huge, 1,000-acre stubble field adjacent to the homestead where Jenny Ganderton now lived with her husband. The surrounding terrain was spirit-level-flat, with the horizon broken only by the tall gum trees lining the road. We nicknamed this 'Kamikaze causeway', as huge flocks of rosella parakeets perched in the trees and would, at the sight of a car, execute high-speed dives across the road. There would always be the sorry sight of freshly killed birds on the tarmac, with their beautiful pink and grey feathers scattered around the corpses.

Our arrival heralded the start of five days' torrential rain. The farmers' delight contrasted with our disappointment at the enforced halt in our plans, while the thunder and lightning wreaked havoc with the ancient eucalyptus trees, setting them on fire or simply knocking them over like skittles. It gave Sarah and me time to ensure we had all the necessary bits and pieces we needed for towing. I had bought the tow gauge and the rope in Sydney, but there were a myriad other smaller items we needed before we were ready. We were daily visitors to the hardware store as we searched out clips, string, radio antennae, elastic cord and a hose reel to wind the rope onto.

The weather finally cleared and less than two days after the rain stopped, the paddock was back in its usual tinder-dry state. Sarah and I prepared for the first tow. I had done some towing behind a static winch before and so knew roughly what to expect, but for Sarah, driving the tow vehicle was completely new. We went over the launch procedure once more:

Pilot: 'All checks complete, take up tension.'

Driver: 'Taking up tension.' (Moves car forward until rope tension reaches thirty-five pounds.)

Pilot: 'Clipping on the microphone.' (The radio is now on permanent transmit for the duration of the tow so the pilot can direct the driver without having to press the microphone switch.) 'All out, all out, all out.'

Sarah would then accelerate as quickly as possible to give a sharp pull to get me cleanly off the ground. She then had to drive straight ahead with one eye on the mown strip in the stubble ahead of her and one on the tension gauge stuck to the dashboard. The ideal pulling strength was the combined weight of pilot and glider and was marked in fluorescent pen on the dial. This would give me plenty of height without putting too much tension on the line, which would risk a 'lockout', where the glider rotates around the tow line and plunges earthwards like a kite.

I lined up behind the car, which appeared as a fuzzy, grey blob in the distance, distorted by the shimmering of the heat haze. All I wanted was for Sarah to be confident enough to handle the car forcefully and give a good hard tug. A timid pull would have required me to run full pelt without the glider having enough speed to lift me off the ground. I need not have worried. I called, 'All out!' on the radio and I saw the puff of dust as she let off the clutch, followed immediately by a strong pull on the tow line connected to my harness. Within four paces I was airborne and watching the car beetling up the field with a dust plume behind it. My vario chirped a healthy climb rate and soon I was 1,000 feet above the field and felt the surge of a strong thermal. I pulled the release lever and watched the rope plummet beneath me as I turned into the rising air.

The landscape was so different from any other I had seen. Vast, square fields stretched one after the other to the horizon, scorched brown by the relentless sun. I flew over a gum swamp and could see the pelicans, spoonbills, herons and black swans all perched on the gnarled tree trunks which protruded from the fermenting mud. I returned to the launch paddock to give Sarah some more practice at towing me, as the weather was still poor. We then returned to the caravan park where we were staying and while Sarah cooked supper, I pored over the map, so that when the normal weather returned with its strong, thermic conditions, I would be ready for the big one.

The forecast, however, remained indifferent, and the world distance record remained out of my grasp for the time being. I had to be content to try to break some of the other records. I took the 'speed around a twenty-five-kilometre triangle' world record within the first week, but even this, which should have been easy, was hard work with such low clouds and pitifully weak thermals.

The weather finally started to improve and dozens of pilots turned up for the annual flatlands competition. The stubble in the paddock now resembled a chess board from above, with the huge number of mown strips, each with its own small batch of pilots and tow car. As soon as the first thermal developed, it became a hive of activity, with hang gliders being catapulted upwards on their umbilical cords. A thick film of dust coated everything as the cars ploughed up and down their strips and it was a relief to circle away from the field and into the cool fresh air at cloudbase.

Now that the thermals were stronger and more consistent, the wind blew from the west, thwarting my attempts to fly eastwards by carrying me straight towards the Blue Mountains, which blocked my path with mile upon mile of unlandable forest. After ten days of frustration we decided to move further away from the mountains, where it would be hotter, drier and even flatter than in Forbes. With our own self-sufficient tow system, it was like having a mobile take-off mountain. Waking early, Sarah and I drove for three hours along dirt roads, then found a suitable big field from which to tow. The houses were sparsely scattered in such an arid area so it was not hard to find the landowner by knocking at the door of the nearest homestead.

It was hard to explain to the outback farmer exactly what it was we were trying to do. However, with the prospect of an interesting diversion to the normal daily routine, he readily gave us permission to use his land, on the condition that he and his family could come along and watch.

There was no time to lose, as the cumulus clouds already looked well formed and the wind was increasing. A flock of emus which were feeding nearby regarded us with supercilious indifference, so Sarah had to drive up and down twice to shoo them from our path. While I rigged the hang glider at one end of the field, she laid out the tow line. The farmer arrived in convoy with his family and two of his neighbours, whom he had phoned to come and witness these 'Pommie Sheilas' who were about to do something involving a hang glider and a world record.

They stood back, watching the proceedings from a distance as I put on my harness and clipped into the glider. Meanwhile, Sarah drove to the other end of the rope. This was out of sight, so all they could see was the hang glider attached to a piece of thin line. They then heard me say the words, 'All Out', and the rope went tight. I took two steps before taking off and rapidly climbed above them. Within one minute I had hit a thermal, released the line and was circling upwards.

Sarah returned to find the little group open mouthed at what they had just seen. They bombarded her with questions, desperate to know how it worked and for her to explain exactly what it was they had witnessed. Sarah was anxious to be on her way as she didn't want to lose contact with me and refused their offer of lunch. Before she left they asked her if we could please come back and fly from their field tomorrow as they wanted to see it all over again.

Meanwhile, I was trying to orientate myself with my map. I could not place my exact position as I couldn't see the town of Bobodah, which should have been one mile to the north of me. I radioed down to Sarah,

'This is a navigational nightmare. Could you please ask the farmer what the population of Bobodah is as I can't see it and I should be almost overhead.'

There was a pause as she put the question to him, then her voice came over the radio as she laughed, 'Bobodah has a population of two, and they're standing next to me!'

The house below was in fact the town so, readjusting the scale of things in my mind, I pinpointed my position and set off downwind. The clouds had changed from welcoming cumulus to threatening towers of cloud. I knew I would be racing against time, as they looked as though they could soon develop into thunderstorms.

Twenty miles into the flight I was struggling low down, having flown underneath a cloud which was decaying. A large field downwind was basking in sunshine and a number of sheep were grazing. I remembered a tip about flying the flatlands. If you are desperately in need of lift over a field, you should try shouting at the sheep. The ground is so flat that there can often be a mass of warm air waiting to rise, only needing a small trigger to break the surface tension and allow the thermal to escape.

I was desperate and prepared to try anything. Feeling like an idiot, I yelled down at the flock of sheep from 500 feet. There was a short delay while the sound of my voice travelled downwards and I rebuked myself for being so gullible and listening to such a silly tale which had obviously been a wind-up. Then, as the sound of my voice reached the ground, the sheep began to run towards the other side of the field. Within a minute, my descent rate slowed and my vario began to chirp once more as a big, smooth thermal broke off the field and carried me to cloudbase 8,000 feet above, laughing all the way.

I continued for another two hours making good progress, but knowing in my heart that it was not going to be a record-breaking day as storms were looming up ahead. I didn't know exactly where I was as the spider's web of roads shown on the map bore no resemblance to the network of sparse dirt tracks below. Many of the individual homesteads marked on the map were now no more than a pile of stones and it was impossible to say from the air whether a building was a house which would be on the map, or a barn which wouldn't.

I was lost and the biggest of all the thunderheads was straddling my path. There was no way round so I radioed to Sarah to tell her I would be landing within the next five minutes. I could give her no clue as to my exact whereabouts, but told her that I would land at the homestead below me and would phone the Forbes Caravan Park from there to leave a message once I had asked the farmer where I was. With lightning and thunder now frequently emerging from the cloud, I was anxious to be on the ground before the gust front reached me. I had watched storm roaring winds uproot the ancient gum trees in Forbes and it took little imagination to realise what damage they could inflict on a flimsy hang glider.

I circled down to land alongside the farm and walked to the front door. I rang the bell but there was no reply except a couple of angry barking dogs. There were two cars parked outside and I couldn't believe there was no one home. I had no option but to hitch-hike into the nearest town as soon as possible to get a message to Sarah.

I rushed to de-rig my glider so that it would not be blown away by the increasing winds and within fifteen minutes I was at the side of the dirt road with my thumb out. I waited, and waited . . . and waited . . .

There were no cars. The heavens opened and I was pelted with rain and hail. I did not want to shelter under a tree as the ground was so flat that they were especially vulnerable to lightning strikes. It was another hour and a half before a car finally came by and stopped to pick me up. The couple explained the mystery of the deserted farmhouse. The annual S & B (spinsters and bachelors) ball was on 'in town' and everyone from miles around was there. In such a sparsely populated area, an occasion to socialise with fellow farmers from the region was not to be missed.

It took half an hour to reach the town of Trangie and by the time I phoned the caravan park it was over two and a half hours since I had last contacted Sarah and I knew she would be worried. The woman in Forbes confirmed that Sarah had phoned several times and she took down the name of the bar from where I was phoning.

An hour later Sarah arrived looking relieved to see me. She had driven through violent thunderstorms and when I hadn't phoned in she feared I had been caught in one. She had been through hell, driving the car along the treacherously slippery dirt roads which were covered in a layer of slimy water. She spent half her time coasting down the road with no traction at all, having to slow to a crawl to avoid sliding clean off the road. She had also hit a dead kangaroo while she was looking at the sky trying to find me.

After a well-earned supper and copious beer for Sarah, we drove back to Forbes. We took a rest day and celebrated by getting sunburned after an hour in the vicious afternoon heat.

Our stay was coming to an end with no sign of the epic conditions which would allow me a decent stab at the record. I had nothing to lose and decided to try to break the 'distance via a turnpoint' world record, hoping that if the weather was right I could go for the open distance record at the same time.

Refreshed, though sore after our day off, we were ready to go by 11.30 a.m. Our well-organised and practised routine ran smoothly as Sarah prepared the car and tow rope while I rigged the glider. The day was disappointingly blue with no clouds at all to help find thermals, but I would have to make the most of it. I replenished my water supply, which I would certainly need on the way, and stuffed two museli bars up my sleeve to keep my energy levels up *en route*.

After take-off I climbed high above the paddock. The wind forecast was wrong and I found myself fighting a headwind trying to reach the road junction which I had declared as my turnpoint. I wasted a lot of time and at one point nearly landed, resorting once again to shouting at the sheep to get back up.

Once I reached the junction and took my photograph to prove it, I could relax a little more and drift with the wind as I thermalled. After the first thirty miles the paddocks gave way to long stretches of scrubland, where kangaroos and wallabies roamed unchecked. I made a point of memorising where the occasional homesteads were so that I would know which way to walk if I landed.

I could not afford to let my mind wander as cloudbase was only 6,000 feet above the ground and with no cumulus clouds to guide me to my next thermal, I was reliant on reading the terrain below to judge the best places to find rising air. I seemed either to be thermalling or struggling, there were no high, happy glides when I could relax and rest my concentration.

An unfailing source of thermals was any freshly ploughed field. The combination of the dark furrows and the movement of the tractor back and forth would dislodge the hot bubble of air above it, rewarding me with more altitude each time.

The batteries in my radio went flat so I switched it off. I was only two hours into the flight and would have to resign myself to a long wait when I landed, as with no radio contact, Sarah would have no idea where I was.

An hour later I again found myself scratching about in a tiny piece of lift above an almost imperceptible hillock. All my concentration was locked into turning as efficiently as I could whilst fighting to stay in the scrappy thermal when there was a loud 'twang' and the glider jolted. My heart jumped as I looked about me to see which part of the glider was breaking. As I glanced behind, pulling out of a dive and emitting the familiar 'Aaarggh' was a large, angry wedgetail eagle. I could have done without his attentions at that moment and I cursed him for distracting me, irrationally muttering, 'If you just leave me alone, I'll be away from here more quickly.'

The more I tried to ignore him, the more furious he became, bouncing off my sail and wires time and again. When he finally judged me to be out of his airspace, he gave one more strike for good measure and with a victorious glance over his shoulder, plummeted back to his abode.

As the sun began to lose its power and evening approached, I had to work harder to find the thermals which were now even further apart. I was so tired mentally and physically that it took all the mind tricks I had ever learned to stay alert and attentive. I knew I had broken the distance via a turnpoint record, but wanted to stretch it out as far as I could to ensure it stood for a while. The distinctive shape of Lake Cargelligo finally came into view with the sun low in the sky behind it and I was soon making a landing approach alongside a small weatherboard homestead next to the main tarmac road.

I had never concentrated so hard for so long and I landed numb with exhaustion after eight hours and a flight which spanned 103 miles. I walked over to the farmhouse and knocked on the door. A slim, middle-aged lady opened it, but I couldn't form a proper sentence to tell her who I was or where I had come from. She didn't bat an eyelid as I, red-eyed, tousle haired and inarticulate, tried to gather my wits and find the connecting path between my brain and my mouth to be able to speak properly.

When I finally managed to explain, she took it in her stride as though hang gliders landed in her back garden every day. She gave me some water and biscuits, which did wonders to restore my powers of speech. I phoned the caravan park to leave a message for Sarah: goodness knows where she thought I was, having last heard from me six hours before.

Two minutes later I was walking back to the glider to pack up when the Citroën hared past on the main road with Sarah at the wheel. I thought I must be hallucinating. I was over a hundred miles from take-off and had had no contact with her; she couldn't possibly be so telepathic as to have guessed her way to exactly the right spot.

Sure enough, ten minutes later, Sarah arrived having stopped to tele-phone in the nearby town of Cargelligo. I was impressed. She had made an inspired guess as to my speed and trajectory from the initial information I had given her before my battery went flat and six hours later had passed my landing place within fifteen minutes of my feet hitting the ground.

We were both shattered by the time we had packed up, so we drove into Cargelligo and found a local pub that did bed and breakfast. We retired to the bar for a well-earned celebratory beer. My shoulders were in spasm after such a prolonged struggle and I had intermittently to massage them as we sat on our bar stools. The men at the bar were dumbfounded at the sight of the two strangers in town and we became mini-celebrities. We weren't even charged for our food and beer.

The following morning we were still tired, but happy as we drove back to Forbes to pack up our things and leave. We stopped off at the towing field to say goodbye to the group of pilots from Sydney who had been sharing our tow strip. Among them was Trevor Gardner, a tall, slim medical student with a big smile. He had taken an interest in my record-breaking flights and was delighted when he heard the news of my new world record. There was a strong attraction between us and we exchanged addresses, agreeing to meet up in Sydney before I left.

Once we had arrived back in Sydney, Sarah dropped me off at the airport to catch a plane to Tasmania. I was going to visit my mother's cousin and her family who had emigrated to Hobart, while Sarah went to see a friend north of the city. I spent a delightful week getting reacquainted with the family I had not seen for years. They were always busy doing something and had a house stuffed full of reference books. Their children, Grace and Helen, were great fun and we spent hours each day walking along the beach and fishing for anything curious in the rock pools near their house.

I was sorry to leave as I had really enjoyed their company and knew it would be a long time before I would see them again. As I emerged at the arrivals gate at Sydney Airport, Sarah wasn't there to meet me as planned. Instead, Trevor stood there grinning and explained that Sarah had gone sailing for three days and had asked him to pick me up. We drove back to his flat, where Sarah had left our car and my belongings. The next three days were blissful, touring the sights of Sydney with a man whom I became more and more fond of. He seemed to know all the secluded and romantic cafés, and we spent hours walking, talking and exploring the hidden parts of the city.

I fell for Trevor with an intensity that I had never experienced, and it was mutual. I knew that I had to see him again as I would not be able to bear walking out of his life for ever in two days' time. He had been thinking along the same lines and had formed a plan. He was in his final year of medical school and as part of the course he would have to serve a period in another country in April; he suggested to me that he should do his elective in England.

Sarah returned from her sailing trip and Trevor drove us to the airport to catch our plane back to London. It was an emotional farewell as I desperately did not want to be parted from him. April seemed like an eternity away, but I would wait as I was sure that his feelings for me were as strong as mine were for him.

CHAPTER 12

Leading the Team

I would have stayed in Sydney, but I had a big commitment in March 1990. I had been selected for the British team to go to the Pre-World Championships in Brazil. I had been chosen as captain of the eight-strong team and it was the first time the job had been given to a woman.

I had a lot to organise, including booking flights and glider transport, reserving accommodation and managing the budget. We arrived in Rio at the beginning of March. It was the most beautiful city I had ever seen, with long, silver, ribbon beaches bordering the turquoise ocean. The sands were strewn with beautiful women wearing the tiniest bikinis imaginable, and bronzed men strutting to and fro in front of them.

There was no time for sightseeing as Pepê Lopes, the competition organiser and one of the world's top pilots, had set up a press conference for me. He was a skilful manipulator of the media and was singly responsible for the high profile of hang gliding in Brazil. An energetic and charismatic man, he inspired everyone around him with his enthusiasm for flying.

It was a totally different ball game dealing with Brazilian photographers. In Britain, newspaper photos of me were generally taken dressed in harness and helmet and about to launch my hang glider. In Rio, the glider served only as a prop on which I was to be draped! They wanted sultry, pouting pictures running my fingers through my hair. They must have been disappointed, as all I could do was laugh each time they tried to get me to do some sexy pose.

As team captain, I was responsible for the entire team budget, some of which came from competition funds and the rest, from the pilots' own pockets. It totalled $15,000, half in cash and half in travellers' cheques, and I was forced to carry it all stuffed into my waist belt until we reached our hotel and it could be placed in a hotel safe deposit box.

We travelled to Governador Valadares, ten hours' drive north of Rio in the province of Minas Gerais, which was to be our competition base. Governador Valadares was a medium-sized industrial town surrounded by small hills and shadowed by Ibituruna, a 3,000-foot mountain which would be our take-off site.

We arrived at the Palace Hotel, which was very comfortable but fairly expensive. It was a rude introduction to the instability of Brazilian currency to find that they were going to put up the price by ninety per cent on 1 March. We moved out and rented a large apartment instead, only to discover that twice nightly a goods train with 150 carriages thundered right past the window!

We drove up the mountain in our two VW Kombis, both of which sounded as though they were on their last legs. The road was impossibly steep as we screamed up the incline in first gear to keep our momentum going.

The spine-back top of Ibituruna was a perfect setting for a large competition with 130 entrants. There was enough space to rig all the hang gliders and once the window was opened, the pilots could take off anywhere along the slope on either side of the mountain. The baking rock faces created the best thermals in the area and it was common for the hill simply to 'empty', with all pilots diving off within twenty minutes. The result was that massive gaggles of gliders would form above launch, creating a rotating jungle of wings.

The seething mass of gliders around me was terrifying and pilots had to be as vigilant as Formula One drivers to avoid a mid-air collision. The three-dimensional chaos would continue all the way to cloudbase and the only way to deal with it was to try and coax the best sink rate out of the glider and climb as fast as possible.

After two nights the team was on the move again as we transferred to another apartment right next to the main road, where trucks and cars passed by all night. We were right alongside a set of traffic lights, which triggered a compulsory hooting of horns by every vehicle that passed. The bar downstairs closed at 3.30 a.m. with much singing and revving of motorbikes followed almost immediately by the cockerel next door, which at 3.40 a.m. began his morning salutations. There was no doubt that Brazil was Latin and LOUD.

It was a haggard and crotchety bunch of pilots that packed up their gear the next morning and moved into a small hotel in the centre of town. It was dirty and hot, but compared with the other options, we had discovered nirvana.

I landed twenty miles from Governador Valadares later that day. I had chosen a pleasant-looking green grassy field below, standing out from the usual brown terrain. The heat intensified as I lost height and as I reached the point of no return and was committed to my landing, I saw an ominous glint of water through the green. It could mean only one thing – a swamp. I cursed my stupidity as I flared and felt my feet squelch into six inches of liquid mud.

By this time, I was soaked with perspiration and ripped off my harness and flying suit. My arms instantly turned black as hundreds of mosquitoes descended. In my panic to put on my suit again, I fumbled with the zips and felt them all start to bite. They were everywhere and I danced about, hysterically swatting them from my face and hands.

Two young barefooted boys splashed through the marsh to help me pack up my glider. It didn't seem to matter where you landed, there were always troops of children who knew how to de-rig a hang glider. For a handful of change, they would fold away my wing, often making a far neater job of it than I could!

They watched my antics with amused curiosity. The mosquitoes did not seem to bother them at all, whereas I could count over twenty bites on each square inch of flesh on my arms. We packed up as quickly as possible and the three of us waded towards the road. As we reached the highway, the mosquitoes disappeared back to their murky quagmire and left me in peace. I happily paid the boys twice the going rate and sat on the verge to wait for the van.

The flying conditions in Brazil were excellent, with consistent good weather allowing daily tasks of three or four hours' duration. I loved the routine of being able to fly every day, coming back to the hotel tired, then eating, sleeping and doing it all over again.

The competition started with a sixty-mile task, in which Robbie Whittall demonstrated his racing expertise by beating everyone. The scoring system for competitions always varies, some rewarding pilots who take risks and fly fast, giving huge quantities of points for a fast time around the course. Others, including Brazil, used the alternative philosophy by rewarding consistency. As long as you arrived at the goal, you scored well, even if you were slow. If you failed to make it, the penalty was such that it was almost impossible to make up the points.

I resolved to fly conservatively to make sure I got to goal each day.

The brown hills around Ibituruna produced good thermals. Heavily eroded through deforestation, the smooth, parched, grassy slopes baked in the sunshine, providing predictable lift. Navigation was easy, with the distinctive shape of Ibituruna visible from the furthest point of any course set. The main hazard lay in landing miles from a main road and having to walk for hours in the heat.

The friendly turkey vultures that I had met in Venezuela were back in force, as scruffy as ever with their legs dangling down. They certainly were ugly, but were excellent thermal markers.

Final glides into goal were always stressful. It was usually the end of the day when the thermal strength was pitifully weak and the goal line gleamed tantalisingly in the distance. It was a great test of patience to circle over the same spot, clawing height inch by inch for half an hour to ensure I had enough altitude to reach goal. There were always a few pilots who landed just short of the line and it is one of the most frustrating feelings to see the goal line rise in your line of vision and to know that you won't make it. You can pull the bar in, push it out, curse out loud or do a deal with the devil for your soul, but it won't help.

Having calculated the height needed and allowing an extra 500 feet just to make sure, it was a question of gliding as straight and efficiently as possible in order to reach the line. With both hands together on the base bar, elbows tucked in and head down to reduce drag, there was nothing else to do at this stage but wait and watch. My pointed toes pushed so hard against the end of my harness that they hurt and my ears were tuned to every frequency change in the vario's sound to fine-tune my speed.

The most pressurised landings would follow an out and return task to the north, with goal back at Governador Valadares. The final approach took us directly over the town, with nowhere to land if you miscalculated the glide and were too low to reach the field. On one occasion, one of our team, Steve Elkins, hit severe sink over the town and landed 200 yards short of the line. His only option was to land on the busy main road and, managing to dodge the trucks and forcing the traffic to stop, he successfully pulled off this stunt. Steve was so disappointed to have missed goal that he carried his glider to the side of the road, took his harness off and lay down in the shade of his glider. He closed his eyes, hoping that the gathering crowd of chattering, excited people would go away.

He slowly became aware of blue flashing lights as police cars and an ambulance converged on the side of the road. One concerned local,

131

thinking Steve was seriously injured, had called the emergency services. Steve's voice came over the radio, tinged with desperation, asking if we could send someone over who spoke Portuguese to sort the situation out.

On Wednesday morning I went to the bank as usual to change the daily requirement of dollars into crusados. Inflation was such that the dollar was worth significantly more each day, making it prudent to change as little as possible. Everyone wanted to be paid in dollars as the value of crusados dropped even as you handed them over. I only ever changed enough to pay for one day's petrol and food bills for the team.

The bank was shut. I went to the foreign exchange but that too was closed and had a notice taped to the door. Thinking it must be a public holiday, I returned to the hotel and asked one of the competition translators.

'The president has ordered that the banks must close for some days,' she stated unequivocally.

I had difficulty understanding that a president could stop the financial systems of a country for an unspecified period. No one knew when things would be back to normal or how much the dollar would be worth when they were. Rumours abounded, but in the meantime we had no usable currency. The formerly mistrusted crusado was suddenly back in favour, but we didn't have any. No one would accept dollars as they had no idea of their value.

We were suddenly plunged into a scenario where the dollar was as unpredictable as a ball rolling around a roulette wheel, never knowing into which hole it might drop. As team manager I felt responsible and fretted about how we were going to keep the vans going with no money for petrol. There was no cash for food, so I arranged credit with the local burger bar, which was run by a hang glider pilot who trusted us.

When the banks finally opened after four days, anyone with a savings account found that eighty per cent of their money had been 'borrowed' by the government for eighteen months in an effort to control the runaway inflation. The dollar was worth less than half of its previous value, which meant that the price of our hotel had more than doubled, rendering my budget completely inadequate.

Each morning I had to put the money worries to one side and turn my mind back to flying. My muscles were really sore and each day they protested violently at being made to work for yet another three-or four-hour stretch. I discovered that one of the American pilots with the nickname of Zoardog had taken out a $20 bet with his friend Jim Zeiset that he would beat me on one task. Jim had happily taken him up, as he had flown with me in India and Australia. It was a curious feeling that Zoardog's only goal in the competition was to beat me on one day. His first question on landing was always, 'Where's Judy?' Towards the end of the competition, many of the pilots knew about his bet and were all willing me on. Zoardog lost his bet and Jim bought me a beer with his winnings!

The Australian team were struggling. They normally had several pilots in the top ten at international competitions, but I was beating them all and I have to confess I felt a tinge of pleasure that the results were being faxed back to Bill Moyes daily.

I consistently made it to goal and my strategy had worked as I was doing well on the scoreboard. I was not the fastest, but those who had really stuck their necks out to try to win had often paid a huge penalty when they blew it and landed early. Both John Pendry and Robbie were way down in the ratings, having won a task each but also failed to make goal at least once.

At the end of the competition, I was thirteenth overall, my best result ever in a championship with such a quality line-up of pilots from all over the world. I was the third placed British pilot, which would surely stand me in good stead for the team selection for the 1991 World Championships.

We drove back to Rio, where we spent two days before flying home. I took the opportunity to fly from the mountain above the city, taking off from a huge wide ramp. We had been sunbathing on the beach and it wasn't until I started to rig my glider that I realised I had not brought any clothes or shoes up with me and had only the swimsuit I was standing in. It was a lovely feeling to run off the mountain with bare feet and to feel the cool marine air down my back.

The statue of Christ which dominates the city rose proudly from its cliff-top perch, arms outstretched. Acre upon acre of high-rise apartments and hotels carpeted the ground below, but the usual assault of such sprawling urbanity on the senses were dulled by the ever-present gleaming ocean gently lapping the endless beaches. I landed on the soft sand and packed my glider into its cardboard travelling box for the journey home.

CHAPTER 13

High Altitude Honeymoon

Trevor was due to arrive in April and I could hardly contain my excitement. He had booked a four-week working elective in Frimley Park Hospital just a stone's throw away from my flat in Camberley, Surrey.

The first League meeting of 1990 was held in South Wales just before his arrival. After all my flying hours in Brazil and my happy frame of mind, I was flying well. On the third day, competition director John Duncker set the most ambitious task ever attempted in the history of the League, which involved a fifty-mile triangle, unheard of in Britain. A local expert laughed in his face, called the task impossible and backed his opinion up with a £20 bet.

Undeterred, John declared the take-off window open and sixty pilots launched from the Blorenge above Abergavenny, to attempt the task. The weather improved with cloudbase reaching 7,000 feet, far higher than I had ever flown in Britain. As I climbed up and up, the area I knew so well took on a different perspective as the huge ridges and mountains became small, interconnected lumps below. I could see the Wye Valley in the distance as I made my way to Hay Bluff, the blunt promontory above Hay-on-Wye. The spring green of the fields below was vibrant and the air was fresh with the scent of new growth.

Glides between thermals were long and fast and I could afford to use only the strongest lift. With the huge ground clearance, it was like flying in the Alps and I couldn't help grinning. Flying in Britain is often so hard as we wait for decent weather and fly cross-country with poor visibility, strong winds and low clouds. It was such a treat to be able to look down on South Wales from a mile and a half above.

Having photographed Hay Bluff, I headed for Pen y Fan, the next turnpoint. The windsurfers wafted slowly along Llangorse Lake in the light breeze, but their loss was our gain as we did not have to confront a strong headwind, which would normally thwart a triangle flight in Britain. I hooked a strong thermal up the inside of the gully in front of Pen y Fan and screamed back up to cloudbase to take my photograph. I met up with six other pilots and started on the home leg.

John Duncker was still on the top of the Blorenge when a cry went up. Someone had spotted us, a tiny cluster of hang gliders in the distance on our way to goal. John ran to the other side of the hill to watch and was rewarded with sight of the first gaggle pulling on speed and whistling over his head to complete a new British triangle record.

I finished third overall after the four-day competition, but as I drove back to Camberley, my thoughts were not about hang gliding for once, but that Trevor would be arriving within a week.

I met him at Heathrow. It was an awkward reunion as we hardly knew one another, yet our hopes and expectations were high. He started work at Frimley Park Hospital while I continued my publicity work with Citroën and each weekend we travelled to a different part of Britain to fly and enjoy the scenery. We fell in love almost immediately and at the end of his four-week stay, Trevor asked me to marry him.

I was completely overwhelmed. I had had my share of relationships, but had never felt this strongly about anyone before. I suppose that until this point I had been 'married' to hang gliding and my devotion to flying had taken precedence over my relationships. This time it was different and, without reservation, I agreed to marry Trevor.

Some of my friends expressed surprise at the speed of our decision; we had after all only been together for four weeks! We had been writing to one another since January and I thought letters were a sure way of getting to know someone. I put their minds at rest, certain that I knew what I was doing.

My parents were delighted as I think they had despaired of my ever finding a partner. The date was set for 24 November 1990 and Mum was like a dog with two tails as she joyfully set about making arrangements. In the meantime, Trevor had to return to Australia. It was very hard separating once again and we resorted back to communicating by fax machines and letters.

My life returned to its normal hectic routine of competitions interspersed with publicity stunts for Citroën. During the summer months I did balloon drops at major agricultural shows, balloon fiestas and county shows. Citroën had a huge video screen which was erected at these events to give the vast audiences a close-up view of the action. When I did a balloon drop, the crowd could watch the take-off in the main arena and then see live footage of the drop, which was relayed from the balloon basket to the screen. I would release, fly around the balloon trailing coloured smoke and land back in the arena.

In May 1990, I was selected to represent Britain at the European Championships. The decision took me by surprise. I had set my sights so firmly on the World Championships in Brazil that I had not considered the Europeans. After the first two League meetings, I was lying in third place and the selectors had unanimously chosen me as one of the top six pilots in Britain. I had made it at last – the first time a woman had ever been selected on equal terms to compete in a world-class competition.

I checked my calendar to find with dismay that the European Championships clashed with the East of England show, which Citroën had booked me for. I had given them my competition calendar at the beginning of the year and they had worked around it, but I had not included the European Championship dates.

I went to see Marc Raven, who had taken over from Jim Mather as head of special promotions at Citroën. He tried his best to sort out an alternative arrangement but the pre-event publicity had been done advertising the drop and there was nothing he could do about it. I had to be there.

I found myself in the awful situation of having to choose between the European Championships and my sponsorship deal with Citroën. After hours of deliberation, I decided to keep my sponsorship and forego my place at the Europeans. The selectors had proved that they wanted me on the team and so I felt that my chances of selection for the World Championships the following February were good. I stuck to my original goal: to be chosen for Brazil.

It was ironical that the only commercially sponsored 'professional' pilot should be the one that was stopped from going to the Europeans by work commitments! As fate would have it, when the selection was made for the team in Brazil that autumn, I was not chosen and I never did get another chance to be on the A-team. Although bitterly disappointed, I did not regret my decision. I had been approached by a film company who wanted to make a documentary about my flying from the summit of Cotopaxi, one of the world's highest active volcanoes in Ecuador. Citroën had agreed to back the project.

The idea of flying from Cotopaxi had originally been hatched by the

Dangerous Sports Club of Oxford University. I had met four of the infamous group back in 1981 in Brian Milton's sitting room as they discussed their forthcoming adventure. I sat there enchanted by the idea, looking at their pictures of the mountain, a perfect cone of captivating beauty, topped with snow.

'We're going to fly off the biggest active volcano in the world,' they told me. However, when the disorganised and unfit group went out to Ecuador that winter, they failed in their attempt to fly from the summit.

The image of Cotopaxi continued to inspire me. No one had ever flown from its 19,600 foot summit, a challenge I simply could not resist. I met with John Gau Productions and confirmed that they wished to cover the flight for the *Voyager* series to be shown on Channel 4. This meant that Citroën would be guaranteed half an hour's exposure on prime-time TV and so they confirmed they would sponsor the project.

The months with the lightest winds were November and December, which coincided with the date that Trevor and I had set for our wedding. We decided to make the trip our honeymoon. Neither of us liked lying on beaches and this seemed like a great adventure with which to start our life together.

Matt Dickinson was the film producer and we arranged to visit Cotopaxi before the expedition to secure the bureaucratic arrangements and permissions we needed. We also had to climb Cotopaxi to investigate the take-off site and filming possibilities. In late September we left the autumnal skies of England and flew to South America. As we flew over Ecuador at 30,000 feet, the sun was dusting the wisps of cloud below with a soft orange light. Far below an active volcano had strewn a plume of smoke across the sky. As we descended into Quito, Matt and I were very excited, hoping for our first glimpse of Cotopaxi. First we saw one snow-capped peak, then another and then, unmistakably, the most perfect volcano poked its nose above the clouds, majestic and beautiful. We both gasped. After so much hard work and anticipation, it finally sat there before us.

Matt is a great travelling companion. His unkempt thatch of black hair has a mind of its own and his bright blue eyes sparkle with good humour at the prospect of a new adventure. He always has a wealth of entertaining stories from his filming and climbing expeditions. As a 'traveloholic', he maintains an infectious, child-like enthusiasm for a new place.

After booking into our cheap and cheerful hotel, we went to the Otavalo market – a Saturday extravaganza. The vibrant colours and bustle of the streets were exciting and I was mesmerised by the striking faces of the

Otavalo Indians. Their dark treacle eyes shone brightly out of broad faces with high cheekbones and wide noses. The men wore their long black hair in pony tails or plaits, always topped with a hat. The women's hair was often wrapped in a brightly coloured woven band, forming a long, colourful sausage. Around their waists, they tied several multicoloured sashes and wore a swathe of necklaces around their necks. They often wore two or more hats piled one on top of the other and the vivid shawls around their shoulders bulged with either their shopping or a baby. They were generally under five feet tall and had an unmistakable aura of pride about them.

We visited the animal market, where the general noise was punctuated by indignant piglets being dragged away from their food, all four feet stuck rigidly forwards, ploughing furrows in the mud and emitting piercing squeals. The following day we drove south to Latacunga town at the base of Cotopaxi. The increasing fertility of the volcanic soil made the valleys progressively greener. Our arrival coincided with a fiesta in town, a street procession creating a typical South American cacophony of noise and colour. The parade was led by an angel on horseback, followed by a prince and several figures wearing hideous masks. A man strained under the weight of a roasted pig which he carried on his back. Around it were arranged cooked chickens, lambs and guinea pigs (a local delicacy). Bottles of wine also dangled from the grotesque arrangement and the bearer's face was puce as he grunted his way down the road.

We drove into Cotopaxi National Park along the track of volcanic ash. Hardy plants thrived in the harsh environment, clinging to the lava. The sparse flowers brightened their surroundings with exotic shapes and colours. The ground crunched pleasantly underfoot and with mist hanging low in the valley we pitched our tents to the sounds of the nearby stream and the croaking of frogs.

We were treated to our first close up view of the mountain when the low clouds briefly drew apart like curtains, revealing the unmistakable triangle of Cotopaxi. The sheer size, the clear snowline and perfect whiteness of the summit were dramatic. I had dreamed of this mountain so many times that to be so close brought a lump to my throat.

The following morning we climbed to the refuge at 15,500 feet, which was a basic but fairly comfortable hut. Although Matt was an experienced climber, I had never done any mountaineering before so Hugo, our guide, took us to the glacier to go through some rudimentary climbing techniques. By the end of the afternoon, I had mastered the basics of ice-axe arrest, crampon use and climbing whilst roped up to someone else. I had also strained both my Achilles tendons and had developed tenosynovitis (a painful inflammation of the tendon sheath).

In spite of the pain in my ankles, I was looking forward to the climb, even though I regarded mountaineering as a rather masochistic sport. The views were superb, but I preferred to take off and climb the easy way, using a hang glider.

We went to bed early as we had to start out for the summit at 2 a.m. One of the effects of altitude is insomnia and none of us slept a wink. Moronically we donned our climbing clothes and tried to force down some breakfast. Our head torches created tiny pools of light as we climbed up the lava slope to the glacier. Due to my inexperience, I was trying to flex my foot when I climbed instead of the correct technique of walking as if in rigid ski boots. My rapidly worsening tenosynovitis was acutely painful from step one and it was a case of practising 'mind over matter' for the following eight and a half hours.

We reached the glacier after an hour of battling with the lava sand, where each step forward saw us sliding two steps backwards. We attached our crampons and climbed onto the snow. Because of the darkness there were no visual distractions from the pain and I found myself wondering incredulously how anyone could possibly become obsessed by this sport – but each to their own I suppose!

After four hours, I was becoming hypoxic. I was climbing very inefficiently, getting frustrated as Hugo and Matt were so fast and I was overreaching myself trying to keep up. First I became emotional, crying with frustration, and then fatigue overwhelmed me. With an air of detachment I observed myself as if from outside as Matt encouraged me to continue.

We stopped for food and drink 600 feet below the summit, sitting in the snow next to a huge rock face with overhanging icicles. I keeled over and fell asleep immediately. It took two hours to cover the final steep, soft, snow-covered slope. I couldn't even manage to take ten steps before having to stop for a breather. I felt terribly dizzy and remote.

Finally, after the biggest physical effort I have ever made, we reached the summit and I celebrated by falling asleep again! I was no more capable of flying a hang glider than I was of winning an all-comers embroidery contest. I was going to have to acclimatise better and learn how to climb properly when we returned in November.

The main problem with the crater as a take-off site was that the slope facing outwards was too shallow to launch from if the wind was light. At such high altitude, my take-off speed would be much faster than normal which, coupled with a degree of hypoxia and deep, soft snow would make it impossible if there wasn't any wind. The inner slope of the crater, however, had an uneven wall with a very steep incline and I estimated that, if desperate, I could take off facing inwards, turn immediately and dive over the lower lip before I sank into the crater itself.

Matt woke me after my third nap and ushered me back down the mountain, where I quickly recovered from my hypoxia. We returned to Quito, and made the necessary arrangements to conform with local bureaucracy. One minute we were dressed in our best bib and tucker visiting the British Embassy to enlist their help, the next saw us in our scruffiest clothes to meet the National Parks authority so that we could plead poverty and not have to pay a crippling fee to film within the Cotopaxi National Park. Once our mission was completed we returned to England to organise our November expedition.

Trevor arrived back in England a week before the wedding and joined in the frenzy of preparation. He volunteered his services as expedition doctor and made sure he had all the supplies he might need to cope with anything from hypoxia to a broken back.

We were married on 24 November 1990 in the Chapel of the Order of the British Empire in the crypt of St Paul's Cathedral. The following morning we set off for Heathrow Airport.

'You're going on your honeymoon?' inquired a bemused check-in assistant. We did not look like normal British Airways passengers, let alone a honeymoon couple. Our baggage comprised a twenty-four-foot folding plywood take-off ramp, ice axes and crampons swinging from our rucksacks and armfuls of radios and electronic instruments, which confused the X-ray machines. Added to this were the two identical hang gliders in their smart new bags.

It was a novel idea to spend our honeymoon with twenty-three other people, and we knew it would not be dull. We spent four days on our own before the rest of the crew arrived, with a ludicrously bulky mountain of gear, and prepared to start filming.

We made contact with the local hang glider pilots who were incredibly helpful, taking days off work to take us flying from Pichincha, the active volcano above Quito. The first day we were taken to the east launch at 12,500 feet. Trevor and I exchanged glances as we saw a forest of antennae directly in front of take-off.

'It's no problem,' assured Bari, the local flying instructor. 'You will clear the top of them.' From our viewpoint, they were almost level with take-off, directly on our flight path and we did not trust this optimistic opinion of thermal reliability. Luck smiled on us and the wind changed, making the less cluttered north launch more suitable.

Given the height of Pichincha, our take-off speed would be significantly higher than normal, but we were blessed with a moderate headwind which eased the problem, though it was noticeable how much faster the glider travelled over the ground. The city of Quito stretched before us. Confined by steep mountains on either side, it was squeezed into a ribbon of sprawling urbanity.

Two days later, we left for Cotopaxi National Park. The convoy included three truckloads of equipment, much of it film gear brought by the two film crews. There were thirteen of us in all (twenty-three with the porters) including Joe Brown, the legendary mountaineer who was cajoled into joining us as 'safety advisor'. A veteran of many expeditions, he was a source of endless entertaining stories, invariably commencing, 'When I was on such and such a mountain in 1956 ...' and usually involving a horrendous accident or someone stuck down a crevasse.

We were to acclimatise at an altitude of 11,000 feet for several days before attempting to venture higher, so we set up camp in the Limpiopunga Valley at the base of Cotopaxi. It looked like the lost world, with volcanic sand and huge boulders strewn around us. Small streams chattered through the rocks, bitterly cold as they flowed straight from the snow cap of the mountain. While Trevor and I checked our gliders and camera equipment, Joe disappeared, returning an hour later with two trout that he'd caught by hand in a nearby brook.

After three days of hiking and sorting equipment, we moved up to the refuge at 15,500 feet, where we were to stay for several days before attempting the summit. Our first day was spent learning more climbing techniques, this time from Joe, who patiently explained the need for me to pace myself and walk in a slow, rhythmical way which conserved energy. He also taught me how to walk in the rigid climbing boots so that I didn't get a repetition of the Achilles strain which had taken several weeks to heal.

We filmed all the climbing scenes which, on the day of the actual climb, would be done in the dark. They also filmed the porters carrying the glider. Although it only weighed twenty-five kilograms, it needed six of them as it was such an awkward shape and was so fragile. The hapless cameraman was lowered into a crevasse to film the porters hoisting the glider over the top of the icy fissure.

For the summit flight I would be able to carry only one camera attached to the glider to ensure my take-off weight was reduced to a minimum, so we 'cheated' and took some extra footage, launching from the lower slopes of the volcano. Trevor and I rigged the hang gliders next to the refuge and attached cameras.

It was a wonderful surprise to take off and fly straight into a thermal and to climb slowly alongside the volcano. While I was giggling and whooping with excitement, Trevor focused his thoughts on tackling hypoxia and was practising slow, relaxed breathing. As I turned, the panorama filed past, with each snow-capped cone in the Valley of the Volcanoes standing proud and alone. I felt privileged to be able to fly so close to the summit of Cotopaxi, the lava fields gleaming richly in rust and chestnut brown contrasting with its snow cap, deeply scarred with blue crevasses. I spent an hour feasting on the view before flying out to land in the valley below. The volcanic plateau is spirit-level-flat, unobstructed and so big you could land a jumbo jet on it. As always, when there are cameras rolling, I messed up my landing by dropping the nose of the glider. The effect of the thin air took me by surprise. There was a moderate breeze blowing and so I gave a good landing flare which turned out to be completely inadequate at 13,500 feet. Instead of stopping all forward travel, I was still ripping across the ground at a rate of knots and ended up doing a highly undignified 'nose in'.

We packed up the gliders, enjoying the warm equatorial sunshine before returning to the relentless cold of the refuge. As I looked back towards the slopes of Cotopaxi where we had been thermalling just half an hour before, I saw the wheeling forms of two condors, circling effortlessly upwards. Their enormous wings appeared to remain motionless as they cruised, fine-tuning their angle of bank using their outstretched primary feathers. I watched spellbound as these majestic lords of the air flew against the perfect backdrop of Cotopaxi with the Andes behind. I desperately wanted to be up there with them, sharing their thermal and watching them at close quarters. An idea for a future expedition began to form in my mind and I resolved that one day I would fly together with condors.

My reverie was broken by the voices of the crew, who wanted to get back to the refuge, where our cook had begun her thrice-daily ritual of preparing a meal for twenty-three people. Hugo, Joe, the film crew, Trevor and I gathered to agree a master plan. An advance base camp was to be established at the foot of the Yanasacha Wall, the large 600-foot rock face at 19,000 feet. All the equipment was to be ferried up there over the next two days. The following day the porters would take the glider, harness, camera and medical gear from base camp to the top and, weather permitting, I would fly from the summit.

My glider left first thing in the morning, carried, dragged and hauled upwards by six of the porters. I rigged the other, identical glider to make one more flight from the refuge with a video camera attached to my wing tip. For two hours we watched the porters struggle up the volcanic sand towards the glacier. They were all seasoned mountaineers, but still had to stop every five minutes for a break as their awkward load made the going difficult.

I wanted to try out the summit 'ramp' that Trevor had spent hours making. The folding masterpiece was made from twelve two-foot-square pieces of thin plywood with webbing hinges and sandpaper strips glued onto the surface so that my feet wouldn't slip. I would certainly need it as on the summit the snow was so soft and deep that without it I would sink to my knees and be unable to run to take off. Joe staked it to the sandy slope near the refuge and it felt solid enough as I ran down it.

Once in the air, I found a thermal and started to climb up the face of Cotopaxi. After only ten minutes I was level with the porters, who were six hours into their Herculean task. They waved and shouted good-naturedly, but were probably totally mystified as to why I should want to fly from the top when I could soar up to the crater so easily and save all the effort. At 18,000 feet I began to worry about hypoxia. I was trying to slow my breathing but with the amount of effort I was having to put into controlling the glider, unbalanced by the weight of the camera, I could not relax. Five minutes later I pulled out and headed for the valley, despite being only 600 feet from the summit.

After one more day's rest we would attempt the summit flight. I fretted in case the weather worsened and prevented me from flying. Although we had a week in hand, I knew how fickle the winds could be, picking up to a howling gale with no warning which would stop me from flying. We didn't have any access to weather forecasts and would have to make the huge effort of getting everyone to the top and hope that it would be flyable when we got there.

I was also nervous about the climb. It had been so hard last time when I climbed with Matt and I felt ignorant, knowing nothing about mountaineering. I could not afford to arrive at the summit in the same hypoxic condition as before, totally incapable of flying a hang glider. This time there were two big differences: I had had time to acclimatise to the altitude and Joe Brown, coaxing me on with his gentle humour and wealth of knowledge had given me much more confidence.

My other worry was the extra speed I would need to take off in the thin air at 19,600 feet. I had spoken to Jes Flynn, an experienced pilot with knowledge of aerodynamics, about the effects of altitude on take-off speed before I left. He sent me a two-page fax giving complicated formulae and figures, the final worrying result of which was that my take-off speed at the top of Cotopaxi would have to be forty per cent faster than at sea level. Jes summarised it perfectly by attaching a note to the end stating, 'This seems to indicate that the R.L.F. technique is required!' (R.L.F. = Run Like F***.)

In spite of my worries, I felt certain that, with the right weather, I could do the flight. The idea that within forty-eight hours I could be standing on the crater's edge, hooked in and ready to launch was exciting and I was impatient to get up there. Trevor busied himself preparing his medical kit to take to the summit. It was hard for him to cater for every eventuality, especially the possibility that I might crash on launch and break a bone or two.

The next day was spent doing some more filming on the glacier, followed by an early night with everyone in bed by 7 p.m. to get some sleep before the midnight start up the mountain. Before going to bed, I walked outside the hut, crunching my way across the lava stones. The sound of laughter filtered through the windows as the team enjoyed another of Joe's stories. I dug my hands deep into my down jacket pockets and looked up to the sky. The stars shone brightly, heralding good weather for the morning. I turned to gaze at the slope of Cotopaxi, standing proud and oblivious to our meagre efforts to climb, fly and conquer its height.

I returned to the refuge to try and sleep. Our group of twenty-three had taken over one of the two bedrooms which had three-tier bunk beds. The ten porters carpeted half the floor space, with the film gear occupying the other half. Nocturnal 'snoring Olympics' resounded around the room as various members of the crew chorused together. I was glad of my earplugs, though they amplified the sound of my pulse which at that altitude, and combined with my nervous anticipation, pounded alarmingly.

I woke before midnight and crept downstairs to check the sky. The stars were obscured by a layer of high cloud and there was no moon to light our way, but the air was still with no sign of the strong winds which would

above The air was so dense above the Dead Sea that it felt like flying through syrup. *(Judy Leden)*

right Yasmin and Ben in Petra. *(Judy Leden)*

left The take off frenzy during a paragliding competion. *(Noel Whittall)*

below Crossing the Rhine during 'Flight for Life'. *(Ben Ashman)*

foot Battling against the storm clouds over the Czech Republic. *(Judy Leden)*

right The 'Flight for Life' team in the rain at Nurnberg International Airport. From the left: Gavin, Judy, Ben and Sid.

below The Blue Mosque at dawn, Istanbul, Turkey *(Judy Leden)*

above Flying above Halab Aleppo, Syria. (*Ben Ashman*)

left King Hussein of Jordan welcomes us after our fifteen day journey from England.

Chris putting my third pair gloves on to guard against the temperature of -87° Celsius. *(Tony Larkin)*

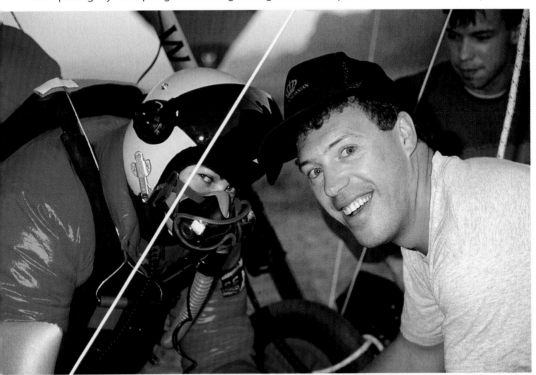

Only another 41,300 feet to go! *(Tony Larkin)*

left Finally on our own, the silence consumed me. *(Tony Larkin)*

below Exhausted and frozen after a two hour descent. (A friend said 'Women only look that bad in childbirth!'). *(Tony Larkin)*

foot Relief, exhilaration and a world record. Per Lindstrand gives me a Swedish bear hug. *(Tony Larkin)*

main picture Waiting for a condor in the shadow of Mt Fitzroy, Patagonia. *(Chris Dawes)*

inset Planning our next adventure. *(Matt Dickinson)*

stop the flight. I woke everyone and we spent the next hour solemnly donning our copious layers of clothing. Inner and outer boots had to be laced and our spare clothes, food and water arranged so that they were accessible in our rucksacks. Although the outside temperature was very cold, climbing is still warm work and it is very uncomfortable to be overdressed and unable to move freely.

It was a sleepy gaggle of people who finally assembled at the door of the hut. Head torches were switched on and without a word we set off in a long, slow crocodile moving upwards. I tried not to think about the gruelling hours ahead as I concentrated on the techniques Joe had taught me. I managed to establish a steady rhythm on the lava ash and we reached the glacier at 3 a.m. After filming us putting on our crampons, one film crew went down to the Limpiopungo Valley in order to capture the landing, leaving the high-altitude cameraman and soundman to document our climb and the take-off.

I followed Joe with the rope between us shortened to fifteen feet so that I could watch him and mimic his steps. His slow, regular pace was easy to copy and I found I could let my mind drift on to other things. The time passed quickly, with far less stress than my previous climb had caused.

As we climbed higher, the wind picked up and the biting cold penetrated my clothing, but the slope was so steep it made it impossible to stop and get my down jacket out of my rucksack. At high altitude, once the cold gets to you it is very hard to warm up again and I began to shiver. The dark climb was relentless, with no ledges upon which to rest and no view to look at. The altitude was making Trevor nauseous and we turned our backs to offer him a little privacy as he vomited into the snow.

At last the sky began to lighten, and by 6 a.m. the shadow of Cotopaxi stretched in a perfect triangle on the top of the clouds below. My steps lightened as the beauty of the morning lifted my spirits.

We met up with the porters just below the Yanasacha Wall. After adapting Joe's foldable mountain stretcher into a sled for the glider, they had made much faster progress. We reached the Yanasacha camp at 7 a.m. exhausted and frozen. Three of us crammed into each tent and we put our sleeping bags over us. I put on my down jacket and managed to recover my energy and body heat fairly quickly.

After half an hour, I stepped outside to see how the porters were faring with the glider. They were climbing the final steep face, dragging the glider behind them on a rope. As I watched, the porter steadying the glider lost his grip on the bag on an almost vertical gradient and it swung like a pendulum towards the rock face, where it would have been smashed into pieces. Everyone gasped, watching helplessly as it slid. Inches from the rocks it miraculously ground to a halt and we breathed again.

By 9 a.m. I was impatient to get going. The glider was at the top and Hugo radioed down to say that there was no wind on the summit. The last 600 feet were cruelly steep and it demanded a huge effort from everyone in our tired group. Every few steps we had to stop and rest, trying to pay back the oxygen debt in order to be able to take the next few steps. Slowly we inched our way upwards, passing the porters who were on their way down to the Yanasacha camp to collect the film gear and safety equipment.

There were several frustrating false horizons on the last stretch and when the crater finally came into view, it took me by surprise. I remembered very little from my previous climb as I spent most of it in the land of the fairies. Sulphur fumes heralded our approach and then the crater appeared, dramatically deep with a ring of snow framing the smoking fumaroles of the black inner crater.

As Hugo had said, there was no wind at the top and the thick silence was broken only by our panting for breath. The clouds formed a broken quilt below us, which was thickening and rising up the slope towards the summit. The snowy peaks of the other volcanoes in the valley formed white islands above a sea of cloud. I hoisted the glider on to my shoulder and walked twenty paces towards take-off as fast as the knee-deep snow would allow. My head began to reel as my body staged a mutiny at the lack of oxygen. I put the glider down and breathed deeply. I began to rig very slowly, trying to keep my adrenaline under control.

The wind started to blow, first a gentle waft, then a steady breeze. Thank God – I really didn't want to take off facing into the crater. Trevor gave me a small bottle of oxygen to clear my head so that I could assess the conditions and work more quickly as the weather had begun to look unstable. If I was going to get off the mountain, I would have to fly soon. As we stood discussing the best take-off spot, a huge gust of wind blew straight up the north face. With an acrobatic leap that belied his fatigue, Trevor caught the glider as the wind lifted it. The breeze continued to blow from the north, the perfect direction. I could not believe my luck.

According to the basic law, you don't get anything for nothing, and the reason the wind had changed direction was that a large and rapidly rising finger of cloud had burst through the sheet of cloud below and was covering parts of the summit. Looking around, there were several very active areas thrusting upwards and they looked threatening. Soon we were faced with an almost solid bank of cloud in front of launch.

'I reckon we've got ten minutes. I want to go as soon as possible,' I explained to the director Karen Bishop as I removed my crampons and outer boots.

Karen grabbed the high-altitude cameraman, who was suffering from hypoxia, and he shakily filmed me getting into my harness. As I walked over to the best place for take-off, I could see the bizarre spectacle of Joe trotting up and down my plywood ramp, checking it was stable after having staked it down. The oxygen was immensely helpful as it allowed me to work at normal speed and to think clearly. Trevor walked with me as I carried the glider, but progress was slow as the snow was so deep, and with each step I sank up to my knees.

The porters were sitting in a straggled row behind the ramp and I turned and thanked them for their efforts. They called out encouragement, half-excited, half-frightened by what I was about to do. I looked outwards and saw the cloud 'wall' looming up in front of me. A tiny gap appeared, allowing me to see the ground below, and I knew it was now or never.

The wind was blowing a perfect ten miles an hour straight up the slope. I discarded the oxygen and put on my helmet. I said, 'Release', and Trevor let go of the glider's wires and ducked out of the way. I ran as hard as I could, pushing the glider through the thin air. Even with the moderate headwind, I ran the whole length of the ramp before the glider lifted me from the mountain. As my feet left the ground the last thing I heard was the porters whooping with delight.

I turned left along the rim of the crater, looking into the very heart of Cotopaxi. Normally clouds would hug close to the mountainside, but these stayed a little further away, leaving a clear corridor between the ridge and the cloud. As I flew down this enchanting passageway, the sun shone through, illuminating the bottomless crevasses and the Yanasacha Wall.

I lost height rapidly and dropped beneath the clouds, where the air became turbulent and buoyant. Looking back at Cotopaxi, the summit was now completely covered in cloud which looked uncomfortably like a thunderstorm. I was still at 16,000 feet and dangerously close to the heart of this powerful monster. If I had waited another ten minutes I would not have been able to launch. I wanted to be on the ground rather than linger in the sort of air which was throwing me about like a leaf in the breeze. All around me the air was being sucked up into the cloud. I had 3,000 feet to lose before I could reach the plateau below me. I pulled on maximum speed and swung the glider into a carving turn which eventually stopped me climbing, and gradually I began to lose height.

Finally, I saw the tiny figures of the second film crew far below in my landing area. Simon, the assistant cameraman, was standing on the truck holding up a windsock. It was horizontal, indicating a strong northerly wind. As I watched, it swung to the east and kept going through south, west and back to north. Terrific! The wind was blowing in circles, and was very strong. I didn't know which way to land in these unpredictable and dangerous winds. I felt like I was playing Russian Roulette.

I took the northerly wind option and hoped it would be my lucky day. At thirty feet above the ground the wind switched through forty-five degrees and I altered my course into it. The direction stayed constant long enough for me to do a perfect landing and collapse in a relieved heap.

I was filled with jubilation as the camera crew rushed over. It had taken me over an hour to fly down. They gave me a radio and I talked to Trevor, who happily told me that he and Joe had had an 'oxygen party', sharing the remaining oxygen, and they felt much better for it.

The whole crowd had waited on the summit so that they could film Trevor's reaction when he found out I had landed safely. The weather was worsening all the time and by now a thunderstorm was imminent. From the valley I could see the anvil of cloud spreading out above them. Lightning, thunder and hail made their journey hazardous as they headed down the mountain. With their hair standing on end and the ropes buzzing, the weary group had to bang their crampons free of cloying snow at every pace.

Climbers are normally advised to be off the mountain by 10 a.m. to avoid the risk of avalanche and the dangers of soft snow underfoot. By now it was past 2 p.m. and they still had three hours to go until they reached the refuge.

Meanwhile, I derigged my glider and with the lucky group at the bottom of the mountain headed for the luxury of a nearby hotel in Latacunga. I ran a hot bath, savouring the feeling of being clean after a week on the mountainside. The realisation that I had finally done it hit me. After all the months of preparation and build-up, it was all over. I lounged back in the steaming water and grinned.

The summit crew arrived with Trevor looking grey and exhausted. They had all been battered and frightened by the storm and were thankful for the peaceful comfort of the hotel. There was a great atmosphere over supper and the champagne flowed freely. Around 9 p.m. the conversation died as we all suddenly felt the effect of the early start, the excitement and the alcohol. Everyone left for their beds, exhausted but with the satisfaction of a job well done.

CHAPTER 14

Honeymoon Lows

Trevor and I returned to England for Christmas and then flew to Australia to start our married life. It was hard leaving my family and friends behind, but it was softened by the fact that I would return to England at least twice before finally moving to Australia. I had a summer contract with Citroën to do some publicity work for them and so would be back within six months.

We rented a beautiful house just north of Sydney, perched on the edge of a cliff overlooking a national park. It was a glorious place to live, teeming with bird life, and we would wake to the tuneful crooning of the carrawongs and the hysterical laughing of the kookaburras.

Trevor started work as a junior doctor at the nearby hospital, working long hours and coming home stressed and tired. I had some money saved and with the guarantee of work in the summer, I decided not to get a job for the four months I would be in Sydney. Instead I used the opportunity to explore the local area and discovered hidden creeks and Aboriginal hand paintings in nearby caves.

I pottered at home, doing all the jobs that Trevor didn't have time for: getting finances in order, fixing his neglected car, cooking and washing. I was happy to support him as he was having to work so hard. I was looking forward to getting to know Trevor. We had only actually spent four weeks in each other's company before getting married and I anticipated an enriching and happy few months deepening our relationship.

After the first two months things started to go badly wrong. It was a slow, grim realisation that the more we were together, the greater the gulf between us became. We were both fairly intense people and Trevor had the additional stress of being thrown into the pressured world of a junior doctor. Our relationship was based on a short liaison and a lot of hope, therefore lacking any fundamental strength to back it up when things were difficult. We had not had time to become friends before getting married and so the whole structure of our union was built on a foundation of sand. It collapsed like a house of cards.

If I went flying it only seemed to exacerbate the problem as he wanted to fly as well but was unable to do so because of work. I stopped hang gliding in an effort to reduce the tension between us.

It was a horrifying realisation that I did not love Trevor. I could not come to terms with having made such a gigantic mistake and chastised myself for ignoring all the signs that were there for me to read beforehand. Two months before Trevor and I were married, Sian had confronted me face to face and said, 'Don't do it Judy, he's wrong for you.'

Her words haunted me as I existed from day to day, not knowing what to do, slowly sinking into depression. I had left my home, family, friends and job and felt I had lost my direction in life. I was desperate to be away from the situation to be able to put things in perspective and think clearly enough to decide what to do next.

Trevor and I had been due to visit England in May for a holiday. I decided to bring forward my departure and fly to Japan to take part in the Shima Seiki competition. It was a tense parting at Sydney airport. We had not made any decisions about the future, but we knew we could not continue with things the way they were.

The contest was to be held in Wakayama, forty miles south of Osaka. I had never been to Japan before and the culture shock started as I landed at Narita Airport in Tokyo. A sea of oriental faces rushed tidily past me in both directions, reminding me of a procession of ants, each with an air of great purpose as they proceeded on their mission.

From Osaka onwards, the journey was more difficult, as there were no signs written in English characters. Luckily, people were very helpful and as I was looking lost a woman came up to me and in her broken English offered to help and made sure I boarded the right train.

Wakayama City was a clean but oppressive concrete jungle, chosen for the competition because it was where the sponsor of the event, Shima Seiki (makers of computers and programmes), had their factories. Beyond the high-rise buildings and countless factories rose the hills from which we were to fly. Every available morsel of space was used either for buildings or for growing fruit trees. There were very few spaces left to land a hang glider. To make things worse, power lines seemed to criss-cross the entire area, creating an even greater hazard.

I have never liked cities and with all the emotional turmoil that was going on in my life, I wanted to be somewhere soothing to the soul. Wakayama City certainly did not fit the bill. The competition entry was by invitation only to encourage the cream of international competitors. I knew most of the pilots there and felt comfortable among friends, relieved to be away from the stress of my marriage.

Shima Seiki were offering good prize money and were challenging the pilots to fly from take-off in the north of Wakayama province to Kushimoto lighthouse sixty miles away on the southern tip of the peninsula. Each pilot was given a piece of paper, which was to act as our 'Paddington Bear' card. It was covered in Japanese writing and we were told to hand it to anyone who approached us when we landed. The first time I had to use this piece of paper, it had an extraordinary effect.

The farmer whose field I had landed in could not speak a word of English and my command of Japanese stopped at, 'Mushi, Mushi!' (Hello). I passed him my piece of paper, he read the contents, nodded sagely and then dashed off. Ten minutes later he reappeared with a car, several cushions and a length of rope. He then placed the cushions on the roof of his car, lifted the glider carefully onto the cushions and tied it on securely with his rope. Gesturing for me to get into the passenger seat, he then drove me to the nearest railway station. He left my glider at the side of the ticket office, helped me buy a ticket and waited until the train arrived. As he ushered me into a carriage, I pointed at my glider, worried about leaving it. Although I could not understand him, his message was clear that I shouldn't worry and I travelled back to Wakayama City, baffled at the impeccable efficiency I had just witnessed.

The following morning my glider appeared on take-off, on time and unscathed. I had to hand it to the Japanese, their organisation was extraordinary. Each evening a truck would drive the length of the course, calling at all the railway stations on the way to collect all the gliders and would then deliver them to take-off the next day.

The people in Japan were always polite, bowing incessantly. There was a business conference taking place in our hotel and I came downstairs just as the meeting had finished. As the lift doors slid open I was confronted by the vision of 200 businessmen all performing their farewell bows to one another. The hierarchy was clear by how deeply each person bowed and how many times they repeated the gesture. Watching the mass of bobbing heads was like stumbling upon a flock of birds in the middle of a courtship ritual.

I was summoned to do an early morning interview, live for breakfast television. I discovered that Japanese TV presenters have a peculiar style of address. They appear to be in a constant state of nervous animation, always smiling and giving the impression of being over-excited and anxious to please. The man who interviewed me appeared normal enough when we first met, but as the moment approached when his live broadcast would begin, he wound himself into a state of agitated hysteria. I watched with detached amazement as his voice went up an octave, increased in volume and doubled in speed. I must have appeared very dull by comparison, as I could not even attempt to mimic his style.

The first two days of the competition were spent doing races along the ridge in front of launch as the weather was not good enough to attempt the lighthouse run. By the third day, the cloudbase had lifted but the wind had also increased. Kushimoto lighthouse was set as our goal. The thermals were rough in front of launch and it took some heavy handling to keep the glider in the core, but I eventually reached cloudbase and turned south towards the next ridge. I arrived at the thickly forested slope just below its summit and was buffeted around before I found a strong enough thermal in which to circle without the risk of being blown back over the ridge and into the rotor behind.

As I climbed, I looked into the next valley. It was steep sided, wall-to-wall with trees and there was absolutely nowhere to land. The only gap in the trees was where a fast-flowing river scythed through the woods. I rose high enough to get a glimpse of the valley behind and it was clear that this, too, was unlandable. The turbulence was getting worse and I was frightened about venturing over such steep gullies in strong winds when there was no chance of landing safely if I went down. I was not prepared to risk it and for the first time ever in my competition career, I abandoned the task. I flew back into the wide valley and went to land at a golf course. On my final approach, the air was so turbulent that I felt I might just as well have let go and allowed the glider to choose its own path for all the difference my control inputs seemed to make. It was not so much a landing as an 'arrival' on the eighteenth green and I was shaking as I took off my harness. I was immediately surrounded by a sea of curious faces as a group of women, all in identical trousers, tunics and head scarves, approached me for a closer look. Giggling demurely, they smiled their welcome to me, glad of the distraction from their tedious work of weeding the golf course by hand.

After packing away my glider, I was taken to the sumptuous club house where I was greeted with courtesy and thinly disguised curiosity. They telephoned the competition headquarters and a car arrived to pick me up. As we tied the glider on to the car roof, I saw a gaggle of gliders spiralling upwards and I felt a deep sense of foreboding that someone might get hurt.

When we arrived at the competition base, I took the meet director to one side and told him that I thought it was dangerous to send pilots over this course when the conditions were so bad. His face remained blank as he shifted me from 'brave pilot' to 'wimp' category in his mind.

I spent the rest of the afternoon at the headquarters, checking off my friends as they phoned in to say the had landed safely. Later that evening as they returned, horror stories echoed around the bar. Phil Haegler from Brazil had done the same as me, but had waited until he was three valleys further on before he threw in the towel. As he tried to land in the tiny field at the bottom of the gully, he encountered such severe turbulence that he was thrown into the river and was lucky to escape with his life. Several pilots landed in the trees, one in power lines and one bent his glider in the air while being thrown around in a particularly vicious area of rotor. The only injuries were cuts and bruises and some bent aluminium tubing, but several pilots had been severely shaken by the experience.

Two days later the same task was set. The conditions were more benign, with lighter winds and weaker thermals and, feeling less at risk, I decided to have a go.

It was slow going as the climb rates were poor and cloudbase low. It was a question of gaining just enough height to squeak over the top of one ridge and head for the next. I tried not to look down, as it made me nervous to think that there was nowhere to land for miles on end.

When I finally lost so much height that my chances of getting back up had all but disappeared, I had no alternative but to pick a tree. The only other options were a river or a series of high-tension power cables, so I selected the smallest and softest looking patch of fir trees and aimed for them. It felt very odd to fly straight at trees and the urge to turn away from them was strong, but I overrode my instinct, kept my course and at the last moment flared hard and closed my eyes. The impact was soft and yielding as the branches enveloped me. I slid gently downwards and with relief I felt the ground under my feet. The trees were only fifteen feet high, without enough space between them to allow me to fall out.

De-rigging the glider was a challenge with it perched at a precarious angle and wedged in between the trees. I eventually managed to zip it into the glider bag, together with half the pine needles from the area. I walked down to a nearby factory, the only sign of civilisation for miles, and presented my piece of paper to the somewhat surprised plant manager. He read it carefully and then barked out some orders which sent his workers scuttling for cushions and rope and I was soon on my way to the railway station.

That night I was woken by a telephone call from Monique Amman, a Swiss pilot calling from her room in the hotel. The tone of her voice shook me to the core.

'Pepê has had an accident, and I think he may be dead.'

I froze with horror, unable to accept the news. Pepê Lopes, my friend from Brazil, was one of the best pilots in the world and silver medallist at the last World Championships. I hurriedly dressed and went down to the lobby, where the small group of pilots who had heard the rumour had gathered. Bewildered and dazed, we sat together in a huddle.

I had driven with Pepê and Phil Haegler to take-off that morning. Pepê had been in good spirits. He had phoned his wife as it was her birthday and had spoken to his two young children. He happily told me about his newly released record, which was his new venture in Rio, and played me a couple of tracks, translating the words for me. I replayed the scene in my mind. I could not believe that this generous, fast-living friend whose zest for life was so infectious and spread to all around him, was gone.

Phil arrived and with one look at the devastation in his ashen face, I knew it was true. Phil was Pepê's best friend and with his voice flat and expressionless he recounted what had happened.

Pepê had been flying alongside Steve Blenkinsop, wrestling for first position. Together with a Japanese pilot, they were flying over an inhospitable series of valleys. When they finally lost height and were forced to land, Pepê chose a rocky slope next to a tiny track and impacted hard, hitting his chest on a rock. Steve and the Japanese pilot landed in the trees nearby and went to help him. It was impossible to get an emergency radio message through to call a helicopter as they were stuck in the bottom of a steep valley, so the Japanese pilot ran four miles up the track to the top of the hill to call for help. Meanwhile Steve stayed to comfort Pepê, who was conscious but in great pain from a punctured lung and internal bleeding. He gradually slipped away over the next three hours and poor Steve could only watch helplessly as Pepê died. If he had been able to be hospitalised immediately, he might have survived, but stuck in a godforsaken valley, he had no chance.

My disbelief turned to fruitless anger about the stupidity of holding a competition in an area without places to land and with organisers who seemed to care so little about the safety of pilots. The gung-ho 'Kushimoto or bust' attitude heartily encouraged by the media had been taken on board by the organisers, who pushed the pilots to fly in areas where they would never normally fly.

In the final reckoning, it is up to each individual pilot to decide whether or not to fly, and we should all use our common sense, but in the heat of the race, the competitive instinct can often override prudence. I feel that competition directors have some responsibility to save the pilots from themselves in situations of probable danger.

The anger gave way to deep sadness at the loss of a friend. The following day the sky poured its sorrow in an endless torrent of rain. I wanted to go home, to be away from the strangeness of Japan and back to the comforting familiarity of England. My emotions were already raw and Pepê's death cut deeply into my soul.

It was wonderful to see Mum and Dad again and to regain my sense of self. Trevor wrote almost daily and said he was missing me badly and I wondered if our inability to communicate could be overcome if I tried even harder. During his visit in May, things improved slightly as I had recovered some strength and was also involved in my work with Citroën. I could not accept failure without giving it another go. By the time he left in June, we had decided to try again and I promised to go back to Australia in August.

In the meantime I started preparations to defend my World Championship title in July. The competition was to be held in Kossen, the heart of my old stamping ground in Austria.

I knew I needed to get back into 'competition mode': I had had so little practice during my months in Australia and my experience in Japan had knocked the stuffing out of me. I had resigned from the League as I felt I was getting stale and needed a year out, so I was ready for an injection of enthusiasm into my flying.

Austria was the perfect tonic. I went out early to practise and booked into a cosy traditional farmhouse next to the landing field. They had a few cows that were milked in the byre which joined onto the house, giving the place a wonderfully rustic smell of cow's breath.

The weather was good, allowing me to explore some of the terrain that I remembered somewhat vaguely from my forays nine years before. I revelled in the heady views of serrated cathedral rocks, highlighted with glistening remnants of snow. The valleys were broad and lush, tended by the same craggy old farmers, their faces ruddy and weathered, with words almost indecipherable through their thick dialects.

As the start of the competition approached, the pilots began to arrive, a total of sixty from seventeen different countries. Hugs were exchanged with old friends and it was a pleasure to see so many new faces amongst the fit and strong-looking batch of women. The rest of the British team turned up and moved into the farmhouse with me.

The smallest pilot in the competition was Hiroko from Japan. She was only four foot ten inches tall and very slightly built. She was flying a Moyes glider which, together with her harness, weighed more than she did. This plucky woman impressed me, though I could not watch her launch as it scared me to see her totter down the slope carrying the whole weight of the glider with her arms as she couldn't reach the control frame apex to support the glider with her shoulders. Once in the air she flew really well, but her landings were a nightmare as, with such short arms, it was impossible to do a decent flare.

Once again, many eyes were on me as the favourite to win, but the pressure did not faze me at all as I concentrated hard. Four days before the competition started, I broke the women's world triangle distance record by flying seventy miles, boosting my confidence and proving to myself that I was back on form.

I had not flown in an all-women's competition for four years and did not know what standard to expect. I was confident that no one had the range of experience I had, but I heard rumours about how strong the Swiss women's team was. The main unknown quantity for me was an American pilot called Kari Castle. All I knew was that she had been competing against men and doing well in mixed competitions. She lived and flew in Owens Valley and a duel between the two of us for first place seemed likely.

I was surprised to find that Kari wasn't due to arrive until three days before the competition as I knew she hadn't flown in Europe before. Although I knew the area I felt that, to be totally in tune with it, I needed a minimum of a week to practise.

There was no mistaking Kari when I first saw her. Tall, blonde and powerfully built, she towered above me. I liked her immediately. She was openly friendly and soon had me howling with laughter with her outrageous sense of humour.

She had been flying in a competition in New Mexico with enormous thermals which were brutally strong, providing fast racing conditions. Although she had done really well, finishing in the top ten, I doubted it would prepare her for the variable conditions in Austria. Her expectations were high as many of her friends had enormous confidence in her, telling her that she would win the Women's World Championship title easily.

The first day of the competition was marked with tiny, feeble thermals and overcast skies. A short task was set round the Kossen Valley and it proved to be a test of patience as I crossed to the north side and used the light wind to soar a tiny cliff edge for nearly an hour, waiting for the sun to come out, enabling me to get to cloudbase and win the task.

The second day the Swiss showed their colours by choosing a different route from everyone else and flying as a team in tricky conditions. Annelise Müller took over the lead, dropping me into second place. Kari had yet to make it onto the score board. She was flying fast, ignoring the tiny pockets of lift, waiting for the big thermals to hit her. She didn't know what she was doing wrong and her confidence began to suffer badly.

The third day's task was a thirty-mile out and return in much better conditions and finally we were able to leave the Kossen Valley. Nine of us got round the course and returned to goal, with Annelise beating me by five minutes. The whole Swiss team were flying well, using their radios to pass information and help each other around the course. Kathleen Rigg came in seventh, holding up the British side. I narrowed the gap between Annelise and me the following day and then the weather turned stormy, preventing any flying for the next two days.

Kari was by now in fortieth place and was looking shell-shocked. I could not bear to see her so distressed when I could see what she was doing wrong and knew how she could pull herself back together. I went round to where she was staying and suggested we talk. It was awkward at first, as I didn't know if she would want my help, but soon she was eagerly absorbing every word as I talked through some basics of sports psychology.

She needed to relax and fly as she normally flew, rather then desperately trying to win each task to make up for her poor scores so far. I left her with my 'bible', a copy of the book *Winning Ways*, and recommended the chapter on self-confidence. She emerged the next day looking red-eyed with fatigue, having read the book until the early hours of the morning.

My parents arrived to watch the competition. Dad had suffered another health crisis, this time with bowel cancer. An operation to remove the tumour was successful, but with a renewed sense of his mortality, both parents were determined to live life to the full and were not going to turn down the opportunity of a trip to the Alps to watch me in action. I booked them into a beautiful, traditional guest house and looked forward to being able to share with them my love of Tirol.

They had not seen me compete since the first women's League in 1981, when I had been floundering around, landing at the bottom of the hill and hauling the glider back up again. As a pilot, I had changed beyond recognition.

I warned them that I would be concentrating fully on the competition and would not want to chat with them before taking off. The following day when I had rigged my glider, I looked around for them but they were nowhere to be seen. Finally I saw two tiny figures sitting on a rock some 500 yards away, so wary of distracting me that they were almost out of sight! That day, despite miserable conditions, I squeaked past Annelise to regain first place. Dad beamed with satisfaction.

'We knew you could do it!' he effused, giving me a hug.

I had to point out that it was far too early for celebration. My lead was small; there were two days left to fly, and anything could happen.

I went to their guest house each morning after breakfast and had coffee with them. They were loving every minute of the excitement, seeing how the scores changed and how the day and my tactics developed according to the weather.

We had a decent racing task at last. The sky was washed a deep alpine blue with crystal clear visibility, showing all the mountains in their full glory. The forty-mile task took me just under two hours and as I steamed into goal as the first to cross the line, the consistent Annelise was hot on my tail, just one minute behind. Not long after I landed there was a loud whoop from above and I looked up to see Kari crossing the line. I could see her grin from 500 feet below! It was great to see her confidence restored, bouncing back larger than life.

I was acutely aware that I must not relax my guard on the last day. I knew that all I had to do was to fly as I normally did and get to goal to win the title. But at the same time, I was also aware of the 'last day syndrome', where people become defensive of their position, and change their style of competing from the formula which has proved successful, losing all on the last day.

The weather forecast was good and we prepared for an early start. Heidi Fawcett was in front of me in the queue to launch and I waited for her to go. The wind felt good, but still she hesitated and her inner struggle was palpable. She is very good at appearing positive to all around her, when in fact she is actually wrestling with inner turmoil. She finally started to run, but from the start it looked shaky. Her left wingtip dropped and snagged on the ground. The whole wing slewed sideways and she hit the slope some thirty feet away.

Several people ran to her and I shouted to Judith Bolton, our team leader, 'Is she all right?'

'No,' came the answer as Judith reached her.

I unclipped my harness and ran to where Heidi was struggling to stand up. Holding her right arm she looked me straight in the eye and said in her best school teacher's voice, which could not be argued with, 'I'm fine. Go and fly.'

Her elbow was dislocated and must have hurt like hell, yet she was able to put on such a brave front as she knew the championship title would be at stake if I was delayed or distracted. I clipped back into my glider and took off. I set off round the course on my own, confident that given good conditions, I could beat most pilots and that I would be better able to concentrate if there was no one else around. I really enjoyed the flight, flying close to the crags on the way back to the goal field at Kossen, working hard to keep my concentration sharp. The last thermal felt wonderful as I banked the glider tightly into the core and kept climbing. I went far higher than I needed to, just to be on the safe side, knowing that all I had to do was to make it over the line, which was now tantalisingly close. With an overwhelming sense of excitement welling up inside me, I straightened up and headed for goal. As I approached and could guarantee I would make it safely, I pulled on full speed and dived over the line to become Women's World Champion for the second time.

I let the glider drift where it wanted as I descended slowly, feeling the exhilaration and relief wash over me. Mum and Dad greeted me in the goal field, beaming broadly. They now knew what it meant to become a World Champion in terms of stress, concentration and hard work. Before long, I had a litre tankard of beer in one hand and a glass of champagne in the other and the rest of the evening remains a blur.

Next morning, I joined Mum and Dad for breakfast, where their guest house host insisted on serenading me by playing 'Amazing Grace' very slowly on a bugle. His bulging cheeks grew red and shiny as he filled the tiny breakfast room with the tremulous wail.

As the time for the outdoor prize-giving ceremony approached the sky turned an ominous black with thunder and lightning to the west of us and it was going to be a race against the rain. I received my gold medal and as 'God Save the Queen' was played over the loudspeaker I did not dare meet Mum's eye. It is from her that I get my emotional traits and I knew that if she was crying then I would start. Towards the end I stole a quick glance in her direction to find her face radiant with pleasure and pride. I was safe and grinned back, raising the trophy high above my head. It was a wonderful moment to share with them after all the help and support they had given me over the years.

CHAPTER 15

Flying to Forget

I returned to Australia with a much more positive attitude. When it comes to competitions, sponsorship and specific projects, I set my sights on what I want and then work hard to achieve them. If it doesn't work out the first time, I put more effort in, perhaps changing tack, working away at it until I achieve my goal. I thought that if I applied these principles to my marriage, I could make it work.

I discovered that no amount of work can repair a relationship if both partners are fundamentally incompatible. What baffled me was why I had ever thought us to be suited in the first place. When Trevor and I met, I had been fanatically involved in hang gliding for ten years, during which time my priority had been flying. I had now reached a stage in life when flying was no longer enough to satisfy me and I wanted a permanent relationship. Trevor had reached the same subconscious conclusion. When we met, this need for someone special was all we had in common.

After four months the situation was desperate again and I had to leave. I left everything behind for Trevor as I could not face the trauma of dividing possessions. Admitting defeat in my marriage was the hardest thing I had ever done. As the plane took off from Sydney Airport, tears rolled down my face as I closed the chapter on my year-long marriage and my shattered dreams. I did not know at the time just how long the road to recovery would be.

From Sydney, I flew to New Zealand where I had been asked to make a film by an American production company. The opportunity provided a distraction from my troubles which proved to be a godsend.

The film was centred around the story of two hang glider pilots climbing and then making the first flight from the summit of Mount Cook, the highest peak in New Zealand. The company contracted to make the film had enlisted American pilot John Heiney to be one of the pilots and he had asked me to be the second. I was looking forward to working with John, who is one of the best aerobatic pilots in the world and who also takes superb hang gliding photographs.

I was told by the film makers that everyone else on the team had mountain climbing experience, and I was worried about my limited knowledge from my two ascents of Cotopaxi. Gavin Wills, the main coordinator of the expedition in New Zealand, booked me in for some intensive mountaineering training with Nick Craddock, one of the top climbers in the country. He was moody and uncommunicative, but with a wealth of useful knowledge. The first day he took me rock climbing and abseiling; I felt as though I was back in the Girl Guides as I found myself learning a dozen different ways of tying a knot. He also taught me how to climb out of a crevasse using just two quarter-inch-diameter pieces of string, though I hoped it was a skill I would not need to put into practice.

The next morning we climbed a snow-covered peak, where I learned more about pacing myself, plodding slowly and rhythmically in Nick's steps. We stopped near the summit for a lunch break, perched high on a ledge overlooking the unspoilt snow fields below.

As we ate our sandwiches, a figure appeared moving steadily up the slope towards us, its dark body lurching drunkenly from side to side. As it worked its way upwards, its shape gradually became clearer. It was a kea, a mountain parrot which lives high in the New Zealand Alps. I could not believe that with a perfectly good pair of wings, a bird would choose to walk up a snow slope, but keas are idiosyncratic birds that seem to approach everything with the absurd air of a clown. As it drew near, its beady eyes fixed brightly on our bar of chocolate and with its comical pigeon-toed gait it sidled up to me. I broke off a chunk and threw it into the snow. The parrot scooped up the morsel with its evil-looking hooked beak, ruffling its olive green feathers with pleasure. When we had finished all the food and the kea realised that there would be no more forthcoming, it flew off, revealing a flash of flame-red feathers under its wings.

The following day I flew to Mount Cook village, where I was due to meet up with John Heiney, the film crew and the guides who would lead us up the mountain. As the tiny propeller driven plane took off from Christchurch, the wide lush plateau with its huge fields gave way to rolling green hills speckled with sheep. Beyond these, the mountains of the dividing range jutted skywards, shrouded in snow. As we flew over the first of these 'foothills', the unmistakable twin peaks of Mount Cook came into view, standing over 12,000 feet tall, way above the surrounding mountains. The whole area looked like a wilderness in its unspoilt vastness. We descended into the valley and caught a glimpse of Mount Cook village, which was tiny, as the plane touched down at the nearby airstrip.

Gavin was there to meet me; tall, gangly and bearded, with humour sparkling in his eyes. Roger Brown the film director was with him and he explained the latest changes to our plan. There was a snowboarding expert, Jim Zellers, arriving with John and he would attempt the first snowboard descent of the face of Mount Cook, together with a New Zealand ski champion, Bruce Grant. It certainly promised to be a 'busy' film.

Gavin told me the latest plan for climbing Mount Cook was to helicopter the gliders high onto the mountain. For the purpose of filming the climbing sequences we would carry dummy gliders of polystyrene, which weighed next to nothing. I was all in favour of this, as the gliders were so fragile and prone to damage. Also, with only three weeks to climb and film the whole expedition, we would not have the manpower or time to carry the heavy gliders carefully up the mountain.

John and Jim arrived that evening. They formed a diametrically opposed pair who seemed to have only an American accent in common. John, thin as a pole and quietly spoken, reminded me of Eeyore in the Winnie the Pooh stories with his self-effacing humour and gloomy, monotone voice. He chose his words carefully, as precise in his speech as with everything else he did. Jim, on the other hand, was muscular, amiable, easy-going and talked mostly in hip California-speak.

Bruce drove up from Queenstown. He was another relaxed, soft-spoken man whose laid-back attitude belied the adventure freak lurking beneath the surface.

The rest of the film crew comprised Roger Brown's three sons, who were acting, in descending order of age, as cameraman, soundman and assistant. The three often bickered among themselves and with their father, which was not conducive to a good working environment. Luckily John, Jim, Bruce and I were staying in a separate cabin and were spared the worst of it.

The following day we were helicoptered on to the Tasman Glacier. Roger kept emphasising the limited film budget, and yet at every opportunity we were shuttled wherever we needed to go by helicopter. I felt like an extra in a James Bond movie with the polystyrene 'gliders' strapped to the skids of the chopper like a pair of rocket launchers.

The blue-grey craggy surface of the glacial ice became increasingly fragmented as we dropped down to land on its surface. It seemed alive as the ice below our feet creaked and rumbled and tiny water streams disappeared down smooth-sided, turquoise sink holes.

We did some further ice climbing training with our mountain guides and were filmed carrying the gliders along the glacier. We then strapped them back on the helicopter skids and flew down to the village.

John, Jim, Bruce and the guides were all great company, with a wealth of stories to tell. John's dour humour had me laughing constantly. When he found out I was a vegetarian, his reply was that it was doing the world a great service to eat creatures as stupid as chickens!

The disadvantage of film making in New Zealand is the unpredictability of the weather. Like Britain, it is assaulted by low pressure systems which come marching in from the sea, dumping their moisture on the land. There is also the risk of strong winds in November and December. The film crew had been lulled into a false sense of security by the perfect weather which greeted them when they arrived. Despite being told it wouldn't last, they frittered it filming incidental shots which could have been done in bad weather. Just as we were ready to start climbing, the weather deteriorated. There was no point in staying at Mount Cook. On the rare occasions when the summit was clear of cloud, a huge plume of spindrift could be seen being blown off the top by the ferocious winds. We moved camp to Queenstown, the 'Mecca' for adventurers where, amongst other things, Roger wanted to film us bungee jumping 200 feet from a suspension bridge at Skipper's Canyon.

I have never felt the desire to go bungee jumping as my fear of heights is so intense. It was amazing to watch the Japanese tourists, who arrived in their droves. Groups of giggling girls would walk onto the bridge, chatting happily with their friends while the elastic was tied to their feet. Having never done anything more adventurous than riding the Tokyo subway, they would then throw themselves off the bridge without a care.

John, meticulous as always, examined all the equipment carefully. 'Hmmm,' he pondered unhappily, 'I don't like the way they've got metal rubbing on metal here.' He pointed to the two interlocking carabiners holding the bungee to the bridge.

'John, would you mind keeping your reservations to yourself? I'm having problems getting to grips with the height and don't need doubts seeded in my mind about the safety of the equipment,' I replied.

The elastic rope was tied to my feet and I shuffled to the edge of the platform. I hated the feeling of standing there with my toes curled over the side. This was the exact position I feared – being on the edge of a drop without being attached to a hang glider. I tried all my mental tricks, but none of them could calm my nerves. I finally had to muster all the courage I could and just lean forwards and let gravity take over.

Once I was committed and my fate was in the lap of the gods, I enjoyed it. The surge of relief as the bungee took my weight was huge and I laughed helplessly as I bobbed at the end of the elastic, being slowly lowered towards the boat in the river beneath.

We were then filmed going down the narrow river in a jet boat. I laughed with exhilaration as the driver aimed straight at rocky outcrops and then swerved at the last minute. John sat next to me, his face expressionless as I giggled. He was thinking of all the things that could go wrong with the boat.

The weather was still poor the following day so we were filmed visiting rare takahe birds at the Fiordland National Park. The eccentric-looking flightless birds had round bodies the size of geese, but the shape of a moorhen. Their heads were iridescent blue and their wings olive green, but with 'hairy' feathers typical of flightless birds. They had bright scarlet, puffin-like beaks with which they made loud clicking noises, and they were full of character and daft antics. We went into their enclosure where we fed them by hand. It was sad to think that such a creature had almost been wiped from the face of the earth. Their numbers had been reduced to fifty before enthusiasts began to guard their nests and their population started to recover.

We moved on to film a meeting with a rabbit exterminator, an old man who spent his life trapping and killing rabbits which, having been imported years ago, are now a huge problem in New Zealand.

I had by now ceased to wonder at the relevance of the film crew's whims. They seemed directionless and would change their minds at the drop of a hat as to what they wanted to film. I began to feel sorry for the editor, who would have to make some sense out of the mishmash of visual images that Roger was collecting.

The weather improved sufficiently for us to fly from the mountain above Queenstown that evening. The sun was low in the sky, glinting on the ripples which covered the wide blue lake below. Beyond the lake rose the imposing rock faces of The Remarkables range of mountains.

We took off together and flew in formation while the camera crew filmed us from launch. We flew out over the lake and, following John's instructions, I flew directly above him only feet away from the top of his glider. He then pulled into a screaming dive and looped the loop directly underneath me. As he appeared upside down directly below me, his body was stretched out as he reached the top of the loop. The sun lit up his multicoloured wing and the control frame gleamed. It was a glorious sight.

The following morning we returned to Mount Cook to sit out the bad weather and wait for a slot when we could climb to the top of the mountain. At last, we were able to take the helicopter up to Plateau Hut, a wooden cabin which provided basic shelter for climbers. John and I were to fly from there down the Hochstatter Ice Fall where the glacier which descends Mount Cook drops into a near-vertical cliff so steep that it rips apart and deep crevasses cleave the ice into a random array of incredible shapes.

Meanwhile, Jim and Bruce had been helicoptered to the Linda Shelf, 2,000 feet below the summit, and were climbing to the top of Mount Cook as the strong winds were not a problem for their attempt to ski and snowboard down the mountain.

John and I rigged our gliders in the morning and then waited while the camera crew changed their minds, deciding to put us on 'hold' and film Jim and Bruce first. We watched as they loaded the camera into the helicopter, then flew up to the summit, staying away from the mountain to capture the action as Jim and Bruce made their first bold move over the edge.

They appeared as two tiny ants as they began their descent. The face looked impossibly steep and their route was often blocked by rocks where the snow could not settle as the gradient was too sheer. Under my breath I wished them well, aware that they were experts in their field, but also knowing from their discussions that no matter how much they looked at the face from a distance, it was only now that they would know the full scale of the challenge they faced. If they fell, there was nothing to stop them until they reached the Tasman Glacier thousands of feet below. The ice axes they carried in their hands were their only protection.

We watched, hypnotised, as the miniature figures slowly carved their way down. It seemed an age before they finally reached the smoother lower slopes just above the hut and it was a relief to see them zigzag safely on to the plateau of snow where we were waiting. They were as high as kites on adrenaline by the time they arrived and the normal laid back drawls were replaced by excited chattering as they relived every moment and related it to us.

John and I then prepared to do a synchronised take-off to fly down the ice fall. By now the wind had dropped to nothing and the snow had softened. On my third step I sank up to my knees in the snow and stopped dead, watching as John just managed to squeak off the hill. I stamped down the snow again, but it was really soggy. I ran as hard as I could, but still could not get enough speed for a clean launch and had to push the glider off the slope, and then pull on speed once I was in the air to get it to fly properly.

It was a relief to be airborne and I headed for the ice fall. I looked into the jowls of the glacier through the bottomless crevasses. Huge towers and turrets of blue ice topped with snow defied gravity as they inched their way down the mountain under pressure from the ice above. The light was angled behind us and the turquoise and white shone brightly. I flew low over the peaks of ice so that I almost touched my shadow before flying out to land on the Tasman Glacier among the 'moonscape' of huge boulders and lines of ice.

We were grounded again by two days of bad weather and on the evening of the third day, we were flown once more to the Plateau Hut to stay the night in preparation for a summit attempt the following day. It would be our last chance, as we only had two days left to complete the film. We woke at 3.30 a.m. and went outside to assess the weather. To our dismay, a huge plume of snow was being blown horizontally from the summit, heralding the strong wind aloft. We had to change our plans to salvage something for the film.

Roger decided to helicopter us to the top of the neighbouring mountain which, at 10,000 feet, was lower than Mount Cook and was sheltered from the strong wind. It was bitterly cold as we rigged our gliders in the snow, with the chilling wind penetrating our clothes.

The wind was strong enough for us to be able to soar the ridge and the view was fantastic. The air was clear and Mount Cook stood bathed in sunshine, having rebuffed our attempts to fly from her summit. The Tasman Glacier descended below, changing from white snow to blue ice and then, as it gradually amassed more debris from the valley sides, blended in with the valley as its surface became littered with boulders. The mountains stretched far into the distance, skirting the valley heading towards Queenstown.

The radio interrupted my reverie as John was instructed to perform some aerobatics above the glacier. I watched, laughing as his glider dropped vertically and gained speed, then swung smoothly into a series of perfect loops.

They wanted to film us landing on the glacier 2,000 feet below, so reluctantly I followed John down and landed to find him shivering with cold. He had landed on a narrow turquoise band of ice in the middle of the white snow to give the cameras a prettier shot, then found to his dismay that the ice was not solid and had sunk up to his knees in the icy water. We had to wait an hour for the helicopter to collect us, only to find that they wanted us to do it again! The appeal of flying had waned in direct proportion to the decreasing temperature, but we obliged and flew just long enough for the cameras to get the shots they wanted, then headed for our landing place on the glacier.

This time they left us for two hours before collecting us, by which time it was 7.30 p.m. and we were both frozen to the bone and very tired after our early start. We couldn't believe it when they said they were flying us up to the Linda Shelf for more filming. We strapped the gliders once more to the skids. As the helicopter climbed towards the small ledge high up on the mountain, it looked frighteningly steep. It didn't look as though you could stand on it, let alone land a helicopter.

The pilot found a tiny level spot and we jumped out, chilled even further by the flurry of snow from the scything rotor blades. It was all I could do to refrain from flattening myself against the snow to avoid 'falling off', as the feeling of exposure was awesome.

Two of the guides had spent the day on Linda Shelf setting up a camp with three tents, which was supposed to have been our final camp before the summit. We had to get into the tents and then emerge, pretending that we were just getting up in the morning. John and I had no problems acting groggy as we were numb with fatigue and cold. I felt a fraud having to pretend that we had climbed all this way up with the gliders, when in fact all we had done was to strap them on to the skids of a helicopter.

We were filmed having a discussion about the wind-blown plume of snow and expressing our disappointment about not being able to fly from the summit so that they could slot it into the film to explain why we had flown from the adjacent mountain and not Mount Cook itself. Finally the helicopter arrived to take us back to our cabin at Mount Cook Village and we said goodbye to the mountain for the last time and returned to the warmth of the valley.

I was disappointed not to have flown from the summit of Mount Cook. I always prided myself on 'delivering the goods' if I committed myself to achieving something. The main error was in the choice of timing, as the filming had been arranged to fit in with production schedules rather than to coincide with the best weather for hang gliding. The other problem was in poor organisation and preparation, which might have hindered the attempt even if we had been granted a small break in the weather. Nevertheless it had been an unforgettable three weeks spent in good company and in an area of outstanding beauty. Jim and Bruce had achieved their goal and the record would stand for ever, as four days after we left the mountain the whole east face of Mount Cook fell away in the biggest landslide in New Zealand's history. The mountain would never be as big again.

I remained mystified as to how a coherent film could emerge from the assorted visual images that Roger had collected. He had not asked us to do any explanations on film, so it was no surprise when a year later I received a panicky phone call.

'We need some more "voice over" from you. Can you go and hire a sound studio today and I will fax you the phrases we need you to record,' Roger asked.

I had to sit in a studio in Guildford a year after the event, and try to re-create the feeling of standing on the edge of the bungee jumping platform. I drew the line at using their phraseology as I could not keep a straight face whilst saying, as they suggested, 'Wow, man, this is totally awesome.'

When the film came out, to my amazement the final result was perfectly watchable and an exciting adventure documentary. In my opinion, the editor deserves an Oscar!

CHAPTER 16

Flight of the Dacron Eagles

Whilst still in New Zealand I received an invitation to join another film trip in Kenya, this time for a BBC documentary for the *Classic Adventure* series. In early January I left for Nairobi to meet up with the rest of the team.

'Flight of the Dacron Eagles' was an adventure dreamed up by Tim Hudson, a relatively inexperienced hang glider pilot from Yorkshire. His idea was to 'migrate' through Kenya from north to south, following the path of the birds through the Rift Valley. Although the expedition would not take place during the migratory season and we would therefore not fly alongside the birds, we would follow the same route.

I had never flown in Africa, but had always wanted to. As soon as I heard about the project, I called Tim and asked if I could join the expedition. Tim's organisational abilities were impressive and his persuasive style soon secured a £30,000 sponsorship deal from Barbour to fund the project.

There were four hang glider pilots taking part and we would be aerotowed behind a microlight to a height where we could find our first thermal. We would then release and fly under our own steam to the next airfield where we would land, ready to continue the next day. A BBC film crew would follow and record our progress.

We arrived amid the hectic scramble of Nairobi and installed ourselves in a cheap hotel to wait for all members of the crew to turn up. We also used this opportunity to ensure all our permits were in order before we set off into the unknown territory of the Rift Valley.

The other two hang glider pilots on the team were Mark Dale, a fellow League pilot from Yorkshire and, to my delight, my old friend Louise

Anderton. She had returned from our trip to Australia and resumed her job in the bank, but was now always ready to seize any adventure opportunity that offered itself. Ben Ashman, the most experienced aerotow pilot in Britain, was to fly the microlight and Richard Meredith-Hardy would fly a second microlight which would act as a camera platform for the film crew.

On the streets of Nairobi we were bombarded with noise, heat and smells, but the people were generally friendly and helpful. Once they found out we were making a film, we were overwhelmed with questions: 'You need driver?' 'You need fixer?' They all knew the necessity of having a local 'fixer' who can smooth out bureaucratic problems.

Richard had arrived a week early and had been spending each day in various government offices trying to secure the release of our six aircraft from customs. Both microlights had arrived but the hang gliders had been 'lost' for a few days. Some years earlier, Richard had flown right through Africa by microlight and his knowledge was invaluable. His persistent harassment of the officials finally paid dividends and the hang gliders miraculously appeared. We were relieved to find all the wings undamaged and prepared to leave Nairobi the following day.

We rented a truck from Encounter Overland, a huge orange 'workhorse' which carried all our belongings, food and water. It came complete with driver, Sarah Ewing, whose normal job was leading safaris in Kenya and Tanzania. She was competent, loud and very funny. Her clothes and skin were permanently covered in oil and she was never happier than when she had some mechanical problem to fix on the truck and could disappear into the depths of the engine.

We had two Land Rovers, one smart and reliable for the film crew, and a more 'functional' model to carry the hang gliders and retrieve us if we landed anywhere other than a specified airfield. Bella and Giles, an easygoing English couple who were travelling through Africa, were employed as retrieve drivers.

Excitement was high as we loaded up the truck. We were to drive directly north for two days to Lake Turkana, where we would start our migration. When we left the mayhem of Nairobi, the glory of the countryside spread out before us. The powerful sun lit up the green plateau below as we trundled slowly along the road at the top of the Rift Valley. Everyone we saw along the way broke into a broad smile and waved, yelling 'Jambo!' in greeting. The welcome in Kenya is genuine and uninhibited and a stranger is embraced with curiosity and friendship.

As we continued north, the cultivated fields gave way to scrubland. Thorn trees with their imposing three-inch darning needle spikes became more common. Finally, the conditions became so arid that even these hardy bushes could not survive in such numbers, thinning out to random clusters in the sand.

After two days of dusty, slow travelling we arrived at our starting point, a beautiful lodge halfway along the shore of Lake Turkana. It seemed more like an ocean than a lake, as it measured 120 miles long and 20 miles wide. We were warned that there were crocodiles in the lake and so we made our first stop the lodge's slimy green swimming pool. Goodness knows what kinds of fauna were lurking in its gloomy depths, but we were so dusty and hot that we didn't care.

The film crew arrived looking fresher than we felt, having stayed overnight in a hotel. It was great to meet up with Matt Dickinson again, who had produced the Cotopaxi film and would be leading the 'Classic Adventure' crew. His eyes were bright with the prospect of a new and challenging project and he looked the part of 'intrepid traveller', sporting three days' growth of beard, matted hair and a good layer of dirt. With him was Sid Perou, a cameraman who wore a permanent smile. Sid was notoriously absent-minded, but had such an amiable nature that it was impossible to hold it against him. He was short and gnome-like, with unruly grey hair, and had no sense of fear whatsoever. He seemed at first glance to possess tremendous courage, but after seeing him at work, it was apparent that he became so engrossed in his filming that he just didn't seem to notice what was going on outside.

With Sid was Gavin Crowther whose official job was soundman, but who rapidly became Sid's minder. He had been instructed by Sid's wife Alison to make sure Sid drank enough water and put on his sun screen, an essential role as, left up to Sid, such irrelevances would have been forgotten.

That evening we began filming. Tim and I rigged our gliders at the water's edge and waited until the setting sun was framed between them. We were then filmed, silhouetted in the burnished orange light as a fishing boat drifted past, scattering the mirror-smooth surface with its trailing ripples. Women walked through the scene with huge baskets or pitchers balanced on their heads. It was so beautiful and the atmosphere was of the Africa that I had always dreamed of.

We returned to the lodge and met on the veranda for dinner. Ben arrived late, an apparition dressed in a full safari suit of baggy khaki shorts, matching shirt, long socks and a pith helmet!

I woke the following morning to find Sarah getting dressed with her T-shirt inside out.

'There's four good sides to every T-shirt,' she said. 'Back, front, then turn it inside out and back and front again.' She had perfected the art of minimalist living having been on the road for so long. On most of her journeys, water for washing clothes was an unthinkable luxury.

Aerotowing was illegal in Britain and Louise, Tim and I had never tried it. We all needed to practise in the calm morning air before we ventured into the turbulent thermal conditions later in the day. Mark had been on an aerotow course in Hungary and went first to demonstrate the technique. One end of the hundred-yard length of rope was fastened to Ben's trike and the other end to Mark's harness. He lined up directly behind and gave the signal 'All out.' The propeller sent a plume of sand flurrying backwards as Ben applied full power. Mark took four steps and was airborne, and together they rose easily into the morning air.

Within three minutes Ben had landed again looking worried. The engine had overheated dangerously and he had released Mark at 1,500 feet. Without radical modification the trike would be useless for the job of towing the hang gliders. If we had no tow plane, we could not fly and there would be no expedition.

Richard's demeanour changed to that of a child with a new toy as the major mechanical problem became apparent. His swarthy face, hidden behind his black beard, heavy eyebrows and unruly mop of hair, lit up with enthusiasm as he delved into his box of tools and spare parts. He and Ben worked on the trike all day, finally plumbing in a second radiator in series with the first, attaching it using bits of camera mount, jubilee clips and a length of hose pipe from the lodge's swimming pool. To everyone's relief it worked perfectly and the expedition resumed.

That evening I tried my first tow. It was nerve-racking to be looking straight into a rotating propeller, unsure of what would happen, but once the trike started to move forward, I was off the ground almost immediately. It then seemed easy; all I had to do was to keep myself positioned behind the microlight, moving and turning in unison.

It was hard to concentrate as the scenery unfolded beneath me as we climbed. The deep green colour of the lake showed why Lake Turkana was known as the Jade Sea. It was peppered with hundreds of birds and tiny fishing boats. A flock of pelicans flew underneath us as we continued to climb to 6,000 feet. As I reached with one hand to release the umbilical cord attaching me to the trike, I had time to survey our proposed route to the south. The vast expanse of featureless desert extended as far as I could see and looked daunting. With the high temperatures and inhospitable terrain, it would be essential to stay within reach of the solitary road which sliced through the sand like a scar. I could hardly sleep that night as I was so excited about setting off on our adventure. Our first goal was to be a thirty-one-mile stretch to Lodwar.

We assembled to rig our gliders the next morning. Tim appeared looking like Darth Vader, dressed in a new black suit, black helmet and mirror sunglasses. The rest of us left our suits in the truck, as due to the blistering heat we preferred to fly wearing only lightweight trousers and T-shirts.

A strong southerly wind was blowing, making headway virtually impossible. The consensus was that it must be a local influence from the enormous lake, so Ben offered to tow all four of us to a small airstrip ten miles away to try to get away from the wind.

I was eager to start off on our journey and was second to be towed up. Once the new airfield was in sight and I had released from the tow, I could not get down as the air was so buoyant. It was also refreshingly cool aloft. When I finally landed, I had to avoid several camels on the runway as they strolled nonchalantly to and fro, picking at the sparse vegetation.

A Turkana tribeswoman approached, unable to contain her curiosity. Lean and beautiful, with glistening skin, her neck was swathed in dozens of colourful necklaces and her body was wrapped in a sarong. Her head was shaved around the sides, leaving only a narrow 'Mohican' strip, plaited and hennaed on top. She was reserved and uncommunicative, unlike the people we had met on the way to Lake Turkana, who were more used to seeing tourists.

The air was stifling as we struggled to acclimatise to the heat, sheltering under our gliders from the glare of the midday sun and drinking huge amounts of water. By the time Ben had towed all four of us to the airstrip, the lake breeze had reached us and the thermals had gone, our chances of reaching our goal under our own steam evaporating with them. We decided to tow up and get as far as we could towards Lodwar and then drive the rest of the way to goal.

The air was very rough as Ben towed me to 3,500 feet. I flew into the headwind in the direction of Lodwar, but it turned out to be little more than a glide with no thermals around. The whole area was so desolate and barren that I made sure I landed next to the road. Having experienced the insatiable thirst that the suffocating heat produced, I had no desire to walk to the road carrying my glider. I de-rigged and waited for Bella and

Giles to collect me in the Land Rover. When all four of us had been collected we drove on to Lodwar to get away from the poor flying conditions of Turkana. It was disappointing not to have made our first goal, but we knew from having seen the excellent clouds further south that conditions would improve.

Lodwar was a sizeable town. By the time we reached the airstrip, the trikes had already arrived and we were billed as the evening's entertainment. Hundreds of people gathered to watch the 'travelling circus' and we had to rope ourselves, the trikes and our vehicles off from the huge crowd to allow us to cook and eat without worrying about souvenir hunters. I felt what it must be like to be part of a chimpanzees' tea party in a zoo. I was self-conscious with the onlookers commenting and laughing at our every move. Gradually the spectators melted away into the night and we rigged our tents, attached the mosquito nets and slept until dawn.

The crowd reassembled as we began 'the breakfast show' and increased steadily as the morning progressed and word spread around the town that activity was increasing at the airfield. We rigged our gliders ready for a late-morning launch. Five thousand people lined the runway and it was impossible to keep them back as Tim prepared to launch. Louise and I walked briskly up and down the side of the runway moving people away from the trike to give Ben enough room to take off. Finally, with a small space visible, Tim called, 'All out', and they took off cleanly amidst the squeals of delight from the crowd.

Louise went next but as she lined up behind the trike, just about to launch, Tim landed having failed to find a thermal. The entire crowd raced over to surround him, jumping over the tow line between Ben and Louise. When the crowd thinned, she managed to take off, but also landed back at the airfield and was subjected to the same mobbing. The excited children had no concept of the danger of a rotating propeller, and each time Ben landed they happily ran straight towards the trike and he had to stop the engine immediately to avoid disaster.

Mark went next while I resumed crowd control duties. He released and found a thermal, climbing quickly away from the chaos below. I rushed to my glider and soon joined him in the relative peace of the turbulent air above the town. We changed our radio frequency to the channel used by all aircraft approaching or taking off from minor airfields in Kenya. A laconic American voice came over the radio. 'Lodwar, this is Red Cross flight 651, currently ten nautical miles south of the airfield, expecting to arrive in eight minutes.'

There is so little air traffic that aircraft never expect a reply to their transmissions, but give their movements just in case there is another aircraft in the area. We needed to let him know our position so that he could avoid us.

'Red Cross flight 651 there are two hang gliders flying above Lodwar at 6,000 feet, two nautical miles east of the runway,' I called.

There was a long pause, followed by, '. . . Um . . . er . . . right.' His cool, laid back tone had gone as he asked me to repeat our position. Despite confirming that we were at 6,000 feet, he obviously did not trust my report as when we finally spotted the small plane he was contouring the hills at less than 100 feet above ground level, just to be sure he would not hit us.

While Mark and I were waiting aloft for Tim and Louise, we were blissfully unaware of the disaster happening below us. Ben tried to land, trailing the tow rope behind the trike rather than releasing the rope before landing. On his approach he flew low over Louise's glider and the metal ring at the end of the rope hit her sail, slicing it almost in half. Louise was terribly upset. It looked like the end of her flying as such a huge rip would need an experienced sailmaker to fix. The film crew were delighted, homing in on Louise's tears, as it provided them with some drama in their story.

Ben remained optimistic as he had been a sailmaker years before and declared it reparable. Together he and Louise took the sail off the glider frame. Ben then stuck the two sides in place using sticky-back sailcloth and set off into town in search of a sewing machine.

The town comprised a network of tiny dirt roads, lined with crude huts roofed with corrugated iron. Ben was a man with a mission: to find an industrial sewing machine. Finally, after a lot of searching, with film crew in tow, he found an old, foot-driven machine that might do the trick. Under Ben's guidance, the bemused tailor sewed the sail back together, his tiny hut full of the bulky glider sail, camera crew and lights, with half the population of the town crowded outside the door. The repair was not pretty, with bright green thread and uneven stitches, but the integrity of the sail was restored and Louise could join us again, though she wisely elected not to fly until the calm air of the following morning.

Mark and I finally flew south from Lodwar at 3 p.m. and headed towards our next goal at Lokichar. We flew closely together, taking advantage of the extra thermal-finding potential of two pilots gliding side by side. The conditions were working well over the desert, but with a moderately strong crosswind and fifty-five miles to cover, we ran out of daylight and thermals after twenty-five miles.

The thornbush trees were becoming more common and they grew in rough parallel lines. I landed in a small space of open sand and then watched as Mark landed like a Grand National hurdler across the rows of thorn bushes, managing to clear two 'fences' before ploughing through the third. His legs were a bloodied mess as he had unwisely elected to wear shorts that day.

Although we were beside the road, this inhospitable place was in the middle of nowhere. There were no vehicles and we had not seen a mud hut for miles. No animals stirred and even the flies gave the area a miss. I had started to de-rig my glider when, twenty minutes later, a small movement caught my eye. Emerging from the thorn bushes were a dozen people. Clad in sarongs with bows and arrows slung around their necks and spears in hand, they kept their distance. These nomadic people endured the harshest of existences and we must have appeared as aliens from outer space with our white faces, strange clothes and colourful hang gliders. After a few minutes observing us, three of them approached for a closer look at us and the gliders, while others warily melted back into the thorn bushes.

Again, we arrived at our goal in the Land Rover but this time we stayed inside a hospital compound, enjoying the luxury of a shower. The feeling of cleanliness never lasted more than an hour, but it was worth the effort to enjoy the brief sensation of being rid of our permanent coating of dust.

Louise's fear was obvious the following morning as she prepared to test fly the repaired glider. We all watched with our hearts in our mouths as she launched. Her take-off was smooth and she landed, smiling, after a short flight, pronouncing it as good as new.

Tim had problems finding a thermal, leaving Mark and me together at cloudbase ready to go. Our goal was Sigor airstrip, fifty-eight miles away. With a three-hour flight ahead of us, we set off. For the first time, there was very little wind and good clouds, so we flew conservatively and stayed high. In the distance we could see the distinct line where the dreaded area of dense thornbush started. Our goal lay beyond a thirty-mile stretch of hostile terrain where it would be impossible to land. There was not even enough space to land on the road as it was overhung with branches of thorn trees. If we lost height and had to land, we would certainly be injured and the scale of bodily damage resulting from a fast landing in the top of an African thorn bush did not bear thinking about.

Flying as a team was working brilliantly for Mark and me and his dry humour kept me in fits of giggles. When flying so closely with someone outside a competition situation, communication becomes almost telepathic. Often all I would hear over the radio was, 'Here we go', and I would be on my way towards him, knowing that he had found a good thermal.

An hour into the flight I was joined by a battleur eagle, immediately identifiable with its jet-black feathers, scarlet beak and legs, and its most striking feature – a mere stump of a tail. They are the most wonderful aerobatic specialists and I held my breath, gazing in awe at this vision, so much more beautiful than the picture in my bird book. He drew ahead of me and barrel rolled, offering me his scarlet talons to grapple. He drew in his wings and plummeted smartly downwards, then straightened up for me to follow suit in his courtship dance. How I wished I could have transformed myself into an eagle for an instant to play with him, but my wings remained rigid and inadequate so I could only watch his manoeuvres. Unimpressed with my non-participation, he turned north and was gone, leaving me grinning stupidly at this brief but unforgettable encounter.

We had originally said that for safety reasons we would land before the thickly forested section and drive the rest of the distance, but the thermals were so good that Mark and I decided to go for it. Before committing ourselves, we stopped for lunch at cloudbase, eating biscuits while we admired the view and gathered our courage. I had flown over short stretches of unlandable terrain in the past and it was always unnerving, but I had never experienced the prospect of such a long period of tension where the penalty for getting it wrong and going down would be so high.

With all our senses on red alert we crossed the threshold from safety to danger. We flew from cloud to cloud, topping up wherever we could, thankful for such excellent thermal markers. I made a big effort not to look down, as the prospect of nowhere to land would distract me and I needed all my concentration to watch the cloud shapes and maximise my climbs in the thermals. There was little idle chatter on the radio as the tension grew. After nearly an hour there was an area of weaker thermals and I was down to 3,000 feet above the ground, but poor Mark had hit some horrendous sinking air and was way below me at 1,500 feet. The situation was looking desperate, when I saw two vultures circling. I flew just above them and hit a smooth, strong thermal. I radioed quickly to Mark as he was in dire straits. 'There's a good thermal on your left.' As he turned I continued to guide him until he was directly underneath me and began to climb. It was a tense moment, but we had got away with it and were soon back at cloudbase.

At last, the small dirt airstrip at Sigor came into view, a small clearing in the forest with the huge 10,000-foot Rift Valley escarpment behind. A surge of relief flooded through us as we approached the safety of our first landing place in almost two hours. Richard flew up to meet us in his microlight with Sid hanging out of the back seat filming our first successful flight to goal. We landed, babbling with adrenaline. We celebrated that night after Tim and Louise arrived in the Land Rover, pleased that finally the dream was happening and the 'migration' had started. We left our gliders rigged and ready for the next day. We hung our mosquito nets from the noseplates and slept under the wings, beneath the endless stars above, undimmed by artificial light.

As the rose glow of the morning began to tinge the eastern skyline, there was activity in the camp as Matt wanted to film Ben flying his trike in the sunrise. The peace of the morning was shattered by the rude roar of the microlight engine warming up. I crawled blearily from my sleeping bag and pulled on a pair of shorts and a sleeveless shirt. Ben was sitting in the trike ready to go. I hopefully stuck out my thumb to hitch a ride and he beckoned me aboard. The cameras were rolling so I kicked off my sandals and climbed barefoot into the back seat.

We lined up along the runway with the silhouettes of the acacia trees lining our route. Ben applied full power and the trike rose eagerly in the heavy, cool air of the morning. We had no helmets and the wind in my hair was invigorating. We headed for the escarpment and climbed to watch the sunrise from above the Rift Valley wall. The tip of the sun's orb appeared over the horizon and soon flooded the cliff face with rich golden light. A thin thread of smoke trailed from a fire outside a small thatched mud hut and the sarong-clad woman tending it stopped to watch as we passed.

We returned to the airfield, cold and shivering. Ben suddenly changed course as he spotted a troop of baboons scurrying across a tiny clearing amongst the trees. Delightedly, we watched their antics from our perfect grandstand viewpoint before landing back at the camp for breakfast.

By early afternoon, the sky looked good, but the air above the runway was sinking and Mark broke all records for the hundred-yard dash as he sprinted to keep up with the trike. Finally airborne, Ben towed him to a large area of lift and returned for Tim who, being a lot heavier than Mark, had to run even harder to get off the ground.

Tim was soon high above the airfield and the radio was alive with his incessant chatter, which was his way of keeping himself calm. Louise was ready to launch but the wind had switched direction, making take-off impossible. Louise and I waited an hour before admitting defeat, reluctantly packing up our gliders and loading them on to the Land Rover. It was so frustrating, knowing the conditions were good but being unable to take off.

The destination for the day was Tot airfield, twenty-eight miles away, and both Tim and Mark arrived having flown different routes, Tim along the escarpment, Mark along the plain. Ben caught up with them as they arrived at goal and was asked by Mark to go and frighten away the lions which were roaming about on the runway. On closer inspection the 'lions' turned out to be a rather harmless herd of cows!

In the meantime, we continued to Tot in the Land Rover, with the road winding its tortuous way over rough tracks and ravine bottoms strewn with boulders. We came across our truck, which had broken down. The cab door was open and from the dark and gloomy depths, Sarah's smiling face appeared. She was up to her armpits in oil and was clearly in her element with an engine problem to fix.

I was first up the next morning and put on my thick flying suit as there was an early chill. I built a fire and put the kettle on to boil. As I sat on a log warming myself and watching the dawn, two bare-breasted teenage girls in tribal dress came walking towards me and squatted down by the fire. They stared at me with undisguised curiosity and I was able to study at close quarters their beautiful faces and their jewellery, so different from those of the tribeswomen in Turkana. The older of the girls had tattoo marks covering her belly (made by cutting the skin with a blade and then rubbing ash into the wounds) and wore huge earrings and a stiff leather 'yoke' coated with multicoloured beads.

Unable to communicate, I made them both a cup of tea. They looked at it curiously, tasted it and then without expression resumed their scrutiny of me, the gliders, trikes and vehicles. I felt privileged to share such a meeting of two worlds which seemed so far apart.

The next section was a fifty-mile stretch to Lake Baringo, famous for its hippos and abundant bird life. Tim had appalling diarrhoea and decided not to fly.

As the ground height was increasing all the time (we were now taking off at 5,000 feet), take-off speeds were getting faster and the risk of crashing on launch was much higher. Mark unveiled his antidote, a home-made rickety metal trolley set on four BMX bicycle wheels upon which the glider would sit and be pulled along until it reached take off speed. It caused much hilarity amongst the film crew, who sang a loud chorus of 'Chitty-Chitty Bang-Bang' and then uttered such irreverences as, 'It reminds me of riding in a pram when I was two', and, 'He must be off his trolley!'

We drew lots on who was to test the trolley and I lost. My glider was placed into the three holding brackets, I clipped in and was ceremoniously wheeled into position behind the trike. Matt was in hysterics at the sight and it was a good job the film crew had a tripod to steady their camera. I attached the tow line to my harness and called, 'All out.' The trike accelerated and the buggy surged forwards, immediately pulling off course to the right and heading for a ditch at the side of the runway. The glider started to fly and as it began to lift the front wheels, I released my grip on the trolley and catapulted upwards in a steep right-hand turn. I corrected my course while the trolley performed a double barrel roll before coming to rest on its back in the sand.

After subsequent flights, we discovered that the trolley's stubborn right-hand turn was a permanent feature. Eventually we learned that if we pointed it at forty-five degrees to the left of our desired course, by the time take-off speed was achieved, the glider would be following directly in line with the trike.

By midday, Mark, Louise and I were circling above Tot airfield and could see our goal, Lake Baringo, in the distance, as well as the vast expanse of thorny scrub in between. There was a fifteen-mile stretch without a road but we had no option except to bite the bullet once more and head towards the lake.

A ridge of hills lay obliquely across our path and we headed for it, hoping they would provide better conditions than the weak, widely spaced thermals over the flat ground. We stuck firmly together, helping each other into any rising air we found. As we reached the ridge, instead of the expected improvement in the thermals, the conditions became even worse and we grovelled about in pathetically weak lift for two hours. The banter on the radio stopped as we realised the severity of the situation. We were 1,500 feet above the ground with nowhere to land and no road for seven miles. With the searing heat and only one litre of water each, it was a bad place to land.

Ben and Richard took it in turns to take off from Lake Baringo airstrip and monitor our positions using the radio. After what seemed like an age, we found a better thermal and clawed our way upwards, flying more efficiently than we had ever done in our lives to gain every available inch from it. It petered out before we reached cloudbase, but we were not prepared to hang about and look for another. We had no height in reserve and set off towards goal praying for buoyant air which would help us to reach the airfield. Our toes were pointed, our heads were down and the radio remained silent as we each willed the airfield nearer. We made it by the skin of our teeth, arriving with only 500 feet to spare, never so glad to reach a goal.

We spent the night at Lake Baringo Lodge, enjoying the supreme luxury of a hot bath followed by supper on the veranda. We then watched the extraordinary spectacle of hippos grazing on the lawn, then had a blissful night's sleep in a real bed.

We awarded ourselves a day off, but the beauty of the lake drew me from my bed early the next morning. I woke Ben who, grumbling at first, soon came around to the idea of an early morning flight. There are few sights to rival hippo spotting from a microlight at dawn, watching them surface, twizzling their ears and snorting. We were almost brushing our reflection in the lake as we followed a small flock of pink flamingos, passing a graceful pelican and a hunting fish eagle. The crocodiles basking on the shore remained as still as statues as we flew past, following us with their eyes while the people collecting water from the lake waved and smiled. We spent the rest of the day enjoying a glorious combination of talking, eating, swimming in the lodge pool and generally recovering our strength.

The next section was supposed to be one of the highlights of the trip. We were to fly twenty-four miles south to Lake Bogoria, approaching in formation over the thousands of feeding flamingos before landing on the lake shore. Matt had visions of repeating the stunning scene from *Out of Africa* in which Robert Redford and Meryl Streep fly their bi-plane along a lake with a 'bow wave' of pink flamingos ahead of them.

The film crew set off early to get into position, ready to film the spectacle on the shores of Lake Bogoria, leaving Sid to mount small video cameras on the wings of the hang gliders. I attached my stills camera to the keel of my glider to ensure I got some stunning photos of my flight with the flamingos.

The cameras and counterweights weighed twenty pounds and this, combined with the thin air, was asking for trouble. My take-off felt wrong from the start. I held the nose of the glider too high and stalled the wing, hitting the runway at speed and skidding to a halt amidst an impressive cloud of dust. I was unhurt, but was shaken and filthy, with the dust having penetrated all my layers of clothing. I needed two new uprights and, while I replaced them, Ben towed Mark and Louise up using the trolley to launch.

After repairing my glider, I was ready to go again, glad of the extra take-off speed afforded by the trolley. I released into strong lift and an hour later approached Lake Bogoria, with its distinctive pink border of flamingos. The formation fly-in had been abandoned as both Mark and Louise had gone down before the halfway point.

I could see the film crew standing next to their Land Rover and flew out over the lake to make my approach towards them. The pink dots became more defined as I lost height. I was entranced by the sight of so many birds. The flamingos in front of me took off in a blur of pink wings as I made my final low glide on to the shore. I landed in front of the camera and then had to perform a wistful 'looking out to sea' pose for the film. Once Matt was satisfied, I noticed that the film crew were even muckier than I was. It transpired that in their efforts to get the Land Rover as near as possible to the desired filming position, they had driven off the road and had sunk up to their axles in hundreds of years'-worth of flamingo guano. Their Land Rover's four wheel drive lever was broken, leaving them with only two wheel drive, and they had no shovel. For the past four hours they had been digging the vehicle out ... by hand!

The day was cursed. The other Land Rover, having collected Mark and Louise, caught fire. There were several jerry cans of fuel for the trikes in the back and, in the heat, the vapour was escaping. Bella and Giles were lighting a cigarette when a tongue of flames shot past Louise's ear. Barely waiting for the car to slow down, she and Mark leaped out of the door and ran down the road. Giles managed to put out the fire with a fire extinguisher before it had time to destroy the gliders, harnesses and the vehicle.

The film crew retired to Lake Baringo Lodge to clean themselves up while we camped out. The following day, Mark joined Tim in the 'sick bay' and there was a general air of apathy. Ben towed me up and after releasing, I joined a flock of circling maribou storks, before setting course for Lows, thirty-three miles away. The flight was beautiful as the desert terrain transformed into cultivated plains. I flew with black kites and was joined for some time by a curious tawny eagle, which flew in tight formation with me.

The airfield at Lows was hard to spot as it was little more than a cow field. We subsequently found out that the last aircraft to land there had done so in 1973! Ben and Richard arrived and we were once again surrounded by a huge curious crowd, although this time there was a marked absence of people in tribal dress. They asked endless questions and wanted to know how everything worked and what we were doing. They listened in reverent silence as we answered, then babbled amongst themselves as they discussed the reply before asking the next question.

It was impossible to launch from the field the next day as the sun had hardened the cow pats, making the runway too rough for the trike. We drove to the local village and found a football pitch to tow from instead. The local school children turned out to watch and while Tim entertained them with endless verses of 'On Ilkley Moor Ba' t'at', Ben and I looked over the field. By now I trusted his judgement and he reckoned the field was big enough ... just. I rigged my glider to take first tow. I backed into the far corner of the field so that we were using the maximum runway length diagonally across the pitch, before reaching the high fence that skirted the boundary. I was nervous, but also anxious to fly as the clouds looked good but showed signs that they might overdevelop later.

Ben just managed to clear the fence and with relief we climbed above the town and I released into a good thermal which took me to over 14,000 feet. As soon as I had launched the crowd flocked onto the 'runway', making it hard for Ben to land without mincing any of the children in the propeller. Mark launched next, but by then the crowd were so over-excited that Ben decided not to risk another tow, so Tim and Louise had to travel by car.

As I flew towards Nakuru, our next goal, Mount Kenya was clearly visible ninety miles away on the eastern horizon. My path to the south was blocked by an enormous thunderstorm, which enveloped the whole area and looked likely to remain for the rest of the day. I watched as a gust front picked up a cloud of dust which rolled off the south end of Lake Nakuru. We needed to change our goal, as to continue towards Nakuru would be unsafe. I spotted an airstrip at Njoro and after a radio discussion with Richard, Ben and Tim, I landed there as it was a suitable site from which to proceed the following morning.

There was a small settlement of mud huts at the end of the runway and by the time I landed, another large crowd had gathered. It always amazed me that no matter where we landed, people would spot us in the air. A hang glider's approach is silent and yet people still saw us. In Britain, folk never seem to raise their eyes to the sky, but in Africa, they are much more observant.

185

Richard and Ben arrived and we were surrounded by a sea of excited, smiling faces. There was a deserted hangar next to the runway and with the storm approaching fast, Richard disappeared to see if he could find the owner. He returned grinning five minutes later with a worker from the Njoro Country Club which was alongside the airstrip. The prospect of a large bar was bliss to the beer-loving Richard. It took a dozen people twenty minutes to dig the grass from underneath the hangar doors so that they could be coaxed open, as it had been unused for years. The microlights and my hang glider were installed inside and we retired to the country club, where we were joined later by the rest of the team.

It was as though we had entered a different time zone. The club was straight out of colonial Africa, with pictures of Queen Victoria on the walls and shelves of musty books around the room. Visitors to the club that evening inundated us with generous offers of hospitality and invitations to land at various farmers' airfields.

After a good night's sleep, Matt insisted on filming some posed scenes around the club. I was fretting as the weather looked as though it was going to repeat yesterday's performance and I felt we needed to get going early.

By the time we assembled on the airfield, the conditions were deteriorating. As my glider was already rigged, I tried the conditions. The take-off was uncomfortably fast at 7,500 feet and there was no trolley to help as the truck had broken down some distance from Njoro with it on board. The air was unpleasantly rough and we decided to cry off and try again the following day.

The next morning everyone was fired with enthusiasm and, wary of a repeat of yesterday, we were all airborne by 11.40 a.m. Mark and Louise went first and were already at cloudbase by the time I launched. I asked Ben to tow me to a stubble fire and, ignoring his protestations and coughing over the radio, I released into a moderate thermal and waited for Tim. As Ben headed towards me towing Tim behind him, he spotted a huge flock of seventy storks thermalling ahead of us. Tim released and we climbed to cloudbase with the huge birds wheeling around us.

Our goal was the far end of Lake Naivasha, forty-four miles away. We had heard from Louise, who had landed after ten miles, but we had lost contact with Mark who was way in front of us as we headed for the escarpment. As we flew southwards, we were frequently joined by beautiful tawny eagles, which took time out from their hunting to escort us, eyeing us closely as they shadowed our movements.

Another thunderstorm was brewing over the town of Naivasha on the east side of the lake as we neared our goal. Tim raced off and went down just before the lake, on the side of a hill in the middle of nowhere, leaving Bella and Giles to try to find him. I spoke to Mark on the radio. He was on the east side of the lake under the storm cloud, about to land one mile short of goal, and worried about the monster above his head. I tried to skirt around the west side of the lake but the wind was increasing by the minute. I could see a gust front creating an angry frothing line on the lake and I knew I had to land as soon as possible. By sheer luck there was a small airstrip ahead and I landed safely, almost on the back of a very surprised gazelle. It stared at me in shock for a full minute before bounding gracefully off into the long grass.

Ben landed alongside me and helped me to de-rig my glider. I would be able to take off from the airstrip in the morning, so we hid the glider in the grass and then he gave me a lift to goal in the trike. On the way, the air became increasingly turbulent and the headwind strengthened. We were low on fuel and I kept quiet in the back seat, leaving Ben to concentrate on navigating through the arguing forces of the wind. Our landing was terrifying, with trees bending over in the howling wind all around us and the turbulence tossing us about like a leaf in the breeze. Ben was swinging his weight from side to side to keep the trike pointing down the runway. Finally, gratefully, we arrived on *terra firma* once again.

Meanwhile, Tim was soaked by the storm and was invited to shelter in a mud hut. I hoped the kindness of his host had not been repaid by one of his renditions of 'On Ilkley Moor ...' Once the storm had abated, just before nightfall, Richard's aerial reconnaissance guided the Land Rover to Tim's hut and by 10 p.m. we were all safely back at camp.

We were woken by the sound of hippos grunting in the nearby lake. Our goal for the day was Mosiro, deep in the heart of Masai country. Ben flew me to the airstrip where I had left my glider and towed me back to join the others. He then towed Mark and then Louise in air which was rough with broken thermals. They both battled for twenty minutes and then went down.

Ben returned to tow me and I knew the air would be turbulent, as he started to sing a Leonard Cohen dirge over the radio – his way of trying to soothe me in rough air.

At 1,800 feet I heard him exclaim, 'Oh shit!'

Instantly my hand hit the release, I turned on a wingtip and headed in the opposite direction. Ben was always so calm when towing us and if he had hit something bad enough to cause him to swear, then I did not want to be on the other end of the tow line. I circled in broken thermals for fifteen minutes before spotting the biggest dust devil I had ever seen. It was coming off a ploughed field which had long strips of plastic covering small seedlings. A dozen of the strips, each fifty yards long, were swirling around in the unruly air, climbing upwards towards me, glinting in the sun. My vario squealed in delight at the powerful lift and thankfully I was soon high above the plain and surveying the route ahead.

The intimidatingly named Hell's Gate National Park lay to the south, famous for its lions. With no clouds to help me locate thermals, I headed for the escarpment to the west. The headwind had increased and I battled against it for two and a half hours in a futile effort to make progress southwards. Between the four of us, we had completed seven unbroken legs of the journey and it was frustrating to have to give up on this section, but it was impossible to win against the wind and I landed next to the road.

Bella and Giles collected me and took me back to Naivasha, where I found that the others had already left for Mosiro. Ben offered me the back seat of the trike for the journey, so we waited for the calmer evening air before setting off. We flew over the magnificent crater of Longenot volcano, which looked like a moonscape with its corrugated sides and sharp edged top. In Hell's Gate National Park we spotted herds of impala, eland, zebra and small groups of giraffe. Navigation was easy, as we followed the solitary road. The greenery of Naivasha suddenly disappeared, replaced once more by the same thorny scrub as in the northern Rift Valley.

There was no airstrip at Mosiro, so an open area near the mud hut village had to suffice. As we taxied to where Richard's trike was parked, we caught sight of the crowd of tall Masai tribespeople. They were statuesque, dressed in red robes and adorned with elaborate, colourful jewellery. A group of smiling women gathered around to examine the newcomers. They touched my plain gold necklace, and allowed me to feel their heavy neck collars and huge earrings dangling from their stretched ear lobes. They dissolved into peals of laughter when I pointed out the tiny holes in my ears, pierced for traditional western earrings.

We were far from the tourist track and the Masai were untouched by corrupting western influences. There was an aura around this camp which was different from any we had experienced so far. I felt that we were on their land and had been made welcome by the Masai. They maintained their aloof dignity whilst enjoying our presence there. The following morning we rigged the gliders under a huge acacia tree while several zebra meandered past. A herd of Masai cows loitered, eyeing us with indifference as the red-robed cowherd leaned on his crook to watch us.

As the temperature rose, thermals started to develop and Tim spotted a small dust devil swirling around menacingly. We all ran to grab hold of our gliders and the film crew were commanded to hold down wing tips and keels, whilst trying to shoulder cameras to capture the drama as the tiny tornado of destruction made its way purposefully towards us.

The dust devil toyed briefly with Louise's glider, which was only saved by four people holding onto the wires. It then seemed to lose strength before suddenly spiralling upwards again and heading for Ben's trike. We watched in horror as it picked the microlight up effortlessly and threw it in the air, depositing it on its back. Its mischief done, the dust devil skittered across the field and was gone.

At first glance the damage to the trike looked terminal, with a broken keel and front tube, a torn sail and bent bolts and plates. That look appeared once again in Richard's eyes and our skilled duo of 'bodgers' started the day-long job of splinting, sleeving and bending the trike back into shape. By early evening, it was ready for a test flight, and the sky, which was washed with the pastel colours of twilight, was too good an opportunity to miss. Ben towed me high into the smooth evening air and we saw our final goal of Lake Magadi in the distance.

When I landed, the Masai chief came up to me, chuckling. He had enjoyed the spectacle and shook my hand in appreciation.

The sky was disappointing the next morning, with sparse cumulus development to the north but no sign of the strong thermals which had been so abundant the day before. It did not encourage us to risk venturing along the route to Magadi, which was road-less and unlandable.

Louise took the first tow using the trolley. A group of Masai were watching the activity in the shade of a nearby tree and were entranced by the sight of Louise soaring upwards. They did not see the trolley continuing on its runaway right-handed course, heading straight for them. At the last moment someone yelled. They scattered in a whirl of scarlet robes and the trolley careered harmlessly into the tree.

Louise found no lift and landed back alongside us. I went next and was down to 700 feet before finding a small broken thermal where I joined a flock of a hundred pelicans which were already circling in it, looking like flying boats with their huge oblong wings.

We were only twenty miles from our destination at Lake Magadi, but the conditions remained poor. We could not gain enough height and were running out of time. We had to admit defeat, de-rig the gliders and drive to Magadi. The journey along the dusty road was arduous and we were all filthy by the time we stopped at the dubiously named Delicious Café in Ngong for supper. Louise and Tim were following in the second Land Rover but they had engine trouble and eventually resorted to driving up the Rift Valley escarpment backwards! We arrived at the soda lake exhausted and slept under the trike wing.

The film crew wanted us to land on the white crust of the soda lake for the grand finale. At low level Magadi had a suffocating smell and looked barren and ugly. Once airborne, the transformation was dramatic. Intricate patterns formed by soda crystals appeared on the surface and the colours changed subtly from palest rose pink to fiery red, contrasting sharply with the muted browns of the surrounding desert.

I released at 5,000 feet and meandered slowly downwards, drinking in the view. A huge herd of cattle were crossing the lake in single file, escorted by Masai herdsmen. Matt asked me to land immediately as the shot of me landing with the cattle in the background would be superb. Reluctantly I wound off my remaining height and returned to the stifling heat of the lake. I did my worst landing of the trip, planting the nose of the glider firmly in the soda, but Matt was ecstatic with the shot. Mark, Tim and Louise followed me in and we lined the gliders up for the final shot. Ben and Richard landed alongside and joined us.

It was 'a wrap'; the adventure was over. There was a huge sadness amongst the team as we had worked together, flown where no one had ever flown before and had overcome most of the challenges that had been presented. Our journey had spanned a big chunk of the Rift Valley. We had soared the escarpments, thermalled with eagles and landed in deserts. We had pushed the boundaries of hang gliding a little further and had had the time of our lives.

CHAPTER 17

Cross Channel Disaster
and Losing my Title

I returned to England in the spring of 1992 to restart my life without Trevor. Leaving Africa had been very hard, as we had had such a fantastic time. It epitomised everything I loved most in hang gliding: travelling, flying with birds, cross-country flying and being with good friends. It was difficult to readjust to normal life back home. With the disappearance of all my plans for married life, I felt directionless and unmotivated. All I could do was to return to the familiarity of what I had been doing before, competition flying.

If I were to draw a graph of my competition successes and failures, they would correlate almost exactly with a graph of my emotional highs and lows. Happiness is good for competition results and it was no surprise, looking back, that 1992 was a poor year. I was back in the League but the magic had gone out of it for me.

The recession had hit the car market badly and Citroën UK's marketing budget had been slashed to a fraction of its previous level by their mother company in France. My sponsorship budget had been axed completely. We had enjoyed a fruitful four-year partnership and we parted company agreeing to review the situation the following year if circumstances improved. I would continue to fly their microlight and, if any publicity opportunities came up, I would still promote their name.

Late that summer a charity flight had been organised, in which forty microlights were to fly from England to France. It was devised by Trevor Jones, who had been a Royal Navy helicopter pilot until he broke his neck in a skiing accident. Paralysed from the neck down with a tiny amount of movement in his arms, he had learned to fly again in a specially adapted three-axis microlight which he controlled with a hand-operated joystick, using his head to activate the modified brakes.

The idea behind the venture was to raise money for the Trevor Jones Trust, which provided funds for people with similar disabilities to allow them to regain their quality of life. It was also something of a personal crusade for Trevor, who wanted to prove that disabled people can achieve a huge amount if given the opportunity.

A friend of mine, Carl Ford, contacted me to ask if I would participate in the flight. He is also quadriplegic as a result of a hang gliding accident several years ago. He ideally wanted to fly as my passenger, but if that wasn't possible, he wanted to raise funds for the trust through my doing the flight for him.

I arranged to take Carl for a flight to see how he would cope. His biggest danger was hypothermia as, with a severed spinal cord, messages from the skin do not get through to the brain, so the ability to sweat or shiver to regulate body temperature is lost. Trevor Jones overcame this problem by flying in an enclosed cockpit, but there was no such luxury on a standard flexwing trike and the wind chill could make a big difference.

We flew from a small airstrip near Carl's house with him swaddled in layers of warm clothing despite the fact that it was pleasantly warm. Our plan was to fly to an airfield forty-five minutes away, but even on such a short flight the risk of hypothermia was high and Carl carried a foil 'space blanket', a mobile phone and a thermometer with him.

The task of manoeuvring a twelve-stone dead weight into the tiny back seat of a microlight was not an easy one, but a team of willing helpers soon had Carl comfortably installed. I then had to strap his limbs to the fuselage to make sure they did not flail into the propeller, and we were ready to go. Carl enjoyed being airborne again, the clouds were growing quickly in the thermic air but the views were good with excellent visibility.

We arrived at our destination and I taxied up to the hangar wall to shelter Carl from the wind. The thermometer showed he had lost four degrees of body temperature, so I wrapped his foil blanket around him and went in search of some hot coffee. Within half an hour he had regained two degrees and was anxious to get back to where his wife would be waiting and he could reheat properly indoors. We took off again, but the big clouds now had cascades of rain dropping from them. I skirted several of them, but ten miles from home we were confronted by a long line of rain extending so far that we could not go around it. We had no option but to fly through it. The shower lasted two minutes, then we were back into bright sunshine, but the rain had lowered Carl's temperature dramatically. When we landed, his body temperature was down by six degrees and he was slurring his words. We carried him to his car, where the heater was on full blast and he was wrapped in blankets. Three hours later he had fully recovered, but wisely decided that he could not risk a flight to France.

The group of forty microlight pilots plus passengers met at Headcorn Aerodrome in Kent on the morning of the big flight. There was a huge variety of aircraft, including one- and two-seaters, both old and new, three-axis miniature aeroplanes and flexwing trikes. The organisation was excellent. We were divided into groups of similar performance machines and told how to maintain contact with air traffic control and what to do in case of emergency. Trevor Jones arrived with his plane and a naval helicopter landed nearby, which was to shadow him along the way. At the appointed time we started our engines and lined up in our groups to take off. I enjoyed the familiar buzz of excitement at the start of an adventure.

We followed our group leader to the runway and took off, setting course for Dover, where we would head out over the Channel. Carl's place as my passenger had been taken by Mick Perrin, a friend from Brighton who was recovering from an operation for bone cancer. The conditions were glorious, with small cumulus clouds dotting the sky, light winds and clear air. We climbed to 3,000 feet as we reached Dover and in a loose formation our group turned for France.

The last time I had flown this route other than by commercial jet, was by hang glider. On that occasion I had sufficient height to make it to the other side. This time was different. I was relying on an engine to get me to France and I was nervous as I did not entirely trust two-stroke motors.

We were halfway across when Peter Keele, flying the microlight directly ahead of me, lost power. His propeller windmilled to a stop and he descended quickly. Instinctively I reduced my power to follow him down. The arrangement was that if anyone landed in the Channel, the person nearest to them would descend to 300 feet to keep an eye on them and to mark the spot for the rescue helicopter. The second in line would stay at 2,000 feet to keep in radio contact with the emergency services.

I saw Peter try to restart his engine, but with no success. He was committed to a sea landing and he headed directly towards a huge tanker that was making its way along the Channel. Instead of landing into wind, he landed alongside the ship and the fast landing flipped the wing over. I immediately buzzed the boat to attract attention, but there was no one visible on its huge expanse of deck. I was in danger of losing sight of Peter, so I turned back to maintain my vigil. He had inflated his life jacket and was clinging to the underside of the trike, which was upside down and mostly submerged.

I called Kent Radar on the radio and informed them of Peter's position and said that he was in distress. I did not like the look of the aircraft as its buoyancy seemed so precarious. They confirmed that Peter had sent out his own Mayday call and that a helicopter was on its way and would be with us in five minutes. I was told to change radio frequency to Calais airport, who were taking control of the situation.

I banked my microlight up and circled above Peter to mark the spot for the helicopter, but it didn't arrive. I called Calais.

'Mayday Mayday, this is G-MVPV, I am at 100 metres above the aircraft in the water. Where is the helicopter?'

'G-MVPV are you the aircraft in the water?' came the confused reply.

'Negative Calais, I am above the aircraft in the water. The pilot needs immediate help. We need the helicopter urgently.'

'G-MVPV ... are you the aircraft in the water?'

Shaking with frustration I controlled my voice and repeated my message in French. It was now nearly half an hour since Kent Radio had said the helicopter was five minutes' away and I knew Peter must be exhausted and cold.

A small fishing trawler appeared, having seen me circling. As they approached, they spotted Peter in the water. Relief flooded over me as I saw the group of fishermen lining the side of the boat preparing to throw life belts. I got my camera out to take some pictures of the rescue, as I knew Peter would enjoy showing them as he recounted his tale.

The boat missed him by fifty yards and turned around for another try. This time they were going to pass very close ... too close. The boat hit the submerged wingtip of the trike. In an instant, the microlight sank, taking Peter with it.

'NO!' I screamed helplessly. 'You bastards.'

I pulled myself together and, with undisguised urgency in my voice, called Calais again.

'Mayday Mayday, WHERE IS THE HELICOPTER – WE NEED THE HELICOPTER NOW!'

'Are you the pilot in the water?' came the reply.

It took every morsel of self-control, which I mustered for Peter's sake, to reply, 'The pilot is now under the water. We need the helicopter immediately.'

I switched to French and repeated the message. The urge to jump in to the water to find Peter was strong, but without even a wet suit, let alone diving gear, it would have been futile.

I sobbed uncontrollably at the horror of the situation. I circled for two minutes, knowing that Peter was dead, but hoping for a miracle. There was nothing more we could do except head for Calais. I called once more on the radio, unable to stop my voice from shaking.

'Calais this is G-MVPV I am now coming to Calais airport.'

'How is the pilot in the water?' he replied.

'The pilot in the water is dead,' I answered, then repeated it in French.

I was shaking with shock all the way to Calais, controlling myself enough to land safely and taxi to where the others were milling around, looking worried having heard the rumours. I gave them the basic facts before being bustled into the control tower to talk to the airport police. I was too numb to be angry, but it transpired later that Calais had diverted the Kent helicopter to a boat on fire, but had never sent another to Peter's aid.

Trevor Jones landed and taxied towards us, his face a picture of triumph and elation at his successful crossing. The TV cameras were capturing his joy when the event organiser ran over to break the news of the tragedy. He was devastated. His own escort, the Navy helicopter, was equipped with a diver and winch and could easily have picked Peter up but were told on the radio that a helicopter had been scrambled and the situation was under control.

I suffered a gruelling two hours of interviews with the police, filling in forms and statements. They were pretty callous in their dealings with me, considering I was still in a complete state of shock. I wanted to go home. I was finally allowed to leave and flew back to Britain with Mick. I was then subjected to an unpleasant wave of media attention as people tried various devious means to obtain my address and turned up on my doorstep to try to obtain some exclusive gory details. I had nightmares for weeks afterwards about the helpless feeling I had when watching Peter sinking out of sight. I was very depressed and needed to get a grip on myself. I needed something to get me going again.

A few months later I was rigging my hang glider at Merthyr Tydfil when Robbie Whittall turned up with his paraglider. In the time it took me to stick six battens in the wing, he had removed his canopy from its bag, put on his harness and taken off. He gained a little height in the light ridge lift and then started a series of wing overs, swooping back towards the hill, just missing the clifftop and then swinging up again in a smooth arc to repeat the manoeuvre. It was almost balletic, but most of all it looked such fun that I felt I had to try paragliding again.

Robbie worked for Firebird, a German manufacturer, who offered to sponsor me with a paraglider. Robbie volunteered to teach me to fly it. The weather was foul during my training week and I did very little flying, but learned a lot from watching Robbie handle his canopy and asking him lots of questions. At the end of the week he gave me a beginner's canopy, a small purple Apache.

The biggest problem I had in learning to paraglide was groundhandling. The inert bundle of material that emerged from the rucksack would suddenly take on a life of its own, and with the force of three runaway horses could drag me through barbed wire fences, cow pats or bushes at will. I loved the sensation of flying a paraglider but I was reluctant to put in the hours of manhandling it on the ground to improve my take-off skills.

I spent most of my early flights grinning, as I enjoyed the sensation of paragliding so much. There were many similarities to hang gliding, but when the wind was light, the more responsive handling of a paraglider made it much more fun to fly. Because of the slower speed, landing on the side of the hill was quite easy. I also enjoyed flying in a seated position after years of flying on my belly. Not only was it much kinder to my back, but also the sense of vertigo that often made me nervous in turbulence was reduced.

I had made plans to visit South Africa in December to try once again to break the women's world hang gliding distance record, which was now held by Kari Castle and stood at over 200 miles. I decided to take the paraglider 'just in case'. The women's world paragliding distance record was within my capability as I had 2,000 hours of hang gliding experience to draw upon. The theory was the same, I just had to learn how to fly the thing!

The long drought which had provided superb flying conditions broke as I arrived in South Africa. Conditions would look fantastic and then, by 3 p.m., huge thunderstorms would develop and block all routes. Again, the hang gliding record eluded me. Based at the small town of Kuruman in the flatlands west of Johannesburg, I was again using a car tow in order to launch.

After two weeks, I moved to nearby Vryburg and joined the paragliding group there who were all chasing records. Having learned to fly my paraglider in the English winter, I had accumulated a paltry three hours' airtime and had not yet tried thermalling. Although I could turn it in circles, it felt monstrously inefficient and I knew that my technique would have to improve in order to cope with proper thermals.

The paragliding courses were being run by Nick Przybylzki, a huge bear of a man who provided tows, retrieve service and enormous meals at the campsite for his groups. I helped out for a few days, driving the tow vehicle to winch the experienced paraglider pilots up and watching them thermal skilfully. I then bombarded them with questions in the evenings about how they turned their canopies so efficiently.

After three days the wind had dropped sufficiently for me to have a flight. Nick always helped the newcomers with their groundhandling and it was a wonderfully secure feeling to have a man of his size weighing me down while I struggled to get the wayward paraglider under control. I was towed up five times but only found one small thermal which I stayed in for a couple of turns before my uncoordinated circles ensured I was thrown out. Although the Apache coped well with my clumsy efforts, I needed to improve my technique before I could use the thermals well enough to climb away from the airfield and fly cross-country.

That night I quizzed the experts about turning in thermals. With a brake handle in each hand as the only means of control, the pressure exerted upon them was critical. Richard Carter, the British cross-country record holder, explained that the correct technique of turning to enter a thermal was to pull down on one brake handle to bank the canopy and initiate the turn. He then gave me a vital clue. It was essential to put slight pressure on the other brake handle as this is what made the turn efficient. Until now I had not realised this. I went to bed dreaming of being a puppet dangling on strings and woke up the following morning to find a perfect looking day, but with a forecast for thunderstorms by 2 p.m.

There was general apathy amongst the group at the airfield, but the sky looked fine to me. Nick agreed to tow me up so I hurriedly put on my layers of clothing in the stifling heat. I had borrowed Richard's 'body armour', a lycra suit with built-in protective plates covering shoulders, elbows, knees and shins. I had seen many of my hang gliding friends hurt during their early dabbles with paragliding and I was only too aware of my vulnerability with only three and a half hours' airtime to my name.

It was 11.15 a.m. when I launched and the tow line pulled me to 800 feet above the airfield. I released as soon as I felt the surge of a thermal and swung the canopy round to stay in the rising air. To my delight, the vario kept chirping all the way round and the altimeter confirmed I was climbing well. With my new knowledge of bank angles and brake pressures the Apache felt much more coordinated and efficient.

I was committed to my first paragliding cross-country flight and I couldn't stop grinning. The sensation of 'dangling' was funny and I felt as though I was sitting in a comfy armchair being propelled around the sky as I reached cloudbase at 6,000 feet above the ground. I flew more conservatively than I would have done with a hang glider; although the Apache climbed well, the glide was poor by comparison. All I had to do was to make sure I stayed in the air, letting the wind help me cover the distance by blowing me along at a good rate.

Within an hour of taking off, a menacing looking cloud appeared to the west which seemed to be growing quickly, exactly as the forecast had predicted. I was having to concentrate hard all the time, as paragliding was so new to me and I could not afford to relax. I was used to hang gliding where I could switch to 'automatic' whilst thermalling, knowing my body would react to the surges in the air to regulate the angle of bank and speed to ensure the best climb rate.

Nick was driving retrieve and whilst gliding between thermals I radioed my position to him. This was made easy by the small GPS (Global Positioning System – satellite navigation) unit I was carrying. In the featureless and often inhospitable flatlands, it made navigating much easier and I was able to give Nick my exact track and distance from my starting point. My map was redundant and I was able to use all the concentration normally needed for navigation to fly the canopy.

The thermals were getting stronger and more turbulent as early afternoon approached. I flew to a rapidly growing cloud and climbed quickly to cloudbase. Without warning, I hit the turbulence on the outside of the thermal and instantly the canopy lurched, half the wing collapsed and the world started revolving in a most disconcerting way. I knew that paragliders sometimes collapsed as they have no tubing to keep the wing in shape, but until this moment I had not experienced a deflation. I didn't know whether the canopy was in a spin or a spiral, and the techniques to reinflate the wing are exactly opposite from one another, releasing the brakes to let the canopy accelerate in the case of a spin, or pulling one of the brakes to slow the wing in a spiral.

I had plenty of height, and resorted to a trial and error approach. I pulled on the brakes but nothing happened and fifty per cent of the wing continued to flap uselessly while I was flung sideways by the centrifugal force. I then concluded it must be a spin and released both brakes. Still no change. I then pulled once more, and with a rustle and a jolt, the wing reinflated and the Apache straightened up, calm and placid as though nothing had happened. My heart was pounding as I struggled to regain my composure. The whole event had lasted less than ten seconds, though it had felt like an age.

The big cloud to the west had now grown even more and was spreading a thin veil of high cirrus cloud in all directions which soon covered the sun, thereby cutting off its thermal-producing strength. The cumulus began to decay as the sky became a uniform shade of grey.

The thermals were weak, but I could still drift along with the wind. I crossed the Vaal river and the barren scrub suddenly changed to cultivated farmland. I checked the cumulonimbus cloud to the west once more and could see a big gust front rolling out from underneath it. It was time to land, as I had seen the ferocity of the winds that such gust fronts produced. I knew I had flown far enough to break the world record but did not have the experience to cope with landing backwards in a strong wind.

I picked out a farmhouse to land next to, and as I approached I could hear the children of the farm workers calling and whistling. I landed alongside the house and packed up quickly. As I zipped the paraglider into its bag the gust front hit, sandblasting me with dust. The farmer plied me with food and drink in the typically hospitable South African way, as Nick found his way to the farm to collect me.

I had flown seventy-seven miles on my first cross-country flight on a paraglider, and had doubled my airtime. I had become hooked on paragliding and could not wait to do more. I had rediscovered the magic which I had felt years before, when I started hang gliding.

I had to switch my concentration back to hang gliding as the third Women's World Hang Gliding Championships were to be held in April and I was determined to defend my title, won two years before in Austria. This year they were to be held in Japan and I was full of reservations after my last trip to Wakayama when Pepê had died.

The venue for the championships was Nanyo City, which was very different from industrial Wakayama. We arrived at the beginning of the cherry blossom season and the trees were laden with flowers. The town was small and full of character, with traditional Japanese houses adjoining tiny, ornate gardens dotted with immaculately sculpted bonsai trees.

The organisation of the competition was so detailed it defied belief. There were hundreds of people involved in the various subcommittees in charge of weather forecasting, film developing, task scoring, retrieve organisation and so on. Thousands of flags waved from specially erected poles, lining every road within a three-mile radius of Nanyo City. They had even lopped off the top of the mountain to provide enough parking space for all the cars, media and organisers' portakabins. All facilities were provided, including packed lunches and the unheard of luxury of flushing, scented toilets on launch. The only thing that could not be organised was the one element vital to a flying competition and that was the weather. We were lulled into a false sense of security by flying almost every day in practice, but it was not to last.

Good weather greeted the first day of the competition. There was frustration on take-off as we watched the cumulus form whilst having to stand in line behind our national flags and listen to endless speeches wishing the competitors, 'Happy frying', and, 'Have a good fright.' Chaos ensued as a crowd of white-jacketed helpers, who did not know how to handle hang gliders, allowed several wings to nearly blow away. These helpers had been instructed to hold the nose wires of each glider while the pilot did a 'hang check' to ensure her harness was attached to the glider. They were so diligent that I ended up being checked three times, as it was easier to do another one rather than explain that I had already done two. We were bombarded with questions and commands from the assistants. 'What is your number?' 'Please do hang check.' 'Hurry up and launch.' 'Please do hang check.'

It was driving me mad. Finally I shouted, 'Release!' which was the signal for them to let go as the pilot was about to launch. Like programmed robots they scattered and I then took a deep breath to compose myself, walked calmly to the edge and took off into the silent air.

The conditions were not brilliant, but adequate for a fifteen-mile task. I flew for two hours in the weak thermals and landed one mile short of goal to win the day. Two TV crews arrived instantly and did a fifteen-minute interview before the army turned up and looked almost disappointed that I wasn't injured and did not require assistance.

A good start was followed by eight days of poor weather when it was impossible to fly a single task. The organisers were getting desperate. For the competition to be valid, we needed to have flown a minimum of four rounds and with one already completed, there were only three days left to cram in the remainder. The Japanese had spent over $1m on staging the championships and creating the hype surrounding it. The worst possible outcome would be an invalid meet with no one on the rostrum collecting their medals.

The next day the conditions were hopeless, with no wind, uniform grey skies and no thermals. In spite of the dismal forecast, we were taken to launch and told to rig. The reason soon became apparent: they set a six-mile task. The round would be valid even if we just flew in a straight line from launch without hitting any lift at all. They were manipulating the scoring system in order to have a task to count towards the championships. I felt insulted that in an event as important as the world championships, we should be told to fly such a farcical task and I could not help thinking that, had we been men, we would not have been given such a ridiculous task.

The conditions were not even good enough to fly six miles and Kari Castle won the day with a five-mile flight, gaining as many points as I had done the first day after a two-hour battle. The main winner was the organisation, who patted themselves on the back for having got another round in and half-completing the championships.

The following day saw a return to decent thermic conditions and no one could believe their ears when at the briefing the organisers stated that the task would be the same as the day before. We watched a wind dummy reach cloudbase time and again on the adjacent ridge, proving that conditions were good.

Nothing I had ever learned prepared me for the feeling of impotence and frustration I now felt. I had spent years learning my skills of cross-country flying and racing in competitions, only to be asked to set it all aside in order to go on an extended glide. I had had enough. I lined up first on launch, took off and pulled the bar in through all the thermals, reaching goal in thirteen minutes. I landed, disgusted with the whole fiasco which seemed to be run solely for the benefit of the organisers. I had blown my chances of winning the championships by taking off first, but I no longer cared. All eighteen pilots who reached goal felt the same way. Françoise Dieuzeide of the French team summed up our feelings when she burst into tears of frustration saying, 'I have spent all winter training for this championship, only to be asked to fly stupid tasks like this!'

The following morning I went to the team leaders' briefing and vented my feelings to the competition organiser.

'I have been flying competitions for more than ten years and have never before been asked to fly such a meaningless task. Half of this "World Championship" has now been decided on two six-mile flights.'

His tight-lipped expression revealed nothing, but I knew of the lower status of women in Japan, and that he would consider my outburst well out of order. By that stage I didn't care.

On the last day, the weather was bad again, but was forecast to improve. My words had obviously not fallen on deaf ears as a decent-length task was set. The sky gradually cleared and we were finally rewarded with good thermals and fine flying. Although I got to goal, it was not enough to retain my title and the World Championship gold went to Françoise Dieuzeide with Kari Castle taking the silver. I had never been to a championships where the morale among pilots was so low. It had stopped being fun and I felt there was little point in continuing to compete. I felt the need for a change.

CHAPTER 18

*'Inshallah'**

Ben Ashman phoned me, tripping over his words with excitement.

'There's a sponsored trip in May to hang glide in Jordan. They will be aerotowing and I've been asked to be the tow pilot. They're looking for an expedition leader, so why don't you give the organiser, Yasmin Saudi, a call?' he blurted, barely pausing for breath.

It was over a year since we had returned from Kenya and I was realising more and more that this is where my real pleasure in hang gliding lay, in exploration, travel and adventure rather than in competition flying.

I met Yasmin, a twenty-four-year-old Jordanian woman who was studying in London. She was delighted for me to lead the expedition. Her long dark hair cascaded in tight ringlets around her face and her bright blue eyes shone with enthusiasm. Her voice was soft and belied the will of iron that I would soon discover lurking underneath. Her preparations were immensely thorough, ensuring everything was organised with the correct authorities. The invitation had been issued by the Jordanian Ministry of Tourism and Antiquities and they were covering the cost of flights, accommodation and transport.

I knew very little of Jordan and pored for hours over a book of aerial photographs of the country and its extraordinary range of archaeological and geological features. The two places that were top of the list to fly over were Petra, an ancient Nabataean city carved from the rock of the Rift Valley wall, and Wadi Rum, a desert valley surrounded by extraordinary rock formations.

Yasmin's motive for setting up the expedition was to hang glide in her

---

* 'God willing' in Arabic.

home country. There was however, a massive fly in the ointment: she had only just finished her initial training and had less than two hours' airtime. Our launches would be by aerotow behind a microlight, totally out of the question for a beginner. Yasmin would have to get a lot more hours in the air before we left.

We arranged to go flying together so that I could teach her on an intensive one-to-one basis. With a good southerly wind forecast, we went to Derbyshire, a good site for beginners. I carried the glider up to take-off while she brought the harness. She flew twice that day and I saw that she needed much more practice. I was happy with her actual flying, but her take-offs were shambolic and landings were more of an 'arrival'. There was a lot of work to do before the expedition in May.

We managed one more trip, this time to Wales, where her take-off technique improved a little. I then left to compete in the League while she returned to London to study for her finals. She was under strict instructions that she had to fly a lot more before we left for Jordan.

We arrived in Amman in mid-May and Ben and I were excited. With us were Niall O'Connor, a university friend of Yasmin's, and Bill Jonganeel, of whom we knew little except that he was a hang gliding instructor.

Yasmin had gone on ahead to spend some time with her parents and all three came to the airport to meet us. Her father, Ghazi, had the same soft voice, tightly curled hair and sparkling eyes, and had a wonderful way of jigging about, high on life, a trait which his daughter had inherited. Her mother, Isa, was Italian but disguised her origin by being very shy. It was only on those occasions when she was severely provoked, usually by one of her two sons, that she would burst into a loud staccato barrage of Italian, gesticulating wildly. The whole family was multi-lingual, speaking Arabic, Italian, German and English with equal fluency. Their house sounded like the Tower of Babel as they flicked between languages in mid-sentence.

The Ministry of Tourism and Antiquities had arranged for us to stay in the lavish Intercontinental Hotel, though we spent most of our first two days at the Jordanian Airforce base at Marka Airport, where we had permission to test our equipment. The immaculate parking area soon resembled a street market as we unpacked our multicoloured wings, and soon a small crowd of uniformed onlookers gathered to watch the entertainment, each welcoming us to Jordan.

Neither Niall nor Bill had aerotowed before so Ben towed me up to demonstrate the technique. The airport control tower gave us permission to take off from wherever we wanted on the taxiway. It was quite bewildering as, with a tarmac strip two miles long and fifty yards wide, we were spoilt for choice as to where to lay our seventy-five-yard tow rope. As the airport had no inbound planes we were given *carte blanche* to fly wherever we wanted.

There was a moderate breeze blowing and I was off the ground within three paces. Ben towed me to 2,000 feet above the runway, where I released into a big, smooth thermal and circled, taking in the scenery. Enclosed by brown, sun-scorched hills, Amman was a sea of cream and beige flat-topped buildings, blending aesthetically with the surroundings. To the west, the buildings stopped sharply as the hills rose to the rim of the Rift Valley where it dropped down to the Dead Sea 4,000 feet below.

Somewhat reluctantly, I spiralled down to help Niall and Bill with their first tows. We were bombarded with questions from the curious onlookers, many of whom were quite at home in fast jets but were fascinated by our tiny, foot-launched aircraft. Ben, never one to miss an opportunity to perform, gave an impromptu microlight flight display, then orbited the control tower so that the air traffic controller could have a closer look.

'Very nice,' came her reply over the radio as she struggled to control her laughter at this unorthodox circus.

The next morning was set aside for Yasmin, and Ben cornered me after breakfast.

'You're the only one of us that has seen her fly. Can she cope with an aerotow launch?' he asked.

The responsibility was awesome. Having been engrossed with studying for her finals, she still only had a total of five hours' airtime and her take-offs were still ropey. In normal circumstances if anyone had asked me whether it would be safe to aerotow a beginner with five hours' experience the answer would be a categorical 'No!' But there were two factors that made this particular case different.

The first was Ben. His experience of aerotowing was huge and he had towed many pilots on their first aerotow who had pulled all the dodgy stunts that it was possible to perform. So far, there had been no accidents as Ben would always fly with one hand ready to pull the quick release attached to the trike which detached the tow line and enabled the hang glider pilot to regain control.

The second consideration was Yasmin herself. Not only was she extremely gutsy in her approach to flying, but she listened well to instructions and did as she was told. The most graphic example of her ability to cope with stressful, rapidly changing situations was to watch her driving around Amman in her mother's truck. She was transformed from the quietly spoken, happy-go-lucky young woman we knew, into an assertive, positive-acting, horn-honking demon of the road. I was impressed with the way she coped with Amman's daunting highway code. I hoped my gut feeling was right as I told Ben that, in my opinion, Yasmin could cope.

Her small beginner's glider had huge pneumatic wheels on its base bar, which Yasmin put to good use on every landing and most take-offs. She and I went through the drill several times until she was as ready as she was ever going to be. She lined up behind the trike and prepared to launch. I could tell she was nervous and I struggled to control my own apprehension on her behalf. As she said, 'all out', Ben applied full power and with her usual awful take-off style she lurched into the air. The nose of the glider was too high and she sailed way above the trike. Ben released the end of the tow line and she flew straight ahead and landed with a belly-flop.

With two more tows her take-offs improved slightly and she was able to pull on enough speed to keep level with the trike, though her path was somewhat erratic. Ben kept up a soothing patter, instructing her as they went, and managed to tow her to 500 feet before she got out of line again and had to be released.

Ben invited Colonel Saudi (a relative of Yasmin's who had been enormously helpful to us) for a flight in the microlight. He had been a fighter pilot for many years and had spent many thousands of hours flying jets. After a ten-minute trip around the airport, Ben touched down with a ten mile an hour crosswind and the trike began to swerve violently from side to side.

In a scene straight out of a Keystone Cops film, the wheel which should have been attached to the right-hand undercarriage came trundling past them. Ben's efforts to control the oscillations were making the situation worse so he took his feet off the pedals which steer the nose wheel. Poor Colonel Saudi was then confronted not only with the wheel of the aircraft having become detached, but the 'pilot in command' relinquishing control by letting go with his feet! There was a grinding of metal on tarmac as the axle dug in and the trike slewed to a halt, allowing the erstwhile steely eyed fighter pilot passenger to emerge pale and shaken. The emergency services bolted into action and an ambulance and fire engine, both with sirens and lights blazing, were dispatched to the scene, dwarfing the tiny microlight. They looked disappointed to find that they were not needed.

The whole of the military engineering department rallied round to repair the damage to the axle, tube, plates and bolts. After two hours, Ben emerged triumphant with all the problems fixed and the trike sporting a wheel procured from a luggage trailer. The hub was rusty and, being a solid tyre, it weighed several pounds more than the former model, but it was a reasonable fit and we were back in business.

Prince Feisal, the second son of King Hussein, came to meet us. He instantly put us at our ease with his relaxed attitude and his obvious love of flying, which he no doubt inherited from his father. He immediately offered us a wheel off the microlight that his brother had bought some ten years before, which they did not fly any more. We could not resist going to investigate and drove to the hangar where the Royal Falcons (the Jordanian aerobatics team) kept their aircraft. The three immaculate planes gleamed, whilst in the corner, in sharp contrast, lurked the motheaten remains of a microlight. The wheels were still intact though the tyres had perished, but the hubs were the wrong size so we left the carcass intact.

That evening, Ben checked the other wheels for damage while Bill provided entertainment as he worked. Bill is an actor and singer with a voice whose volume defies belief. He regaled us with his rendition of 'Summertime', complete with his unique trumpet solo which filled the hangar with deafening sound.

With foresight which proved invaluable, Ben sent me to buy another wheel for the trike 'just in case'. A soldier accompanied me to the engineering quarter in Amman. From the stares of onlookers, it was obviously a novelty to see an un-veiled western woman walking from small shop to small shop in that area. There are no microlights in Jordan, but we eventually found a wheel of the right dimensions on a small cement mixer and, triumphantly clutching my prize, I returned to the hotel. We left early the next morning and headed for Petra. We were driven in an army Land Rover while the gliders were carried in a large blue pick-up truck driven by Harun, a huge amiable bear of a man.

From the village above Petra it is impossible to see the magnificent spectacle which awaits enclosed in the folds of the canyon below. We found a place to tow launch just above the gorge on a narrow tarmac road. As Ben taxiied the trike to the right spot, our luggage trolley wheel fell off, rolled down the hill and over a cliff, never to be seen again. Harun and Ben set to work with Ben supplying the brain and Harun the brawn. In under an hour, the cement mixer wheel was in place and, as the bearing was a perfect fit, it proved to be an ideal undercarriage.

We met some Bedouin tribespeople who still lived their harsh nomadic existence. With weather-hardened features and lean bodies, they kept watch over their goats and gathered around the strange contraption being fixed beside the road.

Bill and I rigged our gliders while Niall preferred to wait until he saw how tricky the landing would be. Yasmin fretted with frustration. Flying into the canyon of Petra would require all the experience I had gleaned after thirteen years of flying and was definitely beyond her capability.

The entire police force of four officers turned out to stop the traffic and keep the crowds back. I was lined up behind the trike and ready to go, but had to wait until a meandering herd of goats had been shooed out of our path before we could launch. Finally we were clear and with a hearty take-off sprint, I followed Ben, climbing slowly into the evening sky.

The whole area was incredibly rocky, spliced by narrow fissures. The rock itself was weathered into smooth domes, like bubbles on top of a milkshake. Suddenly a canyon larger than the rest appeared ahead of us. Nestling in the bottom was the mystical city of Petra.

I released from the tow and gazed in amazement at the incongruous sight of a multitude of dramatic buildings carved out of the sheer cliff. The evening sun threw crimson light on to the rock face, highlighting the intricate colonnade of tombs with pillars and façades surrounding black gaping entrances. The amphitheatre stage was illuminated by the sunshine and its tiered seating cast long serrated shadows as two camels sauntered past, oblivious to its beauty. The scale of the place was breathtaking, with tombs and caves visible at the base of every gully and cliff.

I was losing height and became preoccupied with finding a space big enough to land within the narrow confines of the gorge. So much of the area was covered with enormous boulders which, remembering my 'elbows incident' in Switzerland, would be best avoided. I made my final glide along the line of tombs, swung the glider round and landed on a tiny path which ran up the steep slope opposite.

Bill appeared overhead and landed alongside, wide eyed at the scenery surrounding us. We de-rigged in the dark, jabbering about the incredible views and the matchless beauty of Petra. When we returned to the hotel, we found the microlight in the car park. Ben had managed a landing approach that brought him into the small passageway between the coaches and the trees. He then taxiied to the front of the hotel where he had nonchalantly 'parked' the trike in a vacant spot and strolled into the foyer.

The following morning we flew into the gorge once again. This time I wanted to try out a new camera mount which I had made specially for this trip. It was a long aluminium pole which inserted into the back of the keel and was angled upwards. With the camera on the end, I found my two lead weights did not provide enough counterweight and I had to strap Ben's cordless drill to the nose of the glider before it felt balanced! The glider was so heavy I could barely lift it and was glad of a light breeze to ease the take-off run. The flight was perfect, with the morning sunshine illuminating the city in shades of pink.

On our way back to the hotel, we were taken to see a newly discovered sixth-century Roman church. The vibrant colours of the beautiful mosaics were wonderfully preserved. It made us wonder what other treasures must lie, still undiscovered, under our feet.

There were perfect cumulus clouds developing by the time we had finished breakfast and as we were due to move on to Wadi Rum that evening, it seemed a good idea to fly there if we could. The air was rough and as Ben towed me from the take-off strip, it became much, much worse. It alarmed me to watch Ben swinging his weight from side to side to try and control the bucking trike. We hit one violent gust which made my glider's wires go loose and then twang back into tension once more. I just had time to say over the radio, 'What the hell was that?' before we were walloped again and Ben went up like a train in front of me. I released immediately. It was as rough as hell and I dared not let go with one hand to do up my harness. The wind was incredibly strong and the thermals were being blown to pieces. I dropped back onto the ridge behind Petra and, deciding that discretion was the better part of valour, I slid around the corner to land on the plateau behind.

Four Bedouin tribespeople immediately came to greet me, the welcome in their smiling faces unmistakable and, unfazed by our communication barrier, they invited me for tea. One of the men spoke a little English and kept repeating, 'Welcome, welcome, we happy you welcome in Jordan', followed by a surprising, 'John Major – good.' I responded with a diplomatic (and far more heartfelt), 'King Hussein – good', which was received with beams of delight as the love of the King amongst the Bedouin is genuine and deep.

They took me to their tent, where I was introduced to the rest of the family. The oldest woman's face was patterned with deep blue tattoos and she would not let go of my hand as she was so delighted to welcome a stranger into her home.

Their large rectangular tent, open on one side, was carpeted with colourful rugs and cushions. The pungent smell of goat hair blankets and the smoke from the open fire enveloped me as sweet tea was distributed in tiny glasses. Following their wonderful hospitality, they extracted an ancient pick-up truck from the midst of their herd of goats and gave me a lift back to Petra.

Yasmin's frustration was eased as Ben offered her the back seat of the microlight to fly down to Wadi Rum as his passenger. The wind was increasing, so they waited until the morning to set off, while the rest of us piled into the Land Rover and headed for Wadi Rum, favourite place of Lawrence of Arabia and location for the epic film about his life.

As the Rift Valley escarpment fell away into the painted southern desert, the red rocks of the highlands had been eroded into giant columns that stained the sands below in multiple shades of ochre and red. Thermal winds had dropped white splashes of Arabian sands across these, painting a surreal canvas on the desert floor.

The wind increased as we drove south, and the sand blew in swirling swathes across the road in front of us, eventually becoming as thick as fog, slowing us down to a crawl along the main highway. We could see nothing of the fabled scenery as we reached the Wadi Rum valley and the rest house where we were to stay.

As night fell, the wind dropped and the sand settled once more. The vast silhouettes of the cliffs which bordered the valley on both sides loomed imposingly against the star-studded sky. A half moon rose above the eastern ridge and cast an ethereal silver glow, illuminating the rocks.

After a delicious supper of humus, tabbouleh and pitta bread, Bill entertained everyone within a three-mile radius with his unique rendition of 'La Bamba', complete with ear-splitting trills. The D-string on his guitar broke, unable to cope with the volume, but the show went on as Bill continued his international repertoire with the decibels mounting. When the impromptu concert had finished, the silence of the desert enveloped us as we walked through the cool sand to our tents. I was impatient for the morning to arrive so that I could see in daylight what the tantalising night time vision promised. I woke at 6 a.m. and gasped as I clambered from my tent.

In all my years of travelling, I had never beheld such a scene. The huge vertical crags on both sides of the mile-wide valley towered 3,000 feet above the desert floor and stretched as far as I could see in both directions. The walls of rock were not solid, but eroded into separate blocks like buildings along a street. Deep alleys divided the crags which formed ramparts of redness contrasting with the yellow sand of the featureless desert below. The mountain tops were eroded into contorted shapes, convoluted and bulging, as the early rays of the sun highlighted their patterns in shades of red and orange.

Ben and Yasmin arrived before midday with Yasmin smiling from ear to ear and ranting about the flight. They had had to refuel on the way at the airstrip on the King's Highway, where the runway was actually a widened section of the road. As they approached, Ben could see a long line of traffic snaking miles off into the desert along a track to bypass this section.

'We had better not land there, there is obviously a large aircraft expected,' Ben said to Yasmin, altering his course to avoid the area.

'No, Ben, the runway has been cleared for you,' Yasmin replied.

Still warily keeping an eye out for other aircraft, Ben landed the trike on the road. A policeman approached and politely welcomed them, saying they had been on duty, awaiting the arrival of the microlight, for twenty-four hours. They didn't seem at all put out and took Yasmin to a nearby garage to buy petrol. On discovering that the pumps wouldn't work as the local electricity had been cut off, the police escorted Yasmin to where two workmen were mending a pylon. The police then insisted the men hurry and reconnect the supply as they were holding up an aircraft that was on an important mission!

During the day, the conditions became extreme. The combination of desert heat, baking rock faces and strong winds caused violent sandstorms. We rested, rode camels and walked around the tiny village of Rum, where the Bedouin had set up permanent breezeblock homes. They survived by supplying services to the tourists, hiring out camels or, for the faint hearted, four-wheel drive jeeps to go into the desert.

Yasmin and I were sharing a small tent. She had developed a cough which kept both of us awake until midnight. Finally we fell asleep and the following morning, conditions were much calmer. We rigged our gliders on the small tarmac road which we were using as a runway. Yasmin was to take the first tow before the thermals had a chance to increase the wind strength.

Again, she was nervous, but wild horses wouldn't have stopped her, so determined was she to fly in Wadi Rum. I went through the take-off procedure to refresh her memory, speaking in calm, measured tones which belied my anxiety. As usual her take-off was dodgy. The wheels touched the ground, she scraped her knees on the road, and bounced into the air.

With relief I watched her sail upwards, listening to Ben's calming banter over the radio.

'That's good Yasmin, pull in a little more ... that's right ... a little more still ... pull in hard ... perfect, keep it there ...'

At 1,000 feet, he told her to release and she floated gently down to flop on to the sand nearby. She was radiant as she walked back towards us, and she was lost for words at the beauty of the landscape.

Bill and Niall both flew and returned to earth raving about the scenery. Ben then towed me up alongside the majestic crags. We were two tiny dots joined by an umbilical cord against an enormous backdrop of cliffs. The view from the air was quite different and I felt as though I was a part of the glorious scenery, rather than looking at it from the outside. I released at 4,000 feet above the valley floor, higher than the tops of the mountains. At either end of the valley, the cliffs dispersed into solitary, free-standing lumps eroded into contorted shapes. The desert stretched in every direction as far as I could see. Far below me, a group of camels sauntered along, dragging their long shadows across the sand.

After we had finished flying that morning, we parked our gliders next to the rest house, where Ben was waylaid by one of the Bedouin, who tried to buy his microlight for three camels. The wind did not abate again until 3 a.m. and to make the most of it we were again rigged and ready before 5.30 a.m. I hooked on the tow line and took off behind Ben as normal, blissfully unaware of what he had in store for me. As soon as we left the ground he flew towards a deep fissure which slashed straight through the mountain on the opposite side of the valley. A hang glider on tow is like a dog on a leash and where the microlight leads, so the hang glider must follow.

'Ben ... what are you doing, Ben?' I asked warily as we neared the crack.

'Trust me!' came the reply over the radio. I always hated it when Ben said that, as it always meant he was about to do something guaranteed to scare me witless.

Sure enough, he entered the canyon near the top at its widest part which was sixty yards across, leaving precious little room between my wingtip and the rock walls. My knuckles were white on the bar as I maintained a feverish grip. I made the mistake of looking down and was confronted by an abyss which dropped 3,000 feet to the base of the mountain. The sense of vertigo appalled me. After what seemed like an age we burst into the sunshine on the far side and the air was blue as I repeatedly cursed Ben over the radio. He retaliated in the only way he could, with another verse of a Leonard Cohen lament.

It was Yasmin's turn again, but this time the wind was completely still. Without a breath of headwind to help her launch, her luck ran out. She did an even worse take-off run than usual, bounced hard on the wheels and broke both uprights. Ben stopped instantly, but the short skid along the road had given Yasmin gravel rash on both forearms, which bled profusely. True to form, she did not fuss, but only wanted to know what she had done wrong.

We replaced her uprights, bandaged her arms and left for our next port of call, the Dead Sea. Ben flew the trike across the sun-baked hills with nowhere to land for forty miles. He arrived at Mazara three hours later and landed on the main road in the centre of town. He was surrounded by hundreds of people all welcoming him, wanting to know where he had come from and what he was doing flying such a strange aircraft. He had just started his second glass of sweet tea when the police arrived and 'arrested' him.

One of the officers tried to attach a piece of string to the wheel of the microlight so that he could tow it back to the police station. Ben told him that it would be much safer if he flew the trike to the compound, and after taking his passport the policeman agreed.

The policeman told Ben to follow him as he got into his car and turned left onto the main road. Ben had to face into the wind and so turned right and took off. The policeman, thinking Ben was pulling a fast one, did a U-turn to follow him, just as Ben turned around to follow the police car. Finding himself face to face with the microlight, the policeman performed another about face and drove very slowly back to the station. Meanwhile Ben had to S-turn madly behind the car to avoid overtaking it. He landed inside the police compound where they rapidly discovered that he was a tourist and made up for their mistake by arguing that they had brought him to the station for his own protection. They fed him lunch and copious quantities of mint tea, and by the time we arrived, he was catching up on his sleep in a police cell.

One of my goals for the expedition was to make the lowest documented flight on a hang glider. While the others went to set up their gliders on the shore of the Dead Sea, Ben towed me up from the main road outside the police station. Now our presence had been explained, the police could not have been more helpful. The air felt syrupy as we were already well below sea level and as a result, the trike climbed much faster than usual.

I released near the shoreline of the Dead Sea and descended very slowly in the smooth evening conditions. The sea was as calm as a mill pond, with the sun sinking and casting a golden shimmer across its surface. Looking across the green-blue water and yellow sandbars into Israel, it was hard to believe the political turmoil taking place in the area.

My altimeter read 967 feet below sea level as I made my final approach onto the beach, finishing the flight with a perfect landing, made so much easier by the high density of the air.

Niall and Bill both flew, but Yasmin declined as it was getting dark and she was still a little unsure after her accident that morning. Ben then towed me back to the police station, where the trike was to be parked overnight. It was already dark and the lights twinkled from Mazara, mirrored on the opposite side of the sea in Israel.

I was glad I had memorised where the barbed wire and power cables surrounded the police station as I couldn't see them in the darkness. The policeman in charge was thrilled to see us as he was usually left to hold the fort overnight on his own. He gave us each a bowl of cold water to bathe our feet and a glass of mint tea. After the sweaty heat of the journey and the stifling temperatures on the Dead Sea shore, there could not have been a more perfect end to the day. The Land Rover came to pick us up and we stayed in a hotel high on the escarpment in the town of Kerak next door to a castle built by the crusaders in AD 1142.

We moved on the following day to Jerash, an extraordinarily well-preserved Roman city north of Amman. We arrived in the early evening to find we had the place to ourselves as we wandered around the roads, made from flagstones which were deeply rutted from the wheels of Roman chariots. It dated back to the first century AD, although the area has been populated since Neolithic times. The main colonnaded street opened into an oval forum at the south end. The adjacent amphitheatre seated 3,000 and is still used for the annual Jerash festival.

We found a suitable road to tow from, just above the city, where we rigged the gliders the following day. Again the landing area was very restricted and the take-off was tricky, so Yasmin had to resort to 'crowd control' and doing an interview for Jordanian TV, who had turned up to film her. The city of Jerash looked quite different from above, where the overwhelming impression was of a perfect geometric pattern formed by the streets.

After an unforgettable morning's flying, it was time to return to Amman. Ben went by Land Rover, allowing me to fly the microlight back to Marka Airport. The contrast in the scenery was vivid as the fertile green hills of Gilead gave way to the brown, arid slopes surrounding the capital.

We dedicated our last morning to getting Yasmin airborne. She had been restricted in where she could fly because of her inexperience, but now we were back in Amman, she had the room for error which she needed. I acted as ground control with a radio in either hand, one set to the frequency of the control tower, the other to Ben's channel. This would allow Ben to talk freely to Yasmin on tow without blocking the airport frequency.

We all held our breath as Yasmin prepared for her first launch since her accident in Wadi Rum. We were given the 'all clear' from the tower and she gave Ben the signal to go. Again her take-off was bad, but with a light headwind helping, she got away with it. I could hear Ben chatting to her and she obeyed every command, determined her last flight was going to be a good one. She stayed on the tow until they reached her all-time record height of 2,500 feet above the ground. She released and meandered slowly, feasting her eyes on the stupendous view of her birthplace.

'What do you think of this then, Yasmin?' Ben asked.

'Flipping bloody amazing,' came the reply. We had never heard such language from Yasmin, but then again, she had never flown at 2,500 feet above Amman before.

The tower called me on the radio. 'I have a Hercules inbound arriving in ten minutes, do you want me to get him to hold his position until the hang glider has landed?'

I thought quickly. Yasmin was descending nicely and would be on the ground before he arrived. 'Negative, Amman tower, the Hercules can come straight in,' I replied to him.

The huge plane lumbered into view in the distance and, simultaneously, Yasmin's descent rate seemed to slow down. I thought I had better pre-empt any problem. 'Yasmin, do not, I repeat, do not cross the runway. Stay above the taxiway on your landing approach, do you understand?'

'Yes, I understand,' she replied. 'I will stay above the taxiway.'

She continued to float slowly downwards while the Hercules turned on final approach to the runway.

'Please don't turn and look behind you Yasmin,' I muttered to myself. Yasmin and the Hercules were on their final approach and performed a perfectly synchronised landing. Yasmin had not even noticed the four thundering propellers hurtling past as she was far too busy enjoying her flight.

We sadly packed up the trike and gliders and put them in their boxes to freight back to England. Prince Feisal tracked us down once more to find out how we had fared. He was subjected to a half-hour session from us as we enthused about Jordan. He mentioned that he had told His Majesty King Hussein about our visit and that the King had requested to meet us. We were told to be at the Royal Squadron building at 5 p.m.

I had wanted to meet King Hussein for many years as his passion for flying was legendary. Wearing our best clothes, we were escorted to the Royal Squadron building, where we were surrounded by medal-bedecked, uniformed personnel.

The King arrived with a beaming smile, apologising for being late! He had good humour etched into his face and he put us at ease as he asked about our trip. His interest was obviously genuine and our enjoyment of his country delighted him. It was a small insight into why his people love him so much. He has an extraordinary mixture of strength and humility and impressed us all greatly. After half an hour he took his leave, apologising once more for having to go so soon.

Two weeks had passed so quickly and we barely scratched the surface of this beautiful country. There was so much more to see and flying to enjoy. The Jordanian people had overwhelmed us with their hospitality. There are few countries in the world where pilots are encouraged to fly among the national monuments and parks. The courtesy and kindness we encountered wherever we went was unforgettable.

As we left Amman, Ben and I had no idea that within a year we would be back under very different circumstances and that the bond we had forged with Jordan would last a lifetime.

CHAPTER 19

Courage from Within

The 1993 British competition season began soon after my return from Jordan, and I had entered both hang gliding and paragliding Leagues. I was keen to start flying in paragliding competitions even though I had only twenty hours' airtime and felt I could learn a lot from flying alongside the best pilots in Britain.

I had outgrown my Apache paraglider, so I was given a high-performance Navajo to replace it. During the week preceding the first competition, inclement weather prevented me from trying it, so my maiden flight was the first task! I had been warned that ground handling was much more difficult with a high-performance paraglider, and the odds were stacked against me as this was my biggest weakness. I watched with envy as I saw skilful pilots' canopies appear docile, obedient and predictable. It was by sheer luck that it took me only three attempts to convert my thrashing, wilful mass of material into some sort of flying machine and managed to launch.

The thermals were narrow but strong and I cranked the Navajo into a steeply banked turn using the same force as I had with the Apache. The difference the new nimble wing made was like riding a thoroughbred horse after hours on a plodding, pony-trekking nag. I was oblivious to the glorious view of the rolling Yorkshire Dales beneath as I struggled to get a grip on the new twitchy beast from which I was hanging.

Robbie Whittall was just above me in the thermal and I heard him shout a warning to me. I didn't hear his words. The canopy suddenly lost its 'solid' feel and the world turned at a peculiar angle and began to rotate at an alarming speed. I had pulled too hard on the left brake handle and had entered a spin. I was losing height fast and needed to react immediately to avoid hitting the hilltop 300 feet below.

This time I recognised what was happening and raised both brake handles. The glider recovered quickly, but in just one rotation I had lost most of my height and was shaken by just how quickly things can go wrong on a paraglider if you don't know what you're doing. I recovered my composure and found another thermal. This time I was much more conservative in my use of the brakes and was more respectful of the Navajo. I went on to fly forty miles, the fourth best distance of the day, but the satisfaction was tainted by the knowledge that I still had so much to learn and had come so alarmingly close to a serious accident.

This new paraglider would not tolerate my inexperience, as the Apache had done. Robbie gave me a dressing down later about flying in a danger-ous manner. My only excuse was that my entire experience of paragliding had been gained on the Apache and I didn't realise that different canopies required different amounts of brake pressure. I was humbled and only too anxious to accept advice from anyone who could help.

I was selected to fly for Britain in the World Paragliding Championships in Switzerland in July. Several of the top paraglider pilots at the time had come from the world of hang gliding (Robbie was the current World Champion in paragliding having previously been World Hang Gliding Champion in 1989) so the selectors thought I had a reasonably good chance of doing well, assuming I managed to get to grips with flying my new paraglider. The paragliding championship teams were different from hang gliding, in that rather than have a separate women's competition, teams had to contain two female pilots. They competed alongside the men and the highest placed woman became Women's World Champion. I managed almost to double my flying hours before leaving for France, where the second leg of the British Paragliding Nationals was to be held prior to the world championship.

The alpine light wind conditions were new to me, and although I had plenty of experience of hang gliding in the Alps, I still had a lot to learn about paragliding. This became painfully clear on day two of my stay. On my first high-altitude take-off with the wind flat calm, I did not slow the Navajo down sufficiently. As I ran towards the edge as fast as I could, the canopy accelerated and overtook me. I tripped over a tree root and fell, badly spraining my knee. The doctor in town confirmed a ligament sprain and applied a tensioned elastic strapping, which supported the joint. He told me I should not fly for three days.

After three days, the knee was a lot less painful, so I removed the strapping and went up the mountain to fly. What I hadn't realised was that it was only the specially applied tension plaster that was keeping the knee supported and pain free, effectively doing the job of the ligament. The whole joint felt unstable but I applied my 'mind over matter' expertise and prepared to launch. As I inflated the canopy, a gust of wind blew me sideways and with a cry of agony I collapsed as my knee gave way again. I had learned my lesson and was forced to forego flying in the Nationals to allow my leg to heal in order to be fit to fly in the World Championships in two weeks' time.

The seven members of the British team drove to Verbier in Switzerland a week before the championships. The picturesque ski village was perched on a high grassy ledge, surrounded by huge snow-capped peaks and pine forests. I still could not fly as my leg was weak, useless and painful. The physiotherapist in the village was excellent, administering a daily deep massage of my knee. It was painful, but each day there was a slight improvement which gave me hope. I met an English ski fanatic who lived in Verbier who had sprained both her knees on several occasions. She had a variety of leg braces, which ranged from a rigid plaster cast-style immobiliser, to an elastic bandage with metal strips at the sides. I borrowed an unattractive but sturdy plastic brace which allowed me to bend the knee, but not to twist it.

I knew that my take-offs were still bad and under normal circumstances, I would have gone to the training slope and practised again and again until I had learned the correct technique. With my knee, this was not possible, so I spent my time watching the other pilots train.

Jocky Sanderson was our team manager and helped a lot when I eventually flew again, three days before the competition started. He rigged up a foot support on my harness to take the weight of my leg once I was in the air, and made sure he was standing by each time I launched, ready to hold on to my harness to ensure I was not dragged sideways. I developed a technique of landing on one foot to avoid further damage to my knee.

The paraglider felt febrile in the rough alpine air and I experienced my first big collapses. It became less stressful as I had more of them and began to trust my ability to make the canopy recover. In time, I learned how to feel the pressure in the canopy through the brake handles and literally through the seat of my pants. As the pressure dropped on one side, I found that if I reacted quickly enough, I could prevent it from collapsing or at least minimise the proportion of the wing which collapsed.

It was strange coming to terms with paragliding in turbulence, as it was possible temporarily to lose the canopy completely. It seemed that wherever I looked around the Verbier skies, there would be someone flying with half their wing flailing uselessly behind them, pumping away with their brake handles to recover their full canopy.

The day before the competition, I had another bad launch where I hit my leg on a rock, causing a deep soft-tissue injury. I now had a bi-lateral limp and confused the physio on my daily visit by asking him to work on my other leg instead. He had some fairly exotic alternative ideas and advised me to take tepid salt baths because, as we originally evolved from creatures of the sea, sitting in a salt bath would remind the body molecules of their basic state, thus speeding up the healing process. It was a sure sign of how desperate I was that I actually followed his advice!

I was shocked by the chaotic launch system of a paragliding competition. There were two possibilities: first was a 'ready, steady, go' start where all 125 competitors laid out their canopies within a small space on the hillside and launched together. The first time I saw this, I hung back for five minutes to watch in disbelief. The air became hugely overcrowded as all the competitors flew simultaneously into the same thermal at roughly the same height.

For the second launch option, the pilots took off one at a time, making the launch less stressful, but the queuing system caused a shambolic crush around the three tiny openings in the fence around the launch area. The pilots, already dressed in all their gear, harnesses on and paragliders bundled up in their hands, formed a suffocating crush, pushing and shoving to try to speed their way to launch. It was a relief to take off and be free of the crowd.

On the first day of the competition, I got to goal and was wearing the biggest grin in the landing field. By day three, however, things changed as I took off in turbulent air without enough brake pressure. I had a collapse at fifteen feet and hit the hill hard with my shoulder, spraining all the ligaments. My team mates were humming 'Three Wheels on my Wagon!' as I was now down to one sound limb out of four.

I asked Jocky to accompany me to the nursery slopes and teach me to take off in light winds. Poor Jocky, supposed to be managing the British Team – the *crème de la crème* of British pilots – having to teach me the utter basics of alpine launches. It was an excruciatingly painful lesson for my damaged joints, but worth it as I had no more failed take-offs.

The rest of the competition passed in a haze of pain. I swallowed eight Nurofen a day and it was grim to be able to do so little. Luckily Sarah Fenwick, who had been my driver in Australia several years before and who had now proven herself as a competent paraglider pilot, was the other woman on the team. She helped me to dress and provided a much needed shoulder to cry on when the frustration and pain became too much.

I continued to fly each day, but could not carry my paraglider bag as I could barely walk. On each of the valley crossings, I let go of the brakes, using the opportunity of the smooth air to try and rest my arm and legs. I made it through to the finals, but my results got steadily worse and I finished in seventy-fifth place.

I came home and had several weeks of physiotherapy to get my limbs back in full working order. Once on the road to recovery, I finally made time to do the groundhandling and take-off practice that I should have done a year earlier. Then, out of the blue one morning, came the phone call that would change the direction of my life.

'Judy, it's Ben. I'm afraid I've got bad news. Yasmin has got lung cancer.'

The blunt words were so unexpected they made me reel with shock. Yasmin was twenty-four and a non-smoker, definitely not the sort of person anyone would imagine contracting such an illness.

Yasmin and I had shared a room throughout our stay in Jordan and I had noticed her persistent cough. It was a strange-sounding cough that I had only heard once before in a friend who was suffering from lung cancer. I dismissed this as a possibility at the time, though I had urged Yasmin to go and see a doctor in Jordan. Now, two months later, the diagnosis for Yasmin was as grim as could be.

I went straight to London to see her at the Royal Marsden Hospital as she was due to start chemotherapy the following day. Yasmin was very pale and had lost weight. Her parents were at her bedside but they were no longer the sparkling, animated pair that we had met in Amman. They looked drawn and there was devastation in their faces. Yasmin feverishly pressed the oxygen mask to her face as she was seized by another coughing fit, struggling for breath and fighting the rising feeling of panic. I could not hold back my tears as I watched her face and knew in my heart that she would not survive.

Over the next three months, Yasmin made some progress. She grew very thin and pale, her glorious unruly curls fell out, but the sparkle returned to her eyes. Her mother reflected every slight improvement in Yasmin's condition and fussed around her happily, trying to encourage her to eat. Ben and I went to visit regularly and he amused her by drawing endless cartoons which papered the walls of her hospital room. Often the pictures would gently tease her or her parents, bringing some welcome laughter into the room.

Ben was looking for a new adventure to tempt Yasmin with, to give her something to aim towards and to think about. Roy Castle had by then enjoyed two years of quality remission during which he had achieved a great deal. We hoped for the same for Yasmin, and Ben suggested a three-month trip, flying down the west coast of America in a microlight. Yasmin's eyes lit up, but her parents were against the idea as the trip would be too long and too far away from a hospital.

'How about flying from England to Amman?' I suggested as an alternative. All sides were satisfied with this option and the adventure was christened 'Flight for Life'.

Ben would fly the microlight with Yasmin as passenger and I would help to organise the logistics of the trip. Yasmin was still so weak that the departure date was left vague, scheduled for sometime the following year when she was stronger.

Yasmin was keen to use the flight to raise money for cancer research. I had seen the work of the Cancer Research Campaign in action as my sister, Toni, was working for the Appeals Department of Manchester's Christie Hospital where her husband Peter Stern was head of immunology. His work was funded directly by the Cancer Research Campaign, so Ben and I took Yasmin to the Campaign's head office in London where we devised a fund raising strategy. Ben's creative brain sprang into action and he designed a glossy brochure and busied himself drumming up support from potential sponsors.

One of the biggest obstacles to flying to Jordan was obtaining permission to pass through Syria. In such a politically sensitive area, recreational flying is unheard of and it was not a straightforward matter to fly through the country.

I wrote to King Hussein, telling him of Yasmin's illness and asking him if he would be the Patron of 'Flight for Life'. He agreed immediately and, as he was staying in England at the time, decided to drop round to my flat to discuss how he could be of assistance. I had twenty minutes' notice of his arrival, barely time to panic. I had never received royalty before! He put me at my ease immediately by wandering into the kitchen, offering to help make the tea. We sat down to discuss the plans for 'Flight for Life' and what he could do to ease the bureaucratic problems. He volunteered to write to the Syrian and Turkish authorities to request permission for us. He then asked for Yasmin's phone number so that he could get in touch with her. He was genuinely upset to hear about her cancer and I was struck once more by his great humanity.

Yasmin spent Christmas in Jordan, but by late January was back in hospital in London with a lung infection. As Ben and I walked in, an air of gloom hung heavily as Yasmin lay in bed, skeletally thin with a sparse fuzz of hair where her ringlets had once been. I hugged her gently, afraid of crushing her frail body. Ghazi and Isa were at her beside, their faces once more expressionless with pain. The doctors had discovered another shadow on her lung and each time she coughed she doubled up with pain. She never complained, putting on a brave face regardless, but watching her try to walk across her hospital room, hunched and breathless, made tears well in my eyes as the inevitable outcome of her battle stared us in the face.

It became obvious that Yasmin would never be well enough to accompany Ben on 'Flight for Life'. We decided to bring the departure date forward so that the journey would happen while she was still alive and could meet Ben in Amman when he arrived.

On 1 February, Yasmin's best friend, Nick, phoned me. In tears, he told me that the doctors had said there was nothing more they could do for Yasmin as the cancer had returned in force. Ben and I met him at the hospital. Yasmin was back on oxygen full time, breathing as lightly as a sparrow. Ben plucked up his courage and asked her, 'If you are no longer here, do you want "Flight for Life" to go ahead without you?'

'Yes!' said Yasmin emphatically.

I averted my gaze to hide my tears. She was a woman of great courage.

'Yasmin, if it were possible, would you like to fly once more?' Ben asked her. Her eyes lit up and her ear-to-ear grin spread as she nodded.

Ben arranged to borrow a trike from a microlight school at RAF Holton which was the nearest airfield to London that he could find. Time was of the essence as she was becoming weaker by the day. Yasmin's doctors agreed that she could fly if she wanted to and her parents bravely gave their consent.

Ben drove Yasmin, her parents and Nick to the airfield. I met them there, my car stuffed to the gunwales with every item of warm clothing I possessed. The day was unusually mild for February, but Yasmin now weighed less than five stone and needed to wrap up well. While Ben prepared the trike, I helped her to dress in several layers of fleece, topped with my down jacket, moon boots, two balaclavas and gloves. She exchanged her massive oxygen bottle from the hospital for the smaller portable one which she could use for the flight. Ben lifted her into the trike and climbed into the front seat, stuffing her oxygen bottle down the front of his jacket.

We watched as Ben taxiied to the runway, and as they took off, I could not stop the tears from running down my face. The sky was sapphire blue and studded with cumulus clouds. They swooped around the tops of the clouds, chased birds around the sky and flew low over the hedgerows. Throughout the flight Yasmin remained calm and joyous. 'Now I know what it's like to be an angel,' she told Ben quietly.

Half an hour later they landed and taxiied back to the hangar. Yasmin was beaming, her eyes bright and sparkling. She hardly spoke, but the expression on her face said it all.

As I said goodbye to Yasmin, I knew that I would never see her again. We hugged closely and as I looked into her eyes, her spirit, so vibrant and strong, shone brighter than ever.

The following evening I was on a plane bound for Brazil to compete in the Paragliding World Cup in Governador Valedares, where I had flown in the hang gliding pre-world championships four years earlier. I had booked the flight months before and although it was hard to leave, I knew there was nothing more I could do and now was the time for Yasmin's family to be close to her.

I soon regretted my decision to leave as the daily faxes I received from Ben told of Yasmin's decline. I could not concentrate on a flying competition, it all suddenly seemed so irrelevant. I felt I should be at home supporting Ben, who was now going alone to the hospital.

There was a new face at breakfast one morning when I walked into the hotel dining room. He was already comfortably chatting with some of the British team as I sat down nearby.

'You must be Chris Dawes,' I said, correctly assuming him to be the last of the British pilots to arrive.

He looked me straight in the eye and said, 'Why? Do I owe you money?' and burst into a peal of laughter.

It was Sarah Fenwick who, disturbed by my single state since my separation from Trevor two years before, had talked about Chris with a matchmaking glint in her eye. The very word 'relationship' was enough to send me running into the nearest dark corner to hide, so I ignored her efforts at playing Cupid.

Later that morning, as we waited for the van to arrive to take us up the mountain, Chris enlightened me on the finer points of seaweed farming.

He was a marine biologist, specialising in seaweed cultivation, and managed to make the subject fascinating to someone whose sole experience of the stuff was popping the cells of bladder wrack whilst fishing in rock pools as a child. He seemed very easy-going, with a refreshing lack of hang-ups, and had a disarming honesty about him. I liked him enormously and enjoyed his company.

I returned early from flying one afternoon to find a fax from Ben. He had said, 'goodbye' to Yasmin and had left her family to be alone with her at the end. I felt so sad and numb to think that her death was imminent. Chris saw me wandering blindly down the corridor and took me for a coffee. I blurted out the story about Yasmin and he listened with understanding and sensitivity. He then told me about his grandmother's death, with tears welling in his eyes as he spoke of her relief from the suffering of illness. He hugged me as I cried, and I felt the warmth of someone who understands the need for human contact at a time like that.

Two days later a fax from Ben arrived at breakfast with the message, 'Yasmin has lapsed into unconsciousness. Her fight for life is over.'

I went up the mountain with the others, in a daze. The conditions were very unstable, causing huge downpours out in the valley. I sat alone and watched the dramatic sky with dark grey clouds weeping as I, too, cried. Occasional rays of sun burst through, forming lines of radiance against the gloom.

At one o'clock, a task was set and I went flying, this time for Yasmin. I left the gaggle of gliders behind and flew off on my own. I was soon joined by a big flock of turkey vultures. Instead of the usual circling pattern which they used to gain height, these birds swooped and wove around me, turning tightly, surrounding me, exulting in the smooth air. I felt a strong sense of Yasmin's spirit and her release from pain and landed some time later, smiling through my tears.

I phoned Ben that evening and he told me that Yasmin had died.

I was back in England within a few days and met up with Ben. We resolved that 'Flight for Life' should go ahead according to Yasmin's wishes, and that instead of Ben flying alone, we would both fly to Jordan in separate trikes and each of us would carry a cameraman in the passenger seat to make a documentary of the journey. We both found it incredibly hard to pick up the pieces, as we had lost our main reason for doing the flight. We decided to fix a departure date which would give us a deadline to work towards. We made a pledge that this would be our priority for the year and I resigned from the Hang Gliding League, withdrew from the

European Paragliding Championships and the first leg of the National Paragliding Championships. It was going to take all our energy to organise everything in time for our departure, which we decided would be 15 May.

This gave us two months to secure permission to fly through nine countries, and to arrange for the loan, hire or purchase of two microlights, helmets, intercoms and instruments. We would need huge numbers of maps, a GPS satellite navigation set, tools, cameras, films, sponsorship brochures, a film company for the documentary, spare parts for the trike engines and money to buy fuel, accommodation and landing fees along the way.

It was a tall order, as Ben and I had little emotional reserve to help us through. However, during the next two months, just as things would threaten to envelop us, fate seemed to intervene on an uncannily regular basis. Ben would phone me in the morning with a major problem; for example, we needed spare parts for the motors but could not afford to buy them. By the same afternoon, a totally different sounding Ben would call saying that he had received a call from Cyclone Hovercraft who had heard about the flight and had spontaneously offered to help by supplying spares. It happened so frequently that we became convinced that Yasmin's spirit was around and working with us.

Fate intervened again when I was invited to a party in Dorset. I was delighted to find Chris was there and we spent a lot of time together. His camper van had broken down with a major engine fault and would be in the garage for another week. He had a plane to catch at Heathrow and as I was driving that way, I offered to give him a lift.

The IRA had chosen that very evening to fire mortar bombs into Heathrow. We were confronted by an impenetrable barrier of blue flashing lights and the police were turning everyone away as the airport had been closed. Chris came back to stay at my flat and that evening, in an atmosphere of great gentleness and friendship, we began a relationship which has been different from any I have known and has gone from strength to strength.

It was a shock to my system as, shortly before I met Chris, I had concluded that the part of me that could love a man had been broken by my experience of marriage. I had not been attracted to anyone since my separation from Trevor and had resigned myself to living alone. The realisation had been profoundly depressing, but I was beginning to come to terms with it when Chris burst into my life. He was so different from anyone I had ever met, so honest and open. The man I met over breakfast in Brazil is the same man I am now happily married to. His universal good humour and energetic enjoyment of life are infectious and a joy to share.

My run of luck continued as Citroën stepped in to solve the financial difficulties of 'Flight for Life'. Marc Raven donated the Citroën microlight to the project, saying I could sell it afterwards to fund the flight, with any extra money going to the Cancer Research Campaign. They also gave me the name of a contact at Total Oil who generously gave £1,000 to cover the cost of the fuel.

The film was to be made by Sid Perou and Gavin Crowther, both of whom were with us on the Kenyan expedition. Sid's wife Alison had been suffering from breast cancer, so he had his own reason for wanting to make the journey. We bought a second-hand microlight, which was the same model as the Citroën trike, for Ben to fly. Ben and I divided the work we needed to do before we left for Jordan. Ben dealt with the practical side of things – engines, tools, spares etc. – and I was responsible for all paperwork and permissions.

The job of obtaining permission to enter certain countries was frustrating. Hungary, the Czech and Slovak Republics, and Germany responded immediately and positively. The further east we were to fly, the more difficult it was to find the right person and obtain the necessary pieces of paper. Everything finally came together in the last week after endless phone calls. Colonel Ali Shukri, King Hussein's assistant, called to say permission had been granted by both Syria and Turkey, though the Syrians would not give us visas until two days before we left. Romania sent through the relevant documentation with twenty-four hours to spare, thanks to the last-minute intervention and pushing from the British Embassy in Bucharest. Only Bulgarian permission was missing and I could not get through to the right people. In desperation I called Dimitar Dimov, a friend in Sofia. When he heard of our plight, he took the day off work to sort out the paperwork for us, delivering the information to the Ministry of Foreign Affairs in person. Having seen him in action when I visited Bulgaria in 1989, I knew if anyone could produce the miracle we needed, he could, though it was no mean feat to hurry bureaucracy in Sofia. We would have to leave without permission to enter Bulgaria and trust Dimitar to sort out the necessary paperwork before we arrived at the border.

We would be flying unsupported, carrying all our supplies and spares with us on board the microlights, including Sid and Gavin and all their equipment. We would have no room to carry any food and so would have to refuel the crew at the same time as the trikes *en route*.

227

We had a dedicated support team at home comprising Nick, John Benfield (a university friend of Yasmin's) and my long-suffering parents. We had offers of help from many quarters, one man offering to fly spares out to us in his Cessna if anything went wrong.

Packing clothes was easy. Our limited space and weight allowed one change of clothes, a toothbrush and a comb. We had one tube of toothpaste between us and I allowed myself the luxury of a tiny pot of face cream. This would be minimalist travel in the extreme.

The night before we were due to leave, we gathered at Ben's house. It was packed full with Nick, John, Ben and his girlfriend Chrissie, Chris and myself. I sent a final fax to Ghazi and Isa saying, 'Tomorrow we leave for Jordan, with Yasmin's spirit.'

CHAPTER 20

Flight For Life

The hangar doors groaned in protest as we opened them. Inside, the unsuspecting Citroën trike and Ben's craft, named Spirit of Yasmin, waited in their snug housing. We were to fly the short distance to Blenheim Palace, the official start of our 2,500-mile journey where we would load up the trikes and bid farewell to family and friends. As we warmed up the engines the atmosphere was one of excitement tinged with apprehension at what lay ahead.

Microlights were not my speciality and although I had a hundred flying hours logged, they had mostly been in pleasant conditions above familiar terrain and I was a little concerned about my ability to cope. It was just as well I did not know what was in store over the next fifteen days.

We landed at Kidlington airport near to Blenheim Palace, where a crowd of wellwishers had gathered to wave us off. Ben sighed in disbelief as poor Sid vomited into the grass. We hadn't even started our journey in earnest and he was airsick already!

We had not had a trial run of loading all our luggage into the trikes and despite packing everything tightly together, it wouldn't fit. We had to unload and repack, ruthlessly leaving non-essentials behind. As our first priority, we took a spare jerry can of fuel each, strapped to the side of our trikes, plus a jerry can of good quality 2-stroke oil, tools, spares and a filter-funnel. Next on the list were our waterproof tubs stuffed with paperwork – licences, permissions and registration documents. There were video cameras, batteries and tapes, stills cameras, films and mounts to fit in, sleeping bags were stashed inside the wings and finally, in the tiny space remaining, we stored personal items. It was a huge sacrifice to leave my two books behind, and Gavin's washbag had to be jettisoned with its non-essential items such as hair gel and a dozen assorted potions. By the time we had finished, our microlights were stuffed to the gunwales and they were seventy-five kilograms over the maximum recommended take-off weight.

We posed for photographs and said our goodbyes, then climbed into the trikes and started the engines. Chris held my hand and kissed the front of my visor. He had been so supportive in the build-up to the flight, especially over the past few weeks when the paperwork had driven me into a daily frenzy. There was no time to linger as we were already behind schedule due to our repacking fiasco. We taxied to the runway and after a take-off roll that seemed to need infinity and beyond, we staggered into the air and set course for Headcorn Airfield in Kent.

After clearing customs at Headcorn, our take-off run seemed even more arduous with the microlights bucking and groaning over the rough grass strip as the excessive weight put strain on their undercarriages. The wind had calmed and the clouds melted, leaving a beautifully clear sky as we headed southeast over the English Channel towards France. The late afternoon sun laid a golden path on the calm surface of the sea. My grip was unnecessarily hard and my ears strained for any change in the tune of the engine as I remembered the tragic time I had made this journey when Peter Keele had died.

My relief at spotting Cap Gris Nez was diminished by the huge, black, towering cloud that straddled our path. It was a cold front that had arrived from the Atlantic and we were left with no option but to fly through it. The rain that ran across our visors and down our necks temporarily dampened our spirits, but the sight of Le Touquet Airport, our first day's goal, brought back the feeling of excitement as we entered the first of our list of ten countries.

A friendly helicopter crew who guided us into Le Touquet (the airport control tower was closed by the time we arrived) allowed us to put our trikes in their hangar. They then arranged accommodation for us at a small hotel nearby before taking us to the airport restaurant where we enjoyed a well-deserved meal.

The hotel room was cramped, but we were used to that, having spent the day within the narrow confines of a microlight. Dozens of small, draw-string bags containing all our worldly goods littered the floor. The following morning, I managed to miss one of mine as we loaded up the taxi to return to the airport. I had lost my spare trousers, shoes and T-shirt, not to mention my favourite wide-angle camera lens and our spare Olympus camera.

We were held up for half a day by the French authorities who claimed to have no knowledge of our trip and denied us permission to continue. There followed two frustrating hours of telephone conversations and plenty of muttered curses before we were finally cleared to proceed.

The morning flight across northern France was glorious. The sun was shining, highlighting the patchwork of green fields, resplendent in the brightness of their spring colours. We stopped for fuel and lunch at a tiny airfield, after which we covered the rest of the journey across rural France. As we approached the German border, the cold front which had preceded us from Le Touquet stretched from horizon to horizon. Its tortured black clouds looked threatening and we had to find an airfield nearby. We were soaked once again by the time we landed at a deserted airstrip, and we hurriedly took the wings off the trikes, weighting the sails down with rocks to prevent the wind from turning them over during the storm which was imminent. Within minutes of securing the gliders, the thunder and lightning struck and the wind increased, lashing the trees. We retreated to the shelter and warmth of a nearby hotel, exhausted after six hours' flying.

The cold front had moved further east by the following morning when we refuelled the trikes and packed the bags into their tiny space underneath the seats. We took off before 8 a.m. to fly the short distance to the airport on the German border where we were to clear customs. The air was as smooth as silk and we contoured the wooded hills, flying at low level through mist-soaked valleys full of gently steaming deep-green conifers. We landed before the small airport had opened and had to wait for the customs officials to arrive. We then headed east once more, this time to a totally different type of venue – Nurnberg International Airport.

I had been unduly worried about our reception in Germany as they are usually sticklers for detail involving huge quantities of paperwork and endless rules. It was a pleasant surprise when a German friend of Ben's adopted our cause and arranged a reception for us, complete with media coverage at the large airport in Nurnberg.

The border into Germany is marked by the Rhine river. As it flowed sedately onwards, we flew with our wingtips almost touching, taking photographs and video footage of one other. Ahead of us rose the menacing clouds of our cold front once again. It had now lost its thundery violence, which was replaced with simple, depressing, continuous rain. Not wanting to be late for our appointment at Nurnberg, we pressed on, squeezed into the narrow gap between the low cloud and the ground.

With such poor visibility our maps were completely useless and without the GPS we would never have found our way. As we approached Nurnberg, we contacted air traffic control on the radio and they found our tiny dots on the radar screen, inching slowly towards them, and directed us in. It was intimidating to listen to the amount of air traffic in the sky around Nurnberg and we had to wait for a Boeing 737 to leave before we could land.

A small car with a sign flashing 'follow me' on its roof led us to our allotted parking bay. We were met by a man wielding two fluorescent bats who directed us left and right into the correct spot. I couldn't help laughing at the expression on his face: accustomed to directing jumbo jets, he looked dumbfounded by our tiny machines.

We were welcomed by the airport manager and an assortment of press and TV journalists, who all wanted to hear the story of our flight. Not only were our landing and parking fees waived, but we were also treated to a slap-up meal in the airport restaurant. The mystified looks on the faces of regular passengers were a picture as we strolled through the terminal building carrying our flying suits, helmets and maps.

Ben fell asleep while I went to supervise the refuelling of the trikes. We tried to use four-star petrol whenever we could, but at larger airports the only fuel available was Avgas, which is standard aviation fuel. This meant that our engines ran hotter than was ideal, but they would still function. A huge tanker was dispatched which dwarfed the tiny microlights, only to discover that the dispensing hose was too wide to go into our fuel tanks. A quarter-sized truck then arrived and I filled both aircraft and the spare tanks.

The Citroën trike was playing up and it took over an hour to start the engine. I tried every combination of choke, throttle and sheer brute force, but to no avail. I then handed over to Ben who, even with his experience and extra starter handle pulling power, could not get the thing to start. He became more annoyed and abusive to the trike, which finally gave in to the torrent of insults and spluttered back to life.

We took off from the main runway and headed for the Czech border. By now we were too late to cross as all customs facilities would be closed, so we had to content ourselves with getting as close as possible and then spending the night at a small airfield. A pleasant man who owned one of the hangars kindly offered us the small room inside the hangar for the night. We had originally intended to spend the night sleeping under the wings of our trikes, but as the persistent cold front again caught up with us, we were very glad we hadn't as it poured with rain from midnight onwards.

It was still pouring when we woke the following morning. We were now resigned to the feeling of being permanently damp but we delayed taking off for an hour to allow the worst to pass. We then crossed over the Czech border heading north to Karlovy Vary. I had never been to Czechoslovakia, where my father was born, and I couldn't think of a better way to arrive for my first visit.

Once we had cleared customs, we continued eastwards to the town of Pribram, a special stop for me. My father's cousin Sonia lives there, his only relative besides his father to survive the Holocaust. We arrived at lunchtime and Ben declared a half-day of rest so that he could fix the starting system on both trikes. As his knowledge of engines is infinitely greater than mine, I took time off to spend with Sonia and her daughters.

Ben's modification worked really well. Instead of sitting in the trike seat and pulling the handle (lawn mower style) from near the foot pedals, he had rerouted the system so that the handle was on the outside of the engine casing allowing a much more substantial pull and avoiding the friction of our luggage underneath the seats. It worked really well and solved the problem for the rest of the journey.

My foot throttle kept sticking open, which had caused me some anxiety over the past few flights, especially on landing. Ben had solved this by the less than satisfactory method of disconnecting it completely, leaving me with just a hand throttle.

The mechanical glitches were fixed; unfortunately, the same could not be said for the weather. We were scheduled to arrive in Hungary that afternoon but the headwinds were fierce, slowing our progress to a crawl. Added to this, we encountered severe wave turbulence and as we were flying directly into the wind, we were hit by phase after phase of brutal air that flung us about at will. I was tense and frightened as we fought our way through; I did not trust wave rotor. Gavin sensed my mood and remained quiet, listening to my muffled curses as I fought to keep the trike facing in the right direction. Ben's comments and questions were terse as he fought his own battle with the elements.

Our slow progress had meant a higher than expected fuel consumption and we were forced to stop at a small grass airstrip, whose surface was the roughest we had encountered to date, and I feared for our undercarriages. As we taxiied towards the hangar, several overall-clad mechanics emerged to watch and smiled their welcome as we clambered out, bedraggled and wet as usual.

233

The language barrier limited our conversation with the mechanics, but the shared enthusiasm for flying was obvious as they showed us around their hangar. Tucked away in the back of the building they were constructing ultralight sailplanes, beautiful hand-made works of art. It was only the promise of coffee and lunch in their cafeteria that finally persuaded Ben to climb out of the cockpit of a particularly lovely craft. By the time we had eaten and refuelled the trikes, the drizzle had increased to a downpour and the wind had strengthened. I wanted to wait, but Ben wanted to press on. I lost the argument.

The take-off roll again seemed endless, as the sodden, heavy wings refused to fly. Finally we rattled into the air and I regretted it immediately as the headwind brought us to a near standstill. The Ladas and Skodas on the motorway below us were zipping along by comparison, and the turbulence made the air unruly and unpleasant.

We were aiming for Brno airport on the Slovak border. It was only twenty-five miles away, yet it was well over an hour before it finally came into view. We contacted air traffic control to inform them of our approach and they sounded confused when we said we were three miles from the runway and that our estimated time of landing was fifteen minutes hence. Every five minutes, the controller called us on the radio asking, 'G-MYBW, have you landed yet?'

'Negative, but we are now two miles from the runway,' Ben replied.

I was frightened. I felt I was flying beyond the level of my ability in landing with such a strong crosswind. I had no experience to draw upon. The air was rough and unpredictable and I had no foot throttle to get me out of trouble if I was 'dumped' in the turbulence as I landed. I fought to control my fear, knowing that I had to keep my head together and my reactions sharp if I was going to have any chance of getting the landing right.

I watched Ben land diagonally across the runway ahead of me and I copied his approach. I could not risk letting go of the control bar to keep one hand on the throttle, so I had to trust to luck and my strength to keep the trike level. As the wheels touched, the wave of relief at being on the ground was superseded by the problems of taxing in the howling crosswind. The gusts tried alternately to whip underneath the wing and flip it over, or to push the top of the wing and slam it into the ground. Again I could not use the throttle to help me and had to rely on Gavin to control our taxi speed according to my instructions. By the time we arrived at our parking spot, I was a nervous wreck.

As Gavin helped me take the wing off the trike, I burst into tears with relief at being out of the air and in one piece. On previous expeditions, Ben had seen me as a competent, experienced member of the team, able to match his microlight expertise with my hang gliding proficiency. He had assumed my level of competence in microlights to be the same and was shocked to realise just how out of my depth I felt. He offered to fly the Citroën trike the following morning, as he was far more able to cope with the lack of a foot throttle than I was. We tied the wings down against the ferocious wind and retreated to the restaurant. Our cold front had returned and the worst storms we had seen so far raged outside. We were stuck for the night.

As dawn broke we were back at the airport. The cold front had passed and the air was moist, but thankfully it was not raining. We tipped the puddles of rainwater off the wings and filled out our flight plan to Hungary. We lined up side by side and took off together, climbing in the still air above the banks of low cloud which shrouded the hills. My muscles were sore after my fight to control the trike the previous day. I was getting pins and needles down my right arm due to overworking the shoulder joint. No one was sleeping well and the mental fatigue compounded the strain.

We were looking forward to reaching Hungary, where we knew we would be well looked after. Ben had visited Hungary several times and knew lots of pilots. I still had fond memories of my wonderful trip to the hang gliding competition in 1984. We were being met by Marton Ordody, who is one of the world's greatest organisers, and we knew that if he was involved, we need not worry about a thing.

The last few hills gave way to the plains of the Danube and the river itself which formed the border. We landed at a small airfield, scattered with imposing Antonov bi-planes. We cleared customs and were met by a microlight pilot called Ferenc who through a translator told us he would accompany us all the way through Hungary. A Cessna pilot introduced himself and we were told to follow the two aircraft to Budapest International Airport, where Marton and other friends would meet us.

We flew to Budapest following the meandering Danube, flying at low level and enjoying our first day without being rained on. The cold front had finally departed and we were treated to fine weather for the rest of the trip.

It was a joy to meet up with old friends at Budapest airport, who proved to be as dedicated to our cause as we were. All our needs – food, accommodation and fuel – were supplied free of charge. When the problem of my foot throttle was mentioned, a mechanical wizard was summoned who fixed it within half an hour. The Hungarians impressed me once again with their ingenuity and self-sufficiency, which puts most spoilt western pilots to shame.

We were invited to take part in Hungary's largest air show the following day. We were scheduled to appear 'after the Mig 29'! We sat on the grass to enjoy the display by the impressive formation aerobatics team before the deafening roar of the Mig's engines heralded its arrival. We got ready for our slot, not an easy feat whilst trying simultaneously to stuff my fingers in my ears to reduce the deafening noise. Once the Mig had departed, we did a double lap of honour, escorted by ten Hungarian microlights, while thousands of people waved us on our way. We set course for the south and the Romanian border, with Ferenc in tow. He was meant to be leading the way, but his trike was much slower than ours and we had to orbit every ten minutes to let him catch up. I was glad of the GPS, as the Hungarian plain became spirit-level flat and featureless. It would have been difficult to navigate with our poor quality maps so after the GPS confirmed our course, we could relax and admire the scenery. The wind was behind us, the clouds were benign and beautiful. This kind of flying was made in Heaven.

We arrived at our destination airfield near the Romanian border and were treated to another warm welcome. After unloading the trikes, we spent the evening swooping low over the hedgerows and flying in formation, taking photographs and video footage. As sunset approached, the sky glowed burnished red and we landed to join the barbecue held in our honour. As the Hungarians refused to take any money for all the fuel and accommodation, we made a donation to the Hungarian children's cancer foundation.

The customs officials and local police arrived the next morning to check our passports. We then took off for Romania and the border town of Arad. As we approached, I called up air traffic control, who referred to me at all times as 'Lady', triggering at least three days of mickey-taking from Ben and Gavin. As we taxied towards the control tower, several people approached us, pushing to be the first to shake our hands. The airport dog beat them all by jumping onto my lap and licking my visor.

After clearing customs and refuelling, we moved back into hilly terrain. We were totally unprepared for the staggering beauty of Romania. The mountains were unspoilt and the views spectacular, with deep valley passes and waterfalls cascading down the forested slopes.

The local fuel, however, is often contaminated with dirt, as I discovered when my engine died briefly before coughing back to life. Two seconds without an engine when directly above a network of high-tension power cable seems like an eternity and my heart certainly skipped a couple of beats. As a precaution we landed at a nearby airport to check the engine. Nothing seemed to be amiss and Ben concluded it must have been some dirt or water in the fuel which had now worked itself out of the system. The people at the airport were so keen for us to stay that they tried several excuses: 'The next airport is closed.' ... 'The weather is very bad.' ... We persuaded them that we had to push on and they then gave us lots of help, telling us of features to look out for on the way and a list of radio frequencies of the airfields *en route*.

We were now in the heart of Transylvania and the mountains were stunning. Rocky crags with snow-filled gullies towered above lower wooded slopes. We skimmed the tree tops, chasing our shadows across the leaves. When we stopped for the night at Brasov, we were allowed to stay in the airfield accommodation. Facilities were basic but welcome and for me there was the untold luxury of a separate room in the women's quarters. Our hosts went out of their way to make us welcome, taking us into town for a meal, then driving us back to the deserted airfield before returning to their own homes.

The following morning the petrol which we had requested arrived in a metal dustbin and although we filtered it before pouring it into the trike tanks, some dirt got through and again I had an alarming hiccup from my engine. We had to traverse the Transylvanian Alps and we followed a valley heading directly south. The views were breathtaking, with small chalet villages high in the mountains and alpine pastures brimming with wild flowers.

Tensions soared once more as my instruments failed. My cylinder head temperature gauge showed an alarming but impossible 600 degrees. Ben was worried on my behalf and shouted at me to lose height quickly. He snapped his instructions at a time when I needed some calm reassurance. After twenty minutes, the dial spontaneously dropped down to normal levels and then proceeded to flicker about at will, indicating, as I suspected, a problem with the instrument panel rather than the cylinder head.

We flew on in tense silence to where the mountains dropped away to the plains on the far side, affording decent-sized landing fields again in case of engine failure. I relaxed completely and enjoyed the flight into Ploiesti, a well-organised airfield with a flying club, including a small fleet of Zlins for aerobatic training, several sailplanes and a few microlights.

We were escorted to the office of the commandant of the airfield, an intimidating woman wearing a scarlet skirt with matching nail polish and lipstick. She was shouting into an equally red telephone and was obviously angry. We sat demurely, feeling like children in school when confronted with a teacher in a fury, not daring to speak and averting our gaze. Occasionally she would bark instructions at an underling, who would race off at the double to carry out her wishes. Finally, she summoned someone who spoke English and via him, told us that she had been trying to arrange fuel for us, but it was too difficult to complete all the paperwork. We would simply have to have it free of charge! We were dumbstruck at the generosity. It seemed the poorer the country, the more generous they were. We were humbled by her gift.

We went to look around the hangars, where Ben discovered that to hire a Zlin aeroplane for aerobatic flying only cost $50 for an hour. He calculated that we could split a trip four ways and have fifteen minutes each. He returned to us with the look of a cat that is about to get the cream.

It was a superb experience to be upside down, below wispy clouds, swooping and diving. Sid and Gavin both emerged from their flights looking decidedly green and while Ben and I raved about it, poor Sid had to lie down to recover before we could leave.

The magic continued with the most wonderful flying I had ever experienced in a microlight. As we headed east to the shore of the Black Sea, we met up once more with the Danube which, nearing the end of its journey, was wide and the current was slow. The afternoon air was as smooth as the river's surface and as we flew along with our wheels just three feet above the water, our reflections mirrored our progress. We were below the banks of the river and the fishermen, looking down on us as we passed, waved and smiled. We flew in closer formation than we had ever done before with overlapping wings and huge grins on our faces. As we rounded a corner, a bridge came into view and, laughing insanely, we passed below the main arch. My thoughts once again turned to Yasmin and how much she would have loved to have been with us.

The vast expanse of the Black Sea came into view as we neared our destination at Constanta. There was a lot of paperwork to complete and we had to file our flight plan for the following morning's flight to Bulgaria. Our permission had finally been granted three days before, thanks to Dimitar's efforts. Our landing and parking fees were waived and we were given a courtesy car to take us to a hotel in view of the 'humanitarian' nature of our flight.

We had been underway for nine days, averaging over five hours' flying per day. The constant lack of sleep and cramped conditions were taking their toll on us both physically and mentally. Gavin reckoned he had spent so much time with his legs apart in the back seat that by the time we reached Jordan he would be able to give birth. Sid remained jovial and as unperturbed as always.

We had honed our routine to perfection and each morning we could pack up all our belongings in five minutes. I no longer needed to instruct Gavin in how best to help with the trike as we were becoming an efficient team. While I checked the engine, he would perform the jigsaw puzzle of fitting all the bags under the seats. There was something very refreshing about having a tiny bag the size of a normal handbag with all my worldly goods in it, never having to make a decision about what to wear. Our clothes became more and more oil stained, but we were able to wash them out if we stayed somewhere with a shower.

We woke the following morning to find that, contrary to the forecast, a howling wind was blowing. I knew that Dimitar had driven from Sofia to our destination at Burgas to make sure our passage through the Bulgarian bureaucracy was smooth. He had arranged fuel for us and had the chief Aeroflot mechanic standing by just in case. They were expecting us to arrive at 9 a.m. Meanwhile, we were still at the airport in Constanta, worried about the raging southerly wind. The air traffic controller reported that the wind in Varna, an airport halfway to Burgas, was light. We made the decision to go, hoping that the wind would decrease *en route*.

As we took off it was immediately apparent that this flight would be in total contrast to the day before. The strong winds made the air turbulent and we had to fly very low in the most disrupted air to make any headway at all. The GPS readings were depressing, showing our speed over the ground to be a paltry sixteen miles an hour. It was apparent early on that our fuel situation would be dire if we did not hit the light winds soon. Our fuel consumption was high because of all the weight we carried, and we usually had to stop every three hours. Flying at the high speeds necessary to make progress against the headwind decreased our fuel levels dramatically and it became clear that we wouldn't even make our alternative airport at Varna.

We had to divert into the only airfield within range. Unannounced and unexpected, we approached the huge tarmac runway. From the bunkers around the perimeter, it was obvious that this was a military base and we would be in big trouble for arriving without permission, but we had no option. It seemed deserted as we landed and taxied to the control tower.

As we switched off our engines, a bleary eyed, uniformed man emerged with a look of disbelief on his face. He beamed broadly and shook our hands before disappearing inside. We were confused. This was not the hostile reception we had anticipated. Several men emerged, some with higher ranking stripes on their uniforms and bigger caps, but all with the same friendly smile.

Finally an English-speaking man emerged and we were able to explain our plight. We were taken to the officers' mess and given drinks as we explained our purpose and gave them our brochure. Meanwhile, in the corner, the officer in charge of communications was trying to phone through to Burgas using a telephone that needed winding up before use. He yelled into the receiver for some time before replacing it with an air of triumph. Through our translator he told us that our reception committee was awaiting our arrival in Burgas and that he would arrange transport to the nearest garage so that we could buy fuel and be on our way. We were staggered. Before we left we were told, 'One year ago you would have been arrested, but now, after the revolution, you are welcome as our friends.'

We shook hands with everyone before taking off. The wind had dropped a little, but progress was still slow. At least the sun was shining as we flew low level along the beach before climbing to pass over the mountains before Burgas.

By the time we landed I was exhausted after a four and a half hour battle against headwinds. We now had over forty hours of flying behind us and Dimitar's smiling face was a very welcome sight at the airport. Without any fuss he took care of everything and I relished a rare opportunity to put my brain into neutral as he smoothed our passage through customs, took us to a hotel and found a restaurant for supper. We could not thank him enough for his huge efforts over the previous two weeks. To cap it all, the following morning he took us back to the airport and refused to let us pay for our fuel.

By 7.30 a.m. we were airborne and heading for Istanbul along the stunning Black Sea coastline. Small coves nestled between forested headlands with their golden sands untouched. Little fishing boats dotted the shallow waters, while further out to sea, larger vessels floated serenely, trailing their long nets The sea turned from sapphire blue to bright turquoise as the sun rose higher and shoals of fish were clearly visible through the crystal water.

We crossed the Turkish border and soon had to leave our pleasant aerial meandering to concentrate on our approach into the crowded airspace around Istanbul. A hint of anxiety was unmistakable in the voice of the air traffic controller as she acknowledged our approach. The airport was very busy and we were a difficult item to deal with as our speed was so slow. We did not naturally slot into a pattern with the other aircraft.

'G-MYBW please orbit to maintain your position two kilometres west of the airport,' came the instruction.

This was fun. I had orbited in a holding pattern on board a jumbo jet coming into Heathrow, but never in a microlight. As we circled round and round one another, holding our position, the exotic sprawl of Istanbul lay before us with its eastern skyline of mosques. Our reverie was interrupted.

'G-MYBW you are second to land behind the Airbus.'

We made an unorthodox approach to the runway, cutting straight across the airport to speed up our arrival and to keep us out of the turbulence resulting from the arriving and departing jets. We landed level with the taxiway and scuttled clear as fast as we could. A 'follow me' car was dispatched to lead us to our parking spot, where we were immediately surrounded by people who had come to gaze at the strange spectacle. They arrived in every type of vehicle – catering vans, crew buses, fuel bowsers, baggage carriers, toilet servicing trucks and even a lorry dragging a set of aircraft steps.

With the necessary paperwork completed, we went into town to find a hotel. We spent a wonderful afternoon exploring the city and doing some filming. As evening approached, the muezzin call to prayer wailed from the minarets. The haunting sound immediately brought memories flooding back of our last trip to Jordan and particularly of Yasmin.

The following morning we said goodbye to Istanbul in a blaze of gold as we took off at dawn. The Blue Mosque stood out proudly on the shore, its towers reaching far into the morning sky. The gold tops of the minarets glinted in the sunshine as a thin veil of mist rose over the Bosphorus. It was a sight I shall never forget as we crossed the three miles of water, through the 'Gateway to the East', leaving Istanbul slowly waking from its slumbers.

The landscape turned once again to mountains as we threaded our way through the valleys. We met flocks of storks, gracefully thermalling with their huge wings outstretched, trailing their matchstick legs behind them.

King Hussein had arranged permission for us to land at Istanbul, Ankara and Adana. Unfortunately the distance between stops exceeded the range of our forty-litre fuel tanks. We had filled up our spare jerry cans in

241

anticipation and two hours into the flight, we looked out for a place to land and refuel. Not wanting to alert any police who might be overzealous in their law enforcement, we found a tiny dirt track in the middle of nowhere. The pastures were rich green with their lush summer grass, and a herd of horses grazed contentedly nearby.

Ben descended and checked the road with a low pass before landing. I had never landed on a track before, only on wide runways or fields. It was going to be tricky. There was a steep drop on either side of the track and it would be absolutely imperative that I keep the nose wheel straight. One of the biggest problems I face when flying microlights is that at five feet four inches tall, I can never reach the pedals to keep the nose wheel braced straight for take-off and landing. They are designed by men, for men, and my legs are always at least two inches too short. It became a standing joke as each time we landed, Gavin would push me forwards in the seat. This time it was more important than ever as a slight deviation from a straight line would send us careering down the bank which flanked the track.

'I'll need loads of thrust for this one,' I told Gavin. Luckily he saved his giggles for later as he could tell by the tone of my voice that I was nervous. As we touched down, my fated throttle stuck open again and I couldn't slow down. I blipped it twice, it finally responded, and we rolled to a stop.

Two small motorbikes appeared as three men from the nearby farm came out to see us. They beamed their welcome and through a mixture of sign language and guesswork, we managed to tell them where we came from and where we were going. They invited us for tea at their house which we sadly had to decline as we had a further two hours' flying to do before reaching Ankara. They walked around the trikes, shaking their heads in disbelief, sniffing the fuel and dipping their fingers in to feel its consistency. We shook hands all round and said goodbye, then took off to complete our journey to Turkey's capital city.

The mountains loomed large on either side, but the journey was pleasantly smooth as a thin layer of high cloud prevented the sun from heating the rocky slopes and causing thermal turbulence. As we cleared the final ridge, the farmlands disappeared and there were fewer signs of habitation than at any time on our journey so far.

We landed in Ankara and enjoyed the sensation of the hot sun on our backs. The airport was not very busy and we were met by a group of officials on the parking apron. We feared a repetition of the struggle we had endured at Istanbul, where we had been charged huge fees for landing, parking, taking off, the 'follow me' car and processing. The bill amounted to more than we had been charged during the rest of the trip put together. With every penny we saved on the journey going to the Cancer Research Campaign, it hurt to have to pay so much for one overnight stop.

We couldn't have been more wrong with our fears. We were asked how many tonnes our aircraft weighed as the landing fee is based on aircraft size. When we said '390 kilograms' they roared with laughter and said, 'Your aircraft are too light to charge. We offer you our services free.'

They sent out a small baggage truck and they watched with hilarity as we loaded our copious oil stained bags on to it. They then guided us into the arrivals hall and five minutes later, our strange assortment of luggage arrived on the conveyor belt. We felt like New Age travellers of the sky.

The next day brought the biggest challenge of our flight so far: the crossing of the huge Toros mountains which stood between us and the Mediterranean. There was a valley which cut through the mountains with a high pass at 6,000 feet. This equalled our maximum height capability with our overloaded craft, but we had no choice. We would have to cross in the calmer air of the evening. As a result, we were committed to a long day.

Our climb rate was poor as we struggled to clear the brown hills south of Ankara. We had been told to fly at 13,500 feet to which Ben had agreed, and as we made our way south, air traffic control kept telling us to climb. Ben replied each time saying, 'Negative, we will stay at 1,000 above the ground.'

Finally they gave up on us and we were told, 'Continue to Adana on your own responsibility.'

We emerged above the arid plains of central Turkey, past the blinding crystalline whiteness of enormous salt pans which spread their fingers into the multicoloured earth. The cliffs nearby blended into a myriad different colours as the minerals stained the stone and scree.

We needed to stop and refuel both microlights and crew. A convenient track ran parallel with the main road so once we spotted a petrol station with a restaurant next door, we landed on the track and taxied across the road into the garage forecourt. Once we had refuelled the trikes, we moved into the basic but adequate restaurant where we dined at our leisure, knowing we had four hours to waste before we needed to take off once again to cross the mountains ahead. I wrote to Chris but I could only manage ten minutes at a time as the pins and needles in my arms had become so bad that I couldn't continue.

The air was still rough with thermals as we took off again at 4.30 p.m.

The ground beneath us steadily rose as we approached the foothills heralding the start of the Toros mountains. Ben was uncharacteristically nervous as we approached the awesome 12,000-foot peaks and over the radio we discussed the conditions and the possibilities ahead. I was confident that luck was with us, as there was very little wind and therefore a minimal risk of rotor turbulence. I looked hard into the ravine we were heading for, and all my years of hang gliding experience were brought to the fore as I weighed up the situation. I considered it to be as safe as it was ever likely to be.

Cajoling Ben along, I led the way into the valley. It was intimidating, with near-vertical sides and nowhere to land for miles on end. The serrated spires of rock towered above us and we felt very small. Thankfully, my engine saved its thrice-daily hiccuping until we had passed through the main canyon. We were at a junction where three valleys met and the sea breeze whistled up from the Mediterranean, causing the air to swirl like a washing machine. I stayed high while Ben took a lower route. His trike was pitched violently downwards and Sid, who had loosened his seatbelt, was thrown upwards. He grabbed hold of Ben's shoulders to stop himself and was flung back down into his seat. Ben said later it was the scariest thing that had ever happened to him in a mircrolight.

No sooner had Ben recovered from his scare than I found myself in trouble. The high pass seemed beyond the capability of my trike. The throttle was set on full power and I was pushing the control bar out to ensure maximum climb rate, but the ground was rising faster than I was. Gavin lapsed into nervous silence in the back as I alternated prayers and curses at the labouring machine. There was nowhere to land as the terrain was carpeted with trees. The only possibility was the motorway which carved through the pass. I was eyeball to eyeball with the truck drivers as they came over the brow of the pass and I don't know which of us looked more frightened. Finally, with my wheels almost brushing the trees, I drew level with the highest point and, with a huge sigh of relief, we found ourselves in smooth sea air above descending ground which dropped away to the Mediterranean coast. The banter between us began once more as the tension disappeared. We followed the GPS reading towards Adana airport, where we were met by some friendly members of the local flying club who invited us to drink cold beer as the sun set in a fiery sky.

We enjoyed a luxuriously late start as our flight to Halab Aleppo airport in Syria would only take us three hours. Sid and Gavin's cameras were stashed under the seats as we were specifically forbidden to film or photograph from the air in Syria. We filed our flight plan and took off into uncomfortably rough air, heading east towards the Syrian border. There was a great deal of confusion with an air traffic controller, who was convinced we were flying north. Ben confirmed that we were adhering to our flight plan and heading east, only to be told that we should head north to Ankara. It had taken a whole day to get from Ankara to where we were now and we certainly did not want to go back there. The conversation went back and forth, with the controller still having no idea of our intentions, despite our filed plan and our persistent confirmation that we were flying to Syria. Finally in exasperation, Ben said, 'I am sorry, your transmission is broken and I am not receiving you clearly. I am changing frequency and we will continue to Syria under our own responsibility.'

As we reached the coast, the air became smooth and we enjoyed some low-level flying along the beach, chasing our shadows along the sand. We had one more range of mountains to cross before we entered Syrian airspace and this time we cruised easily over the pass and on to the vast, sun-burned plains beyond. The fields of grain had been harvested, leaving a landscape of square fields in varying shades of brown and gold. Our maps were even more useless than usual as whole towns appeared where nothing but wasteland was shown on the map, and where a village should have confirmed our position, there was nothing visible below.

We contacted Halab Aleppo air traffic control who asked for our permission number before we proceeded further. We were flying at 4,000 feet and all our documents were in screw-top, waterproof barrels beneath our seats. Ben explained that our aircraft did not have a cockpit and that we would show them our papers when we arrived. Thankfully, they understood and allowed us to continue our approach.

The heat hit us like a blanket as we landed. A crowd of men gathered around us, intrigued by our aircraft and faces. I drew particular attention as the concept of a woman flying an aircraft, especially of the 'flying motorbike' variety, was unheard of.

A five-hour wait to clear customs was both unexpected and unwelcome in the sweltering heat. We were left in a tiny room sitting in a row looking like the Raggle Taggle Gypsies-O without being told what was happening. Each enquiry was met with a smile and the soon well-worn phrase, 'Please wait, not long now.'

People wandered by, looking through the windows, watching our every move with uninhibited curiosity. A huge crowd gathered to meet a flight returning from the annual haj pilgrimage to Mecca. The atmosphere grew more oppressive as the crowd's excitement grew and they ran en masse from one end of the terminal building to the other.

Finally our passports were returned to us and we realised that the people we had thought officious were actually on our side. They were inhibited by the Syrian immigration system, which is simply not geared up for welcoming tourists who enter the country flying their own aircraft.

The city of Halab Aleppo was fascinating, with friendly people, many of whom stopped us in the street to welcome us to Syria and to ask us if we needed help. The Arabic script on the road signs reminded us just how close we now were to our final destination.

We did not want to fly over the Syrian plains in the heat of the day, as the turbulence would probably be severe, so we were packed and ready with engines running by 6 a.m. the following morning. We had to wait for the air traffic controller to make his bleary way up the stairs and into the control tower to give us permission to take off. We had not filed a flight plan, but we told him our destination was Damascus.

We took off and headed due south, enjoying the smooth air. The mountains to the west formed the border, beyond which lay Lebanon. The endless plains in shades of gold stretched out before us. Syria's ancient heritage was visible from the air, with large castles looking like wheel hubs of circular towns around which smaller grey, flat-topped dwellings radiated outwards. We were smitten by Syria's arid beauty.

Our mood changed suddenly as we spotted a missile base below us. From our perspective at 6,000 feet it looked like something out of a Thunderbirds film, the classic red-and-white striped torpedo shapes pointed straight at us. The radar dish scanned the skies looking for aircraft and I felt extremely vulnerable. Although we had permission to fly to Damascus, I considered that if they spotted us, they might act first and check their facts later. Like the proverbial sitting ducks we crept slowly past, but did not relax for the rest of the flight.

As in Turkey, the distance we had to travel was greater than our fuel tanks would allow, so we landed after an hour on a narrow, secluded road to top up from our jerry cans. A small gathering of shepherds and farm workers arrived, some in curious agricultural vehicles, some running across the fields. They all smiled and welcomed us. Aware of the sensitive security surrounding our visit, we took off again in under ten minutes. The northern farmland gave way to desert sands and small rocky hills. We had arrived in the biblical lands of the Middle East.

Damascus Airport was quite the opposite to Halab Aleppo. The facilities were impressive and it seemed every airport worker found some excuse to be in our area to look at us and our aircraft. Our passports had hardly left our hands before they were stamped and we were free to go. We stood bewildered at their efficiency before gathering our grubby belongings and piling into a taxi.

Ben and I had both been tense during the morning's flight. Fatigue was accumulating and there were ever more reminders of the reason for the flight. We showed our one remaining brochure time and again to explain our journey and each time, Yasmin's beautiful face shone out of it.

That night we ate Arabic food once more and it hit us that at the same time tomorrow the trip would be over. Ben was feeling a huge weight of responsibility now that we were only two hours from Amman. Aware that he must not let Yasmin down, he felt that he was bringing her spirit home to Jordan and that tomorrow he would have finally to let her go.

We were due to arrive at Amman airport at 11 a.m. so we returned to Damascus airport early in order to prepare the aircraft with plenty of spare time in case of hold-ups, although we were totally unprepared for the scale of delay we were about to encounter. As we filled in our flight plan, we were at last able to write 'Amman, Jordan' in the box marked 'destination'. Gavin and Sid were then left sitting in a room while Ben and I were led away by two officers and taken upstairs to a large office full of uniformed men with lots of stripes on their sleeves and guns in their holsters. The atmosphere was tense and we knew we were out of our depth.

The head of the Aviation Authority then appeared, carrying an aura of hostility with him. He made Saddam Hussein look like Winnie the Pooh. We were interrogated for two hours about why we had not filed a flight plan in Halab Aleppo and why we had landed on a road without permission. Goodness knows how they had found out about our landing, but they were furious. They had figured out from where we had landed that our flight path had taken us over several of their sensitive missile bases.

Ben deserved an Oscar for his performance as he answered their questions, explaining that my aircraft had had a spark plug problem and that we had landed to fix it. They had no experience of microlights and asked why we had not sent out a Mayday distress call. Ben's placid explanation that our engines were almost human in their temperaments and were designed to land almost anywhere softened their anger a little. The final thing that secured our release was showing our brochure once more. Yasmin's face worked the necessary magic as it finally sank in why we were making the flight, and that the beautiful woman in the brochure had died of cancer. A glint of humanity showed through a chink in his armour and we were allowed to leave.

We were given our flight instructions by air traffic control. We were to fly at a speed of 240 knots at flight level 245 (24,500 feet) and to make a 200-mile detour into the desert to the east of Damascus before turning south to Jordan. To argue with these impossible demands would have meant that we would have been stopped from flying, so Ben signed the flight plan, we collected Sid and Gavin and went to our aircraft. Ben drew me aside and spoke quietly. 'Don't talk about what just happened until we're in Jordan. Let me do the talking to air traffic control. Don't speak to me on the radio and don't even risk using the intercom to talk to Gavin. Just follow me and do what I do.'

I passed on the message to Gavin and with the tension palpable, we climbed into the trike and took off. As instructed, we set course to the east and Ben gave regular updates on request.

'G-MYBW is now five miles from Damascus heading east, passing through 3,000 feet on our way to 24,500 feet, increasing speed to fifty knots.'

Once out of sight of the airport, Ben descended rapidly to 50 feet above the desert floor and changed direction to the south. As instructed I said nothing and followed suit. Together we contoured the barren and hostile rocky terrain, flying as fast as our machines would go. We would not have seen any military installations until we were on top of them so we were just hoping that our path to the south was clear and that we could reach the sanctuary of Jordan without further hitches.

We were below the radar now and Ben kept up his calls to Damascus tower, reporting our position as flying east, and climbing through 10,000 feet and beyond. Meanwhile, the flying was brutal in the turbulence of low-level thermals, but our adrenaline was pumping as we fled for the border. We were given permission to contact Amman airport and, confident that our tiny, slow-moving specks on the Damascus radar screen were no longer visible, we climbed to a more comfortable height above the exquisitely patterned, pastel desert.

'Amman tower this is G-MYBW,' Ben radioed ten miles before the border.

'G-MYBW this is Amman tower. You are clear to fly direct to Amman. Welcome to Jordan.'

A thin line ran from horizon to horizon marking the border and as we passed it tears rolled unchecked down my face. The relief at having made it to Jordan was mixed with a sense of grief and a sense of honour at the tribute we were paying to our friend. The sight of the city of Amman brought more emotion as we approached Marka airport. We could see a large crowd below and we did a circuit of the airfield before lining up to land on the taxiway. My trike had the last laugh as the throttle once again stuck open as I landed and I had to switch off the engine and suffer the indignity of being pushed the last 100 yards to where our reception committee was waiting.

Ben and I hugged each other and sobbed uncontrollably. We struggled to control our raw feelings and turned to face the crowd who had gathered to meet us. Filthy, red-eyed and exhausted, we shook hands with Prince Ra'ad, King Hussein's cousin, before an emotional reunion with Yasmin's parents, whom we had not seen since her death. After speeches of welcome, we were taken to the Intercontinental Hotel, who did not turn a hair at our bedraggled appearance. Nick and John had arrived with clean clothes and within an hour we looked and smelt like different people.

It felt so strange to stop. We had been living on our nerves for fifteen days, relying on adrenaline to drive us when fatigue threatened to over-whelm us. We had experienced great exhilaration at each warm welcome from every new country, but also intense fatigue after the physical pain and pressure from bad weather, engine problems or over-zealous bureaucrats.

We spent the following week touring Jordan to finish off the film. Wherever we went we were greeted with affection and hospitality. The people we met were touched that we should have undertaken this journey in memory of a Jordanian woman. We spent two days in the spectacular scenery of Wadi Rum, flying around the awesome peaks at dawn and flying in formation, chasing our shadows along the desert floor. We returned to Amman via the Dead Sea and Jerash, where again we flew with our wingtips almost touching. In Amman, we gave talks about our adventures and did several interviews with the Jordanian media. We arranged to do a day of 'joy rides' for the people of Amman whereby they paid five dinars (five pounds) for a short flight and all the money would go towards the new cancer centre being built in Amman. We anticipated that a small group would take up the offer, but on the day 500 people turned up wanting to fly. Only the early arrivals were able to buy tickets.

King Hussein arrived at midday and came for a flight with me. His security guards looked anxious at the prospect of him flying in this tiny, flimsy-looking craft, with a female pilot at the controls. The King himself took it in his stride and enjoyed the ten-minute fight around the airport. He then invited us for lunch at the officers' club, where a sumptuous picnic had been laid on. After four hours of flying in the heat of Amman, Ben and I were dusty, sweaty and grubby. The beautiful, pressed linen tablecloths and serviettes contrasted sharply with our stained shirts. His Majesty, as usual, treated us with kindness and courtesy, entertaining us with some flying stories told, as always, with great humour.

After an hour, we were getting anxious about the crowd of people who still wanted to fly. The King accompanied us to the microlights and spent the rest of the afternoon at the airport, talking to people. Within half an hour we heard the unmistakable thrumming of helicopters and three huge Super Pumas arrived on the taxiway. King Hussein did not want people to go away disappointed and in a typically generous gesture had ordered the helicopters to take up all those who wanted to fly.

Ben and I flew forty people each that day and were exhausted. The King finally stopped us, saying we had done enough, and told us to taxi to the hangar where his aircraft were kept. His mechanics helped us dismantle the trikes for their voyage home and they were loaded with great care onto palettes. King Hussein was flying to England the following day and had invited us to fly back with him aboard his Tristar. The contrast between our outbound journey and the speed and comfort of the return plane flight could not have been more marked.

As we took our leave of Amman the following morning, none of us spoke. We were deep in thought about our unforgettable journey and the friend to whom we had now said our final goodbye. We had cemented such a solid link with Jordan as a result of Yasmin. It had been a great adventure and a fitting tribute to a wonderful woman.

CHAPTER 21

Stratosfear

It was great to be home again with Chris. Although we had been living together for only three months, it felt as if we had always been a couple. It was so easy being with him, life was full of energy and humour and there was no doubt in my mind that I had found my partner for life. I felt very lucky to have found someone who enjoyed the same things in life and who shared the same values.

We both enjoyed having new challenges to get our teeth into and when I got home, there was little time to rest and relax. My next project was scheduled for the autumn and it required more preparation than anything I had ever done before.

I had wanted to break the world balloon drop altitude record since 1983, when I had done my first balloon drop. A year later, in 1984, the record had been broken by Englishman, Rory McCarthy. I had seen the TV film of the flight, watching spellbound as he was towed to 34,700 feet. I was inspired by the pictures taken from his wing mounted camera, as he was towed high above the clouds by the balloon. I longed, one day, to be able to see that same spectacular view for myself.

Whilst sponsored by Citroën, I had performed many balloon drops and the prospect of the world altitude record had really begun to gnaw at me. As Per Lindstrand had agreed in 1988 to join me in the project and tow me to an altitude sufficient to break the world record, all I needed to make it happen was a film company to record the attempt and a sponsor to finance it.

At the beginning of 1993, I approached Matt Dickinson, who was now working as a film producer for National Geographic. He confirmed he would like to film the flight and as we now had a fifty-minute documentary to sell to a sponsor, the project was on.

I approached 'Sega' computer games and after several meetings, they agreed to sponsor the attempt by providing a balloon, a hang glider and all the other equipment necessary. Having been adorned with daisies and branded with tampon logos for the sake of a sponsor in the past, I was aware of the potential pitfalls of the branding exercises associated with sponsorship, but nothing could have prepared me for what Sega had in mind.

Sega's artwork department were put to work to create a design for the balloon and hang glider. Two weeks later, Matt and I were summoned to the Sega offices for the ceremonial unveiling of the drawings. We went to the artwork offices where two ponytail-sporting thirty-somethings led us to their easel. Resting there was a canvas with a picture of hang glider dangling from a balloon. Fighting disbelief, I saw that the balloon had been designed as an enormous bottom, sporting a black lace G-string. The hang glider was painted to match.

I was convinced it was a joke until I saw the rough drawings scattered on the desk and realised they were serious. Matt looked appalled. The National Geographic film company covers adventures that push the limits, but not in this way. They want things to be visually exciting, and interesting scientifically, but following a 240,000-cubic-foot flying bottom to the edge of the stratosphere did not fit their image. As far as I was concerned, if anything were to happen to me during what was to be my most dangerous project to date, I did not want to meet my maker whilst attached to a hang glider painted as a rear end. We sent the artists back to their drawing board.

The second design for the hang glider and balloon was not subtle, but was a big improvement, with a grotesque skull and crossbones logo. They then completed the artwork for my harness, painted my helmet with Sonic the Hedgehog and gave us a deposit as a sign of commitment.

We steamed ahead getting contracts drawn up, started filming and had the hang glider made with its skull logo screenprinted on it. I attended twenty meetings with Sega, their advertising agency and their PR company. Three weeks prior to leaving for Jordan on the Flight for Life trip, everything went worryingly quiet and I couldn't get a straight answer from anyone. Two weeks later I learned that the three top marketing people had been headhunted by BSkyB and the new manager had axed all ongoing projects.

Losing our sponsorship put the whole project in jeopardy. National Geographic became nervous and we were in danger of losing their commitment if we couldn't find a new sponsor. We knew the package would be perfect for somebody, as a fifty-minute documentary is worth a great deal in promotional terms. It was just a case of finding them.

My financial situation looked bleak. Because the deal had seemed certain, I had been buying essential equipment for the drop, spending more than double the amount that Sega had given us as a deposit. I had very little in the bank with no imminent income as I had committed the next month to Flight for Life. I was absolutely determined to fulfil my promise to Yasmin, but as I left for Jordan I was very worried.

King Hussein had taken a keen interest in the balloon drop record from the first moment he heard of it and at the end of our stay in Jordan, he asked me how the project was going. I told him that Sega had withdrawn their sponsorship and that the attempt had been indefinitely postponed. Within hours he returned with fantastic news. Royal Jordanian Airlines would sponsor the project. I was speechless with surprise and gratitude. Not only would I be able to do the drop, but at the same time I would be promoting a country that I had grown to love.

Per had flown a balloon in Jordan the previous year and had the inspired idea of doing the record attempt in Wadi Rum, which would make a perfect backdrop for the film with its spectacular scenery. I asked His Majesty for permission and he not only agreed, but in typically generous style, immediately offered assistance in the form of transport, accommodation and helicopters. The expedition date was set for mid-October 1994, when the winds in Jordan would be light and the skies clear. This gave us just four months to prepare, so we had to move quickly.

We were hoping to reach 40,000 feet and would need sophisticated oxygen equipment. Per has great contacts with the Swedish airforce and they were unreservedly helpful in providing us with training and equipment. We flew to Linkoping air base in southern Sweden to be fitted with fighter pilots' pressure suits, helmets and masks. The helmets were made to measure, moulded to our heads and faces for a snug fit. It was so exact that there was even a furrow built inside the back of mine where the ridge of my French plait slotted in. The mask fitting was lengthy as it had to form a perfect seal around my mouth and nose to avoid the oxygen leaking. The multitude of tiny straps were minutely adjusted one by one, secured temporarily with surgical clamps while the patient technician tested and retested the seal.

Above 38,000 feet we would have to 'pressure breathe'. At this height the atmospheric pressure is so low that the oxygen supplied through the mask would not be absorbed through our lung walls, and we would suffer oxygen starvation. Pressure breathing increases the pressure of the oxygen entering the mask, thus forcing it into the bloodstream. I tried this in the laboratory in Linkoping and the effect felt very strange. Instead of inhalation being an active manoeuvre requiring muscular expansion of the ribcage, it became passive and it was the exhalation which required effort. It felt as though someone was holding their hand in front of my mouth and, as I tried to breathe out I had to force the air out against the pressure of this hand.

As the pressure of the incoming oxygen increases, the lungs are inflated, like attaching an inner tube to a garage pump and pressing the button. To brace the torso against the pressure of the incoming oxygen and to help restore atmospheric pressure to the body we would need to wear pressure suits. Visually, they are unattractive garments unless you are into bondage. Made from green canvas, they cover the whole of the torso and legs and have small 'bladders' covering the chest, abdomen, thighs and shins, tightened to ensure a close fit by means of a complex network of straps and laces at the back. During the fitting of the pressure suit, mask and helmet, it became glaringly apparent that this would not be a comfortable flight.

The film crew turned up and caused mayhem at the well-organised Swedish Airforce base. Their powerful lights set off the fire alarm and then blew all the fuses. Somehow the long-suffering airforce staff maintained their good humour and we took home our box of goodies.

The hang glider had to be built quickly. I would be carrying a lot of extra weight with the oxygen system alone weighing over twenty kilograms. I had to move up a size to a medium glider and chose an Airwave Klassic. As I studied and planned the flight, I became aware of two potential hazards which would need to be taken into consideration. Firstly, I was almost certain, having watched Rory McCarthy's drop, that if a hang glider were to be taken any higher, the rotation when released from the balloon would be so severe that there was a high risk of it rotating past vertical, tumbling and then breaking. There just wasn't enough density in the air to slow down its rotation at the height from which we were proposing to drop.

Secondly, assuming the tumble could be prevented, the chance of a structural failure would be increased due to the tremendous speed that the glider would reach in the subsequent dive through such thin air. I gave Airwave a free rein to do any modifications they thought necessary to strengthen the glider. Having made the necessary calculations, they reinforced the glider's keel and pulled up the back of the sail slightly.

I was convinced that the way to reduce the glider's rotation was to hang it with its nose pointing downwards at forty-five degrees instead of dropping with the glider horizontal as I normally did. What I needed was a way of altering the angle just prior to release, as taking off with the glider's nose already down was impractical and would have been uncomfortable.

Having established a basic model using a potato peeler and string to illustrate the design, I recruited the help of a friend, Simon Lawrence, to make a life-sized version. Although not a hang glider pilot, Simon's grasp of how the release system was to work and his powers of invention were to prove invaluable. His engineering skills and initiative produced a multitude of pulleys, extra rigging wires, straps and rope. I spent several evenings dangling from the rafters of a local barn, testing the system, but the proof of the pudding was to be at the Bristol Balloon Fiesta. Suspended underneath the British Gas balloon, I was surrounded by dozens of other balloons of every shape and colour, with the Clifton suspension bridge spanning the River Avon directly underneath me.

At 3,000 feet I pulled on my rope, tilting the glider to forty-five degrees nose down in preparation for the drop. Matt and the film crew were orbiting us in a helicopter as Per gave his unique countdown: '1,5,3,2,1.' It worked! The glider dipped its nose and started to fly without the usual violent rotation. I landed to find that some concerned Bristolian had called the police to report that, 'A microlight is stuck under a balloon and a helicopter is trying to rescue it!'

The next stage in my preparation was to have all my old fillings replaced, as any air trapped in them could have caused at best, extreme pain and at worst, a shattered tooth. It was gruelling to return to the dentist's surgery day after day with my jaw still aching from the previous day's new filling. My dentist, Rob Nichols, was a fellow paraglider pilot and was in as much discomfort as I was as he had suffered a crushed vertebra a few weeks before in an unorthodox 'landing'. We winced in unison as I underwent my seven hour-long appointments. Each filling was done with immense care to avoid any air pockets inside the tooth. I emerged with seven new fillings, a sore jaw and a firm resolve never to eat chocolate again.

Airwave made me a harness, adding a container in front for my emergency parachute, side bags for the camera recorders and batteries, and numerous attachment points for the oxygen cylinder, emergency bottle and regulator.

I had to plan what to wear extremely carefully as the temperature above 33,000 feet would be minus fifty-five degrees, which would feel even colder with the wind chill once I had released from the balloon. Never has a woman fretted so long about an outfit. I consulted everyone I could think of – cavers, mountaineers, trans-Everest balloonists and extreme parachutists. Two days before we left, I had spent a small fortune on gear, but was finally happy. Working from the inside, I had thermal underwear, a pressure suit, two fleece jackets, fleece trousers, down jacket and trousers, three pairs of gloves, two balaclavas, two pairs of ski socks and a pair of moon boots.

We arrived at Heathrow on 16 October 1994 with enough equipment to sink a battleship. There were sixteen of us: six film crew, two balloon crew, a stills photographer, Anders Forsloff (a Swedish oxygen expert), Simon Lawrence, Ben Ashman, Per, Chris and myself. Jules Wigdor, a veteran of several of Per's escapades, was the project manager and the final member to join us at Heathrow.

When we landed in Amman, we were met by several palace officials, whisked through customs and into waiting vehicles which took us to the luxurious Intercontinental Hotel as their guests. The following day we loaded the trucks with all our gear and headed for Wadi Rum. As we entered the valley, the familiar cathedral rocks towered 3,000 feet above us in the haze of the midday sun. We drove up to the rest house at Rum Village passing camels which ambled by with their lazy, long eyelashes and belligerent mouths. The Bedouin looked on as we unloaded our strange-looking equipment, forever bemused by the antics of westerners. The army had erected a tent village for us and a huge Bedouin tent with the floor strewn with mats and cushions. There was always tea on the fire, and a host of army personnel had been drafted in to help us.

The oxygen cylinder I would need was huge, as it had to last for up to six hours, keeping my pressure suit and me fully inflated. It was attached to the back of my harness and stretched from my shoulder to my knees. The implications of landing with this contraption had been worrying me, as it weighed over twenty kilograms and any mistimed landing involving tripping in soft sand, could result in a hard thump to the cylinder and spell disaster – I could have been sent straight back into orbit without the help of the balloon.

I decided to invest in a pair of wheels to avoid landing on my feet. I was lent an enormous set of beginner's wheels, which would withstand even the heaviest landing. My first test was aerotowing behind Ben's microlight, taking off from the road in Wadi Rum. The trike pulled me easily from the ground and we climbed in the gentle morning breeze. The beauty of Wadi Rum once again took my breath away; the vibrant colours of the angular cliffs glowed as we rose through the inversion into the crystal air above. Ben towed me six miles to the hard salt flats at Disi, where the huge circular fields of an agricultural project stand out incongruously green among the mixed browns of the desert.

I released and lined up for my first wheel landing, fighting the urge to rotate myself into the normal upright position. As I descended, it felt strange to have my face so close to the ground. However, I touched down smoothly, bounced three times and rolled to a stop, swerving round through ninety degrees. I was greeted by Ben and Chris, who were whistling the *Dambusters* tune and I acquired the nickname of Barnes Wallis, 'Barney' for short.

Simon worked on the pulley system during the day and in the evening Ben towed me to Disi once more. After another successful practice run, we took off to return to Wadi Rum just after the sun had set. As we climbed, the sun reappeared again above the silhouetted cliffs and the full moon simultaneously appeared behind us. Ben and I were lost for words, marvelling at the sight as the scene imprinted itself indelibly in our memories.

We landed back in Wadi Rum to be confronted with both good news and bad news. The good news was that Miranda Creed-Miles had arrived. Miranda had helped with the organisation of the Flight for Life expedition. She knew about the balloon drop and, thinking I could use some extra help, had bought herself a ticket to Jordan and turned up in Wadi Rum. Her creative needlework skills and unfailing good humour were to prove invaluable.

The bad news was that a major problem had arisen with the oxygen system. Per and I planned to carry emergency back-up cylinders, and one of them had been accidentally set off while Anders was cleaning it. The other was indicating 'empty' and we couldn't risk using it. Anders was rushed to Amman airport to catch the Royal Jordanian flight to Amsterdam. He then had to get to the Airforce base in Sweden and exchange the cylinders. All he had with him were Per's credit card and a toothbrush and it was a tribute to his initiative that he arrived back, albeit pale and exhausted, within forty-eight hours, carrying two new cylinders.

The following morning we did our first practice balloon drop. The purpose was to test my new release system. During previous drops, I had always been released by the balloon pilot who leaned over the edge of the basket and used a knife to cut the umbilical cord connecting us. For the high altitude drop, I wanted to be able to control my own release if something were to happen to Per and he couldn't release me or in case the radio failed. The forty-five degree nose down attitude was also uncomfortable to hold for any length of time so when I was ready to go, I wanted to drop straight away. My release system was operated by a rope handle which I pulled to separate the hang glider from the balloon, but Per would still carry his trusty Swiss army knife just in case my new device didn't work.

We rose at 5 a.m. and rigged the glider. It seemed to take for ever to fasten the video cameras to the wing, but we were finally ready to go at 7.15 a.m., long after the sun had risen and the penetrating heat had started. The lift-off was clean, though the initial ascent was slow, giving me a long look at the sheer rock face as we rose. When we reached 5,000 feet I pulled my rope to tilt the glider to forty-five degrees. From the resulting nose-down angle, I was looking straight down the cliff below me.

Per made the balloon descend in order to decrease the glider's rotation slightly and also to reduce the distortion of the balloon when the weight of the hang glider was released. He radioed to me to release when ready and I gave a count down to warn the film crew to start the cameras rolling. I pulled my release handle and was delighted with the effect. The glider gathered speed and converted the energy into a swooping climb up above the balloon. Trailing coloured smoke for the cameras, I circled around Per, drinking in the scenery.

One more problem had been solved leaving only one more to go: would I be able to fly wearing all the kit and the oxygen system necessary to keep me alive at 40,000 feet? The next and final test would be a full dress rehearsal at 10,000 feet.

I spent the morning with Miranda making a face mask as this was the only part of my body which was as yet unprotected from the cold. Equipped with copious amounts of neoprene and fleece material, it was just a question of fitting it to my goggles and oxygen mask to block any gaps where the flesh-freezing air could enter. With endless patience and good humour, Miranda produced a masterpiece, which fitted together like a jigsaw and covered all the exposed areas.

Chris busied himself with the oxygen equipment, becoming familiar with the set-up. Now that the drop angle had been sorted out, the thing that remained most likely to kill me was a problem with the oxygen supply. He and Anders agreed to double-check all the connections to minimise the chances of a mistake.

Meanwhile, I developed a sore throat. I had been told that if I had a cold I would not be able to attempt the record as such a fast ascent and descent with blocked sinuses would guarantee permanent physical damage. With this in mind I had been taking massive doses of vitamin C for three weeks prior to our arrival in Jordan. Incensed at the very idea that a common cold would dare to strike me now of all times, I rationalised that the sore throat must be due to the dry desert air.

I spent a restless night thinking about the drop. I wanted to get it over and done with. I felt better about the release itself but I was still worried about how uncomfortable the pressure breathing had been at the airforce base. My throat felt worse and I began to sneeze.

The following morning I climbed groggily from bed at 4.30 a.m. and started dressing. Per had been to high altitudes before in a balloon and so didn't need to put on all his gear for the rehearsal. I had to wear everything that I would have on for the actual attempt and it was stifling. My down jacket sealed in all the heat and I felt like a roasting turkey. A doctor specialising in high altitude medicine was present every time we flew, courtesy of the Royal Jordanian Airforce, and after I confessed to him that my sinuses were blocked, he squirted a spray up my nose which cleared them immediately.

We were delayed again, this time by a valley wind which wafted down the Wadi for a short time each morning. With such a big balloon, conditions needed to be calm, so we waited for half an hour. By the time we took off, I felt very weak through overheating and claustrophobia. The mask was tight on my face and I couldn't move. I put on my goggles just before launch and they fogged up immediately.

As we took off at last, two hours after donning my super-warm clothing, I just hung my arms over the bar, desperately needing to cool down. By the time we passed 2,000 feet, drops of sweat were gathering in the goggles and I couldn't see anything. I took a glove off to wipe them and was rewarded with a magnificent view of the Sea of Galilee, the Dead Sea and the Red Sea. I was still unbearably hot in the cooler air at 10,000 feet and had taken the goggles off completely so that I could see what was going on. I then cut away for another problem-free drop. I followed the balloon down and as Per landed in the middle of the desert, vehicles appeared from every direction. A helicopter landed alongside, Ben arrived in his microlight, our lorries and the film crew descended on the site like the cavalry. My landing was smooth, but I was exhausted by the heat. Chris and Simon raced over and pulled off my harness and thick outer layers of insulation. The relief was immense as the cool air reached me at last. I was soaked through with sweat and suffering from heat exhaustion.

All the tests were now complete and we were ready to go for the record. Chris and Anders went over the oxygen system once more, Simon made a sealed, temperature-proof cover for my instruments with a perspex window so I could see the altitude and climb rate. Miranda modified the face mask after the morning's test and Jules disappeared to confirm our intentions to the Jordanian Airforce, the air traffic controllers and the meteorological office.

My sneezing grew worse and my sinuses felt like concrete. I knew in my heart that I would have to delay the flight. I walked away from the group, who were discussing the logistics for the following morning, and found Anders working alone in the Bedouin tent. I told him of my symptoms and he endorsed my decision, confirming that permanent damage was guaranteed if I were to climb to 40,000 feet with a cold. In tears of frustration, I took Matt aside and told him of the situation. I then went to bed stuffed full of antihistamines, decongestants and nasal spray.

The following morning, Chris and I were dispatched to Aquaba for a two-day rest. We sunbathed on the shore of the Red Sea and walked around the town, relaxing after the hectic activity of the previous week. The dust-free coastal air, together with the drugs given to me by the doctor, did the trick in clearing my sinuses and I was able to breathe freely once more.

We returned to Wadi Rum, where Jules met us with the forecast for the following morning. It was perfect, predicting fifty-knot southwesterly winds at altitude. The temperature at 40,000 feet had dropped to minus sixty-two degrees Celsius but it was as good a forecast as we could ever hope to get. The crew were ready, and the green light was given for the following morning.

That night Chris held me in his arms. We both knew the risks involved and the fear we both felt was left unsaid. Now that we had found each other, our lives had been so enriched and the thought of losing that was unbearable. My love for him was stronger than ever, as I realised what he must be going through. I prayed that he would never do the same to me as I would not be able to face it with such strength. He spoke softly against my hair. 'All you have to do tomorrow is survive.'

My diary, 25th October 1994:

I shivered in the early morning chill as I dressed with immense care, aware that everything had to be right. I felt refreshed after a surprisingly good sleep, all the tossing and turning had been done by our three new helpers enlisted yesterday who are so nervous for me that they haven't slept a wink. Miranda coated my back with talcum powder to absorb any sweat, which would freeze at altitude.

Chris and Simon rigged the hang glider as Anders connected my pre-beathing system to my mask. I put on my helmet and pushed the mask's bayonet attachments into their slots, securing it to my mouth and nose. For the next five hours I inhaled hundred per cent pure oxygen. I could hear nothing except the rhythm of my own breathing through the snug earphones that cut off all sound.

By 4.30 a.m. I had been 'pre-breathing' for one and a half hours to avoid getting the bends during our rapid ascent which might cause nitrogen bubbles in my joints to expand and cause major damage and even death. By inhaling oxygen for two hours before the ascent, all the nitrogen should have been eliminated from our bodies before we set off.

My mind returned to the job in hand as Miranda brought my clothes piece by piece and helped me into them. She tightened the laces of the pressure suit so that it fitted closely. Two hoses protruded from the left-hand side of the suit. These were connected to the regulator – the 'brains' of the oxygen system which controlled the onset of the pressure breathing. The regulator was attached to the side of the harness and there was a hole in the front of the harness for the hoses to go through after they had passed unobstructed through each layer of clothing in turn.

I dressed slowly and calmly, allowing Miranda time to check each layer. I felt surprisingly calm, concentrating on the challenge ahead. In my mind, I went over the emergency drill which I had arranged with Per in the event of radio failure. We were to give each other a series of different 'jolts' to indicate that either 'descent has started', 'release speed attained', 'release when ready', or 'I have an emergency, descend immediately.'

The minutes moved interminably by. Chris and Simon finished rigging and checking the glider, conscious that my life depended on their thorough preparation of the equipment. The balloon was being inflated and cameras were being attached to both balloon and hang glider.

Miranda helped me to put on two balaclavas after I removed the helmet, holding the mask to my face. I held my breath, removed the mask and pulled them over my head, replacing the mask before breathing again. Just one breath of normal air at this point would have introduced nitrogen back into my body and joints, risking the bends, and delaying the flight.

Chris brought my barograph for me to set, the 'black box' which would record our flight as proof for the Guinness Book of Records. Miranda finished dressing me with a final layer of down jacket, down trousers and moon boots and I moved into the pick-up truck which had its air-conditioning on full blast. I was desperate to avoid the debilitating effects of overheating which I experienced during the practice drop so I lay down on the back seat with my oxygen cylinder and tried to stay still, mentally rehearsing the drop sequence for the umpteenth time.

Per, cool as the proverbial cucumber, sat apparently unperturbed by it all. Finally he joined me in the truck and we were driven to the balloon. A surge of excitement tinged with fear thrilled me as I took in the scene. The huge sphere stood turgid and steady, the gold Hashemite crown, emblem of Royal Jordanian Airlines, shone proudly in the early light. The cliffs behind were black, as yet untouched by the impending dawn. The sky above was deep blue, heralding the rise of the sun.

Per opened the door and I watched as he waded over to the basket. It was smothered in people checking and double-checking tethers, cameras, instruments, propane, oxygen and hydrogen. Finally we drove to the hang glider. Dwarfed by the monstrous balloon and dripping with ropes and pulleys, it sat patiently in the sand, unaware of the long, cold flight ahead.

Anders tapped on the door and beckoned that it was time to go. Slowly, I walked to the glider, turned, and reversed into the harness. I was so bulky in all my clothing that my arms had to be guided into position as Simon supported the weight of the oxygen cylinder and Chris fastened the zip and buckles.

Anders came close to shout instructions to me as he changed my oxygen from the pre-breathing tank to my personal cylinder attached to my back. Under his guidance, I held my breath, while he disconnected one and reconnected the other. I became a self-sufficient unit with my own life-support system.

Miranda checked my neoprene mask, ensuring all the exposed flesh was covered. My goggles were around my neck, waiting until I was high and cold before putting them on so they didn't fog up again. I had wiped them with alcohol and stuck silica sachets to them in the hope of keeping them clear.

I lay down in the harness for Chris to check that my oxygen tank was correctly attached. He helped me on with my gloves, liners first, then huge gauntlets. I was cooking already and wanted to go. I felt restricted, with umbilical cords attaching me to oxygen, camera recorders and sound wiring. We did a radio check – the sound was crystal clear through the headphones.

It was time to attach the hang glider to the balloon and as I could not get up with the weight of the cylinder on my back, Chris and Simon wheeled me backwards towards the basket. I was blind, deaf and mute. I could only look straight ahead and had to put myself entirely in the hands of my helpers. I could only hear the intermittent dull roar of the burners as the balloon was readied for take-off.

Chris's disembodied voice came over the radio. 'OK Per, let's go.'

I knew he was aware of my overheating and silently thanked him for speeding things up. I sensed an increased urgency amongst the people around me. Simon disappeared behind me to connect my glider to the basket. His face reappeared in front of me and he gave me the thumbs up and shouted that the connection was complete and all ropes were tangle free.

As all the others moved clear, Chris was there in front of me and carried out the last task, which was to connect my emergency oxygen handle as the balloon took my weight. I reached out my hand and he held it to his face and kissed the palm of my thick gauntlets. He pushed me gently away, willingly releasing me to do what I had to do.

We started to climb and the tethers were released. Finally on our own, the quiet consumed me. We rose into the clear skies above and I felt a fatalistic peace wash over me. We were fully committed and within four hours it would be over, for better or for worse.

Down below, the crowd cheered, then fell silent. Chris (a non-smoker) drew heavily on a cigarette.

We climbed fast, drifting southwest to start with, then passing back over Wadi Rum as we contacted the southwesterlies at 10,000 feet. I was lost in the spectacular landscape below. For a moment the record was forgotten as I watched the reds and golds of the desert glow, the long shadows of the crags retreating, scurrying away from the heat of the day.

The green circles of the Disi fields were clearly visible and provided an excellent landmark. Ahead lay Iraq – miles away but directly on track if the jet stream should be stronger than forecast. The Red Sea came into view and with it, Egypt and Israel. There were some clouds to the west but we quickly rose above them.

The silence was eerie. There were six people with radios on the ground but no one spoke. Per was busy coaxing every ounce of performance out of the balloon. The noise of the burners was constant and I knew that he must be heating the envelope to its limit. We passed through 34,000 feet and a spangling shower of ice crystals came streaming past me as we left a vapour trail.

At 36,000 feet the oxygen felt strange. I was acutely aware that if something went wrong with it at this altitude I would only have forty-five seconds to act before lapsing into unconsciousness. I massaged the exhaust valve on the mask to stop it icing up. The oxygen system has been tested to minus thirty degrees and we were already down to minus fifty-five degrees. I monitored my breathing closely. I was aware of a slight pressure on my body as I realised, with surprise, that pressure breathing had kicked in; not the extremely uncomfortable suffocating experience I remembered from Sweden, but a gently increasing pressure which allowed me to function normally despite the rarefied atmosphere.

Fifty minutes after take-off we were above the ice crystal layer of cirrus clouds. The sky above was dark and the curvature of the earth was clearly visible as we reached eight miles high. The temperature had been a bitterly cold minus sixty-two degrees for the past half hour, though I felt surprisingly comfortable – the thick layers of clothing were working well. Only my face felt cold.

I tried once again to put on my goggles. They fogged over immediately and I despaired of them, leaving them dangling and instead used the big visor on my helmet which came right down over my face, keeping it just warm enough. Above me Per was having problems. The propane was so cold that it was coming out of the cylinder as 'snow', igniting and falling on his head in flaming lumps. He switched off the burners and radioed to say that we had reached the maximum altitude possible and that he would start the descent. He sounded clear but a little breathless due to the difficulty of talking against the pressure of the oxygen.

There were two minutes to go before I dropped and I focused my concentration on the release. I pulled on my rope to crank the glider's nose down. I pushed my body as far over the bar as possible and I had no option but to look straight down. The air was so clear and the desert so featureless that the perspective was hard to judge. My only guide was the tiny line of pimples which were the huge cliffs of Wadi Rum.

My heart was racing and fear coursed through me. I suddenly thought, 'I wish I'd taken up knitting instead.' But it was far too late for second thoughts. Per spoke again. 'We are at descent speed, release when you are ready.'

There was no time to hesitate. We were descending fast and a short delay would lose us the record. I grabbed my release handle, held my breath and pulled. . . .

Nothing happened.

I pulled harder. Still nothing. The release mechanism had frozen solid. I called Per. 'Cut me now.'

I knew he was ready, as we had arranged, with his knife poised.

He cut the rope. Instantly I felt the glider fall and rotate around me. It was at least vertical, maybe past vertical. I was in freefall, harness straps slack. My feet hit the keel and I felt the oxygen cylinder catch in the back wires. Still the glider fell.

'Fly, please fly!'

The air didn't catch me, but eventually the glider stopped rotating and I realised that it probably wouldn't tumble. At last the glider responded and with a smooth surge, it pitched upwards. My oxygen cylinder 'pinged' clear of the wires and I was flying.

The rush of relief was immediately replaced by pain. The wind whipped up under my visor making my eyes water. I blinked and immediately my eyelashes froze together and I couldn't see anything. I was flying at the same height as commercial airliners and was completely blind! I felt the skin on my face burn with cold as my flesh froze. I shoved my padded arm against my face, trying to block the gap under the visor where the wind was coming in. The cold was all-consuming. The wind chill factor had brought the temperature plummeting to minus eighty-seven degrees. Everything was frozen – harness zip, compass, feet and hands – but it was my face that felt it. And it hurt!

After a few minutes, I started to think more clearly. I didn't know exactly where I was, but with a stiff breeze and a super-fast ground speed due to the thin air, I realised that I might be heading towards Iraqi airspace. I turned the glider and found the brightness of the sun through my still frozen-shut eyes. I continued until I sensed the darkest part of the circle and straightened up. At least I knew I was then heading west and back towards Jordan.

It seemed like an age before my eyelashes finally thawed, allowing me to open my eyes. I squinted in the bright sunshine and could not keep them open for more than a couple of seconds at a time as it was still unbearably cold, but I knew it would get warmer as I sank towards the desert seven miles below. I could hear no one, but I felt as though I could see to the ends of the world.

'God, I'm cold!' I thought to myself. I needed to find out where I was and looked around. I was surprised to see the green circles of the fields at the Disi agricultural plant below and deduced that we were only fifteen miles past it, rather than fifty miles away, as we had thought from our calculations.

Suddenly I caught sight of Per, a tiny orb miles below me, having made a fast descent back to the warmth of the desert within thirty minutes. An even smaller white dot was circling him and I knew Ben had found him with the microlight. I tried again to zip up my harness to try to defrost my feet, but it was locked with ice. I needed a distraction from the cold and looked once more at the panorama below me.

The road from Jordan to Saudi Arabia was clearly visible, and the desert stretched as far as I could see to the east. I could see a giant shadow close to the balloon and realised he must be about to land. He touched down lightly and the balloon stood proud for a moment, then deflated, sprawling across the sand, lifeless now its mission had been accomplished.

At 10,000 feet my hands thawed and with the returning feeling came the 'hot aches'. They had been numb for one and a half hours and I banged them against the base bar to ease the pain. I detached one side of the mask, letting it hang, releasing the oxygen into the wind. The feeling of freedom was wonderful as I inhaled deep breaths of the fresh desert air. Finally, I managed to zip up my harness, though it made no difference to my still-frozen feet.

I began to see detail in the desert floor below. Per had landed in a rough area with uneven ground scattered with rocks, adequate for a balloon, but less than ideal for me. I elected to land cross wind along the rough channels on the ground. I couldn't see a smooth area and I knew it was going to be a case of making the best of it. The helicopter landed and the film crew spewed out onto the sand and hurried to their positions.

The ground rushed up, I focused what concentration I could muster and touched down right on a bump, bouncing me back into the air momentarily, before the glider settled. It was over, we were OK, and we had broken the record.

I slumped with fatigue and relief. I couldn't move – the harness pinned me to the ground and I was connected to everything via pipes and ropes. I was aware of people around me pulling, disconnecting and freeing me from the equipment. I felt the weight disappear and Chris helped me to my feet. I leaned against him as he took off the down jacket. (One of my friends commented afterwards that women only look as bad as I did then during childbirth!)

Per came over and gave me a bear hug. He was bubbling with excitement and we jabbered together. When he cut me free, he had been on the floor of the basket peering through the camera viewing hole. He saw me plummet but didn't see the glider recover. For a moment he was worried and then he saw me circling at the same level as him and he happily descended. He hadn't realised that I was flying blind – it would have been embarrassing if this had resulted in the only two aircraft flying at 40,000 feet colliding in mid air!

My height recorder displayed a maximum altitude of 41,370 feet. The exact drop height was later confirmed at 38,900 feet. Simon had to leave the glider in the sun for half an hour to defrost as he couldn't fold the wings in. I had mild frostbite on my face and so my nickname was changed from Barney to Frosty.

Chris and I flew back to Wadi Rum by helicopter, arriving at 9.30 a.m., just as the late risers were emerging from their tents. As I washed my face, a woman, still in her nightdress, joined me at the sinks and stared at the swollen and angry-looking red blotches on my cheeks. 'What bad sunburn – you have to be so careful in the desert,', she exclaimed.

'Actually,' I replied, as nonchalantly as I could, 'it's frostbite', and smiled to myself at her confused expression.

We threw a wild party that night. Tony Larkin, our stills photographer and night time picture editor for the *Sun*, had been looking for a headline for the drop. He stood up and triumphantly gave us his title – 'Danglin' Doris in Daring Desert Dive!'

The whole team had worked so hard to make it happen and celebrated by drinking the rest house dry. I lasted until 10 p.m. before the day's excitement, coupled with such an early start, caught up with me. Chris and I sloped off, scuffing through the sand as the moon rose over the ridge into the star-studded sky. The elation had been ousted by fatigue and I felt only relief that it was all over. I climbed into my sleeping bag and was asleep before my head touched the pillow.

CHAPTER 22

Flying with Condors

During the time we spent in Jordan after the balloon drop, Chris and I discussed the possibility of having a baby the following year. This was an idea that I had never seriously considered before I met Chris. As we both worked from home, we had been in each other's company almost constantly during the year that we had been living together. We grew closer each day and, both being in our thirties, we were in no doubt how lucky we were to have found one another.

Chris has always loved children and my perspective had changed since we met. I had never felt maternal, but the idea of sharing a child with Chris, who would play such an active part in the child's upbringing, was a different matter. It would take some adaptation after my self-centred years of competitions and projects, but I was ready to make that commitment. Over the years I had changed, and felt more settled than I had ever been. I had lost the constant restlessness that drove me so relentlessly. I had done almost everything that I really wanted to do in flying except ... flying with condors.

My dream of flying with the biggest bird of prey in the world had started more than a decade before when I had first flown with vultures in India. Since then, I had been inspired to fly with them after watching the BBC film *Flight of the Condor*. The images of the magnificent birds soaring above the stunning mountains of the Andes captivated me. With their wingspan stretching up to ten feet across they have had to perfect the art of thermal soaring. Flapping their wings would require too much energy as they are the heaviest flying birds in the world, and gliding is therefore more efficient. This increased the feeling of affinity I had with them as, flying hang gliders and paragliders, I did not have the option of 'flapping' and was restricted to using wind and thermal currents to keep me aloft.

Chris had spent a lot of time working in South America and had seen condors occasionally, and together we shared the same dream of flying with them. We decided that before starting a family, we would make a pilgrimage to the Andes together. We scheduled our expedition for January 1995 to coincide with the fifteenth International Seaweed Symposium which Chris was due to attend in Chile.

'I know how to show a woman a good time!' he laughed as we walked into a lecture on 'Exudates from *Gracilaria chilensis* stimulate settlement of epiphytic ulvoids'.

Once the symposium finished, we packed for our expedition. We had a huge amount of equipment, the bulkiest part of which were two para-motors – engines that strapped to a paraglider pilot's back. We had decided to use paragliders, rather than hang gliders, which would have been heavier and more cumbersome. We were worried about being unable to take off where the birds were flying. We expected the condors to be flying in fairly remote terrain and the chances of finding a convenient mountain that was both accessible and suitable for taking off with a paraglider was unlikely, and to be stuck on a ridge within sight of the birds, but unable to reach them, would defeat the whole idea. Having motors on our backs seemed to provide an obvious solution. We could use them to take off from flat ground and climb the initial 1,000 feet, allowing us to find a thermal, switch off the engine and then use natural lift. If we could restart them in the air, it would also enable us to fly to where the condors were without having to rely on thermals, or worry about landing on hostile terrain below us.

We had bought the motors the previous summer and had spent some time learning to fly them. The 210cc Italian-made engines attached to the harness of the paraglider. They arrived accompanied by an explanatory video which appeared at first glance to be more like a fashion show than an instruction manual. It showed an immaculately dressed pilot with mirror sunglasses looking smoulderingly into the camera as he started the engine. With the merest tweak of the paraglider, the canopy obediently inflated and positioned itself perfectly above his head. With one more sultry glance into the lens, he applied power and within three paces was airborne. It looked easy.

It therefore came as a huge surprise when we tried the same technique and it didn't work! Chris managed to get off the ground on his second attempt and instantly acquired 'expert' status. When I tried, the canopy insisted on transforming itself into a 'bag of washing' and obstinately refused to fly. Seven attempts later, I managed to iron out enough of the teething problems in order to inflate the paraglider and increase the engine power. Slowly, slowly, more power, keep running, more power, longer strides, more power, keep running, full power and ... airborne! Sweat poured off me as I finally launched, but I felt triumphant.

I did not feel comfortable with an engine on my back like a rucksack. I could feel the vibration going right through me and the noise, generated within inches of my ears, was deafening. The coordination of adjusting the throttle lever in one hand together with maintaining the pressure on the brake handles, took some getting used to. Chris often teases me about my inability to do more than one thing at a time, and launching a paramotor seemed to require half a dozen simultaneous variable actions. However, by the time we left England, and after many more frustrating learning sessions, we had more or less mastered the technique of taking off.

Finding the birds would be our first major problem. Although wide-spread in the Andes, condors are by no means common. They nest on high rocky ledges, often at heights of 10,000 feet. We had three weeks in which to find a suitable place, assess the terrain and fly with condors. Several people had been very negative about our chances of flying with these elusive birds and had thought it extremely foolhardy to set off into the wilds of the Andes without any guarantee of finding them. In response to these pessimistic taunts, Chris philosophised, 'Well, if it was easy, I suppose everyone would do it.'

We decided to head for Chalten, a tiny village in southern Patagonia, where a climbing friend had seen condors flying. Although this did not guarantee they would be there, or that we would be able to fly with them, there was no substitute for a positive sighting, so we borrowed a twin-cab pick-up truck and set off.

The sky was blue, fair weather cumulus clouds hung high above, and the Andes spread out before us. As we drove through the Nahuel Huapi National Park, which straddles the Chilean–Argentinian border, the scenery was beautiful. Exotic-shaped skeletons of huge trees, bleached by the sun, were covered in fine hair-like strands of epiphytic air plants. Clear blue lakes appeared around every corner, the sun spangling on the surface of the water, while high above towered serrated rocky ridges streaked with snow and randomly splashed with grey, cream and orange.

Our exhilaration was broken by the unmistakable smell of petrol. We pulled over to discover that one of our spare jerry cans had leaked copiously in the back of the truck, soaking our food, cooking pots and, worst of all, our bedding. The frequent stretches of dirt road were so dusty that we seemed to be constantly stopping either to strap our mattresses to the roof to get rid of the smell of petrol, or to whip them off again to avoid them being covered in dust. Finally we decided that dust was the lesser of the two evils and left them on the roof for the remainder of the journey.

We drove south from morning until night following the spine of the Andes, visible at a distance as we continued parallel with the mountains. Huge cattle ranches gave way to the brown, deserted monotony of the Puna. Only occasional glimpses of wildlife broke the tedium of hour upon hour of straight dirt road. Flamingos stalked the small lakes and giant ostrich-like rheas ran away at the sound of our truck. Groups of guanacos, members of the llama family, stopped their grazing to survey us haughtily as we passed. Just to ensure we couldn't relax whilst driving, the roads were punctuated intermittently by bone-shaking pot holes or ridges over which we would become temporarily airborne.

We camped by a stream, but instead of a romantic evening in a new and wonderful country, we were forced to eat petrol-flavoured pasta whilst sitting in the truck to avoid swarms of biting horseflies which descended on us thinking it must be Christmas. A high speed tent construction followed and we triumphantly zipped up the fly screens against the marauding hordes.

We made an early start and drove across the Puna, stopping only to change seats when one of us tired of driving. There were often gaps of three hours or more between tiny villages. We felt vulnerable when, just as it was getting dark, we had a puncture in the middle of nowhere. We drove very gingerly after that, in the knowledge that we didn't have a spare.

As we neared Chalten that evening, the views were magnificent. There were glaciers visible in every direction with huge blue lakes at their bases, into which enormous chunks of ice would periodically crash. Above the village, a long, low ridge stretched to either side and above this the summits of the two prominent mountains, Fitzroy and Cerro Torre, reached skywards.

The wind was strong, ruffling the sparse vegetation and as we stopped to admire the scenery, a big black condor circled overhead. We were very excited. We had driven for three days, having only the word of a climber that there were condors in this area. We had taken a gamble on finding

272

them here and it had paid off. The evidence was circling leisurely above us on jet black wings.

We made straight for the Chocolateria, a legendary café which serves huge slabs of sticky chocolate cake, our first non-petrol flavoured food for two days. After a long shower and a big supper, we opted for an early night. The evening was still and quiet, and the star-studded sky was full of promise for the morning.

I woke up in the early hours of the morning feeling terrible. The tent was spinning in a most alarming and nauseating fashion. I crawled outside and staggered up the track trying to clear my head. I was then violently sick, which helped to ease the nausea, and after an hour I went back to the tent and slept. In the morning I felt dreadful. Whatever I had eaten had now given me diarrhoea as well as vomiting and I was incapable of coherent speech, let alone flying.

I went with Chris to a small slope facing into the prevailing wind and it proved a perfect take-off site. The wind was calm and the view was stunning. I could only watch with envy as he put on his flying suit and laid out his canopy. His launch was perfect and he cruised over to the nearby rock face and switched off the engine. A black form appeared above him as a condor took off from the cliff face. Enchanted I watched as the two came closer, then the condor turned towards the high mountains and left. Chris landed some time later with an ear-to-ear grin, babbling incessantly. I went back to bed and did not emerge until the evening, when we were told by several local people that such days were really rare with such light winds. I was pig sick – literally.

By the following morning, I had recovered and was keen to fly. The wind was a lot stronger than the previous day and we would need to keep a careful eye on it. I was nervous about the take-off, but once in the air, the awkwardness of the engine on my back disappeared. At 1,500 feet, the thermals were strong and I switched off the engine. I felt much more comfortable as a familiar silence surrounded me. The view was magnificent. A long meandering turquoise river flowed down the valley and into an enormous lake. Fitzroy and Cerro Torre were revealed in all their glory with dark, rocky, pointed peaks. Glaciers embraced them, cascading down both sides. They split to reveal their turquoise interiors and finally melted into crystal blue lakes at the base of the mountains. The colours were vibrant, with rich green forests on the slopes of the lower valleys and multicoloured cliffs on the mountains.

There were no condors around, but as Chris came up to join me we thermalled together and took pictures of each other against the spectacular backdrop. The thermals were strong, coming out of the valley below and rocketing us skywards. As I reached the clouds, the lake below me was being whipped into wavelets by the wind, indicating that the breeze was increasing. As I watched, they intensified and powerful gusts teased the surface into forming peaks. I radioed to Chris. Without doubt it was time to land.

We descended vertically as the wind increased by the minute. The front of Chris's canopy deflated twice as he hit low-level turbulence, and he was forced to restart his motor in order to make any progress. His landing was tricky, requiring lightning reactions to avoid being pulled over backwards in such a strong wind. Having watched his arrival, I elected to land at a helicopter base which was more sheltered and made the landing easier. We were both very thankful to be on the ground.

The weather in Patagonia is generally very windy. It is, after all, just a stone's throw from the infamous Cape Horn. That night, the strong wind became ferocious. The tent thrashed constantly and we didn't sleep much. Any lull in the gale was filled by the noise of fighting cats or noisy neighbours in the overcrowded camp site.

The following morning we moved camp to an isolated glade in the middle of a forest, only to find that it was populated by huge quantities of insects and an even greater number of obnoxious plants which liberally transferred burrs to our clothing, which then found their way into our bedding and the inside of our socks. As we put up the tent we saw three condors circling overhead, confirming that we had found the right spot to fly, once the wind dropped.

It was the ominous start of a whole week of unceasing gales. Occasionally, in the mornings, it would lull just enough to deceive us into unpacking our flying gear, strapping on our cameras, warming up our engines and attaching our paragliders. Only then would the wind start to blow, making it impossible to take off.

Meanwhile, we still saw an occasional condor, penetrating the wind apparently without effort. We were treated to a regular display of wildlife, with parrots conducting low level fly-pasts, dodging the trees and squawking simultaneously. Woodpeckers scolded one another from the branches above us, resplendent with their black-and-white striped wings and rakish curly crests.

Despite the beauty of the area, our frustration mounted as the days passed. One afternoon, we met a couple of hikers in the village. They were from Buenos Aires and told us that the previous year they had seen condors near Bariloche – two days' drive north. The way they described the sighting, from the top of a precipice where the birds nested, we knew they must have witnessed the birds at close quarters. They showed us the place on the map and from that moment, as each unflyable day passed, the temptation to move became stronger.

After ten days we could bear it no longer. As a parting gesture on the final night, the wind increased even more. The tent thrashed, the trees thrashed and we thrashed. By 8.30 a.m. we had packed up and were on the move once more. The wind had whipped the lake into a frothing, seething mass and the dirt road was periodically obscured by dust. We resigned ourselves once more to the endless Puna ahead. As we drew nearer to Bariloche, two days later, we saw ten black birds circling. Chris, in his usual optimistic style, declared them to be condors, whilst I remained sceptical, assuming they were turkey vultures. We agreed to differ.

We drove to the end of the track at the base of Mount Tronador – 'Thunder Mountain', so named because of the noise of huge chunks of ice which break off the glaciers, crashing thousands of feet into the valley below. We could see in the distance the ridge that we had been told about, but the valley below it was thickly wooded and the only take-off possibility was a tiny field thick with horseflies, where we fuelled up the paramotors.

Murphy's Law seemed to govern the direction of the wind, as it blew from behind regardless of which way we faced. Lugging six stone weight of gear from one end of a field to the other in sweltering heat and pursued by voracious horseflies is guaranteed to leave you in a filthy mood. Chris was 'sweating for Europe' and we were running out of water. After we had each tried four times to take off, without success, a national park guard arrived and told us we were not allowed to fly there anyway.

We conceded defeat once again and called it a day, returning to the campsite to replan our attack. The good news was that the guard confirmed that there were indeed condors on the precipice and that a track led up to a small mountain refuge on the top. We decided that if the condors could find enough lift to fly there, then so could we. We left our paramotors in the guard's garage and arranged for our paragliders, cameras and meagre living provisions to be taken up by mule. We walked up the trail, harassed to the point of insanity by the marauding horseflies.

As we finally emerged above the tree line onto the ridge, a shadow momentarily obscured the sun. Looking up, we saw a condor, thirty feet above our heads, ridge soaring in the late afternoon breeze. We stopped, speechless, and watched in awe as its black wings changed shape and shrugged off the turbulent air. Its primary feathers, like outstretched fingers curved upwards, moved imperceptibly as it changed course. It sank below the edge of the precipice, giving us a perfect view of the bold white stripe along its back, contrasting with the glossy black of the rest of its body.

We were euphoric. We had finally found the right place, there were no signs of impending bad weather and the setting was perfect. The summit of Mount Tronador stood proud on the skyline and beyond lay snow-capped peaks as far as we could see, stretching into Chile. We were standing at the top of a two-mile long precipice where the condors nested. The cliff face dropped 2,000 feet to the narrow, boulder-strewn valley below. The glaciers which draped the mountains in all directions cracked and split as they neared the precipice.

The small wooden refuge was basic, but the people were friendly and it provided a roof over our heads. The condors were obviously not frightened by people as the bird we had seen had flown uninhibited, so close to us. It was ironic that we should have taken so much trouble to buy, transport and learn to fly paramotors, only to find that we wouldn't need them after all. It felt right to me that we should not use engines as, in my dreams when I was flying with condors, it was never with a motor. We went to bed feeling like children on Christmas Eve, knowing that the following morning our dream would come true.

We were up with the dawn, too excited to sleep. The air was clear and still and we were ready to fly by 8.30 a.m., but there was no breeze and no condors, so we had to wait. The edge of a glacier in front of us hung over the precipice, and occasionally there would be a resounding crash as a chunk of it lost its battle against gravity and crashed into a myriad shards on to the rocks below.

At 11 a.m., we saw a small black dot skimming the cliff below us. It was joined by three others and the dots got larger and they gradually climbed up to our level. The shape was unmistakable, as they cruised to and fro. Our condors were awake and coming out to play. Chris and I inflated our canopies using the light breeze which had picked up, and launched into the same thermal as the condors. To our disappointment, they did not immediately rush over to join us, but rather timidly went to land at their roosts on the cliff face below. We continued to fly along the cliff edge, and after half an hour, they decided that we weren't going to offer any threat and they took off again. Within minutes there were twelve birds in the air and we were surrounded as they moved in for a closer inspection of the two strange, colourful creatures in their midst.

The adults looked dapper with their bold markings, as if they were 'dressed for dinner in their tuxedos', as Chris put it. The white band on their backs and white 'clerical' collar were well defined. The juveniles were still plain dark brown and were much more curious than the older birds, gradually venturing closer.

Our climb rate was better than theirs, but the condors' glide speed was much faster. They came cruising past our wing tips, peering hard at us. Before long they came so close that we could see the colour of their eyes – green for males, red for females. Bolder still, an adult bird arrived for a close-up inspection. I caught sight of her as she approached from behind me, less than three feet above my canopy. Fixing me with her red eyes, she flew over the top of my paraglider. I watched as her shadow moved forwards over my wing. She emerged again, blocking the sun, bending her head right under her belly in order to keep watching me.

Most of the condors stayed thirty feet away from us, but occasionally one would come much closer, to within ten feet. For two hours we played with them, thermalling and ridge soaring, chasing and being chased. I have no idea what they made of us. Presumably, anything that floundered around as much as we did on take-off could have meant 'imminent supper' to a hungry condor.

It was fantastic to watch them fly from such close quarters, seeing how their wings changed shape and the huge difference between the clumsy efforts of the juveniles compared with the adults' regal mastery of the air. I could not help but laugh at the young birds; it must be hard to be born with enormous, unwieldy wings and several seemed to be having problems in getting to grips with handling them. When they hit turbulence, their legs would swing down and their wings wobbled about as they tried to regain control. They looked for all the world like paragliding beginners enjoying themselves, but not quite at ease in the air.

The wind suddenly increased. Chris and I both sensed it and went to land immediately. With its craggy cliffs and hostile landing areas, this was not a place to be taken lightly. We landed in a snow field near the refuge and I took off my harness in a happy stupor. I could not believe that after so many years of dreaming of doing this, it had come true and was far better than I could have imagined. As Chris ran over, the daze was replaced by exhilaration and we danced together in the snow.

We packed up and returned to the refuge with euphoric grins on our faces. We celebrated with yet another huge bowl of steaming pasta before going for a slow ambling walk in the afternoon sunshine. After a good night's sleep, we rigged up our canopies and cameras once more and waited. Sure enough, as soon as the thermals started, the dots appeared far below us. The wind was stronger and as we took off, the air felt more lively, so we kept a more respectful distance from the cliff edge.

This time the condors were much less shy, moving straight towards us and sharing our thermals. Curiosity got the better of one juvenile as it approached me head on. Confident that it would miss me, I held my course, enjoying the unique view straight into the eyes of the magnificent creature. Our closing speed was fast as the condor flew straight at me, absorbed in its observations. At the last moment, it realised the severity of the situation, pulled in its wings and plummeted below me. In a wonderful display of control, it swooped up again behind me and returned for another look.

Another shattering crash rent the air as an enormous slab of ice broke off the glacier and fell. We were flying at the same level as the glacier, peering into its deep blue interior. Waterfalls cascaded in threads of silver down the cliff face, joining forces to create bubbling streams which flowed into lakes of every colour.

On this occasion, we only had an hour in the air before the wind increased and, combined with the already boisterous air, sent us scurrying down to land in our snow field. As lightly as feathers we touched down amidst the silent shadows of the condors flying past. In a dream-like trance, we sat in the snow and watched as they circled in the cool mountain air.

We slept on the mountain for four nights, flying each day with condors at our wingtips. Every flight was different, some with strong winds, others with weak thermals. The condors handled the changes with easy grace, expert aviators with their endless wings.

We had to return to Chile as our holiday was over. Sadly we packed our bag of provisions and bedding and sent it down the mountain by mule. We prepared to take the scenic route and fly down to the valley. The wind was being awkward, refusing to blow up the slope. Without a breeze to help it was impossible to launch as the snow was too soft to run on. We had to walk back to the edge of the tree line before we were far enough away from the influence of the glacier for there to be a gentle waft of air up the mountain.

I took off first and dropped like a stone, barely having enough height to make it round the side of the cliff. I was in rotor and the canopy bucked and rustled as I fought to keep it inflated. At thirty feet above the ground, I had lined up to land in the strong valley wind, when the paraglider deflated completely and I plummeted to earth. Luckily, the area was boggy and as I squelched bum first into the swamp, my relief was superseded by disgust as the thick, brown, syrupy quagmire engulfed me. Horseflies descended with a vengeance and it took me an arduous half hour to pack up my canopy, wade to the track and then walk back to the guard's hut where our truck was parked.

Meanwhile, Chris had waited twenty minutes for a good thermal to come through and had climbed high above the mountains and saw from his lofty perch the white streaks of the condors' backs heading off in all directions looking for food. As he watched, an old bird, resplendent in his gleaming plumage of black and white, flew underneath his boots, missing them by less than three feet.

I went straight to the river and sat in it, washing away the mud that so liberally coated me. Chris landed nearby and we collected our paramotors, packed the truck and reluctantly turned our backs on Thunder Mountain and our friends, the condors. As we left with heavy hearts and unforgettable memories, we knew that someday, we would be back for more.

Epilogue

During the twelve months since the condor expedition, I have won the Women's World Paragliding Championship, had a baby and suffered my first broken bone in seventeen years of flying.

The World Championships were held in Japan and despite my resolve never to return there to fly, I found myself not only competing, but standing on the rostrum with the gold medal around my neck.

Making the decision to write a book and actually sitting down to write it are two entirely different things. The publishers contacted me saying they wanted to produce the book, but that wasn't enough to induce the discipline I needed to sit at a desk for hours. In the end, the solution found me in that I broke my lower leg in two places when I was five and a half months pregnant. I spent the following six weeks in a plaster cast, unable to do anything other than sit at my computer and write.

Just after Christmas 1995, our daughter was born and we named her Yasmin in memory of Yasmin Saudi, in the hope that she may grow up to have the same zest for life as her namesake.

Although life is still hectic with a dozen projects on the go at once, I have a feeling of deep contentment and a level of happiness that I never thought possible. My thirst for adventure remains strong, as there are many things I still want to do. Now that we are 'a family', Chris and I will involve Yasmin in our travels and hope that her perspective on life will be enriched as a result. She will have been to beautiful places and I hope we can help her to follow whichever path beckons, so that she too can reach for the sky.

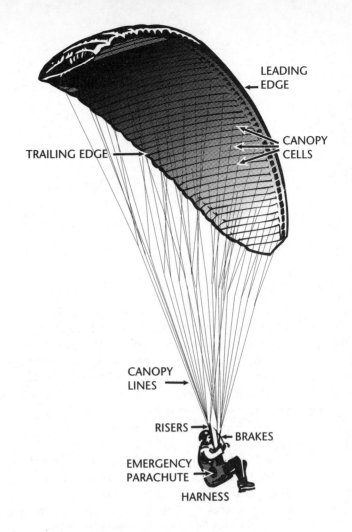

LEADING
EDGE

CANOPY
CELLS

TRAILING EDGE

CANOPY
LINES

RISERS

BRAKES

EMERGENCY
PARACHUTE

HARNESS

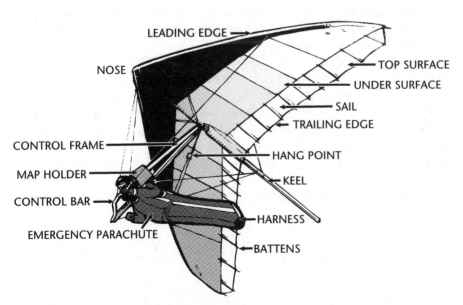

LEADING EDGE

NOSE

TOP SURFACE

UNDER SURFACE

SAIL

TRAILING EDGE

CONTROL FRAME

HANG POINT

MAP HOLDER

KEEL

CONTROL BAR

HARNESS

EMERGENCY PARACHUTE

BATTENS

Glossary

Aerotowing – method of taking off where a microlight tows a hang glider.

Altimeter – instrument displaying height.

Balloon drop – a hang glider is suspended underneath a hot air balloon with a 30-foot length of rope. The balloon then tows the hang glider to the desired altitude where the rope is cut and the hang glider is released.

Barograph – an instrument which records height gain and time. Necessary for setting world records when it is sealed by an official observer to prove that the claimed flight has been made.

Battens – see diagram, hang glider

Cloudbase – the base of a cumulus cloud, usually the top of a thermal.

Control bar – see diagram, hang glider.

Control frame – see diagram, hang glider.

Cross-country – a flight using thermals and the wind to cover distance.

Cumulonimbus – cloud associated with thunderstorms.

Cumulus cloud – fair weather 'cotton wool' clouds marking the top of a thermal. The crispness of the outline and shape of the cloud will indicate the strength of thermal underneath.

Dust devil – visible sign of a powerful thermal setting off. The twisting, rising column of air picks up debris from the ground and can be powerful enough to pick up and crush a hang glider.

Flare – A manoeuvre performed to land a hang glider or paraglider, when the wing is deliberately stalled to halt all forward motion as the pilot reaches the ground.

Flexwing – hang glider-type wing with aluminium tubing and sailcloth.

Glide – to fly in a straight line.

GPS (Global Positioning System) – instrument used for navigation using satellites.

Gust front – The start of a strong wind, for example, on the edge of a thunderstorm.

Handling – effort required to turn a hang glider i.e. a glider which handles well requires little physical force.

Keel – see diagram, hang glider.

Leading edge – see diagram, hang glider.

Microlight – powered aircraft with a hang glider-shaped wing and a three-wheeled trike unit beneath.

Nil wind launch – a take-off performed when there is no wind, requiring the pilot to run fast.

'Over the back' – flying cross-country (going 'over the back' of the hill from which you have taken off).

Ridge lift – when the wind is forced upwards over a hill, it causes a band of rising air which hang glider pilots can use to stay aloft.

Rotor – an area of turbulence behind an object such as a cliff edge or building, where the air cannot flow smoothly over it.

Spin – half the paraglider wing is stalled and the other is flying. The canopy will then rotate violently and significant height may be lost.

Spiral – caused when one wing tip deflates in turbulence and the pilot takes no corrective action, resulting in the canopy entering a steep continuous turn.

Stall – where the glider is slowed to the point where the airflow breaks away from the wing and no longer produces lift. A hang glider will then rotate until it is pointing downwards and will dive until the airflow has been restored and the wing starts to fly again. It can then resume its normal flying attitude. A paraglider stall is caused in the same way, but the canopy, having no rigid structure, will collapse and fall behind the pilot. Significant height may be lost before the wing reinflates.

Tasks (competition) – a course set by the competition director which the pilots must follow. It may vary each day, depending on the weather. Tasks may be:

  (a) 'open distance' – fly as far as possible. The one who flies the furthest wins.

  (b) 'declared goal' – fly to a specified place. Pilots must then cross a finish line. The fastest wins.

  (c) 'triangle' – fly around two turnpoints and back to the start. The fastest wins.

  (d) 'declared goal via one or more turnpoints' – fly to a specified place, passing nominated turnpoints on the way. The fastest wins.

Thermal – a column or bubble of warm air caused by the sun's uneven heating of the earth. These warm columns then rise. A hang glider will be carried upwards in this ascending air, staying inside the thermal by turning in circles.

Tow – Method of taking off without using a hill. The three types are:
  (a) aerotowing (see above).
  (b) car towing – the hang glider is pulled up into the air by a car. A rope is fixed at one end to the rear of the car and the other end to the hang glider pilot's harness.
  (c) winch towing – a hang glider or paraglider is pulled by a wire attached to a drum which then 'reels in' the line, like flying a kite.
Trike – microlight (see above).
Turnpoint – A point along a course that a pilot must pass, which is specified before take-off. Proof of having reached the turnpoint is by taking a photograph of the landmark. Churches, road or river bridges and prominent buildings are often used as turnpoints.
Uprights – see diagram, hang glider.
Variometer/Vario – instrument measuring how fast you are climbing or falling. It has a visual display, but also an audio function so that the pilot does not need to watch the dial. The pitch of the tone increases with the climb rate.
Wave – the wind is forced upwards over a hill or mountain and this rising movement of the air can be amplified by the next mountain which the wind hits, setting up a standing wave. This phenomenon will only happen in certain conditions, depending on the wind strength and direction, and the stability of the air. Large height gains are possible in wave conditions.
Wave rotor – When the wave pattern is slightly out of phase, severe turbulence can result. Wave rotor may also be encountered beneath established wave.
Weight shift – The movement of the body required to steer a hang glider or microlight.
Winch (see 'towing').
World records – These are divided into several disciplines:
  (a) open distance – the furthest distance, measured in a straight line from take-off to landing.
  (b) out & return – pilot must nominate a turnpoint before launch, fly to it and back again.
  (c) distance via a turnpoint – pilot specifies a turnpoint before launch, passes it, then flies as far as possible.
  (d) triangle fly – pilot specifies two turnpoints before launch, flies around them and back to the start.
  (e) declared goal – pilot specifies a goal before launch and must reach it.
  (f) altitude gain – biggest gain of altitude from take-off or lowest point of flight, to highest point.
  (g) hang glider balloon drop altitude record – highest point at which a hang glider has been released from a hot air balloon (see 'balloon drop'.)